DOCUMENTS IN WORLD HISTORY

Volume 1

The Great Traditions: From Ancient Times to 1500

SECOND EDITION

Peter N. Stearns
George Mason University

Stephen S. Gosch
University of Wisconsin, Eau Claire

Erwin P. Grieshaber
Mankato State University

 LONGMAN

An imprint of Addison Wesley Longman, Inc.

New York • Reading, Massachusetts • Menlo Park, California • Harlow, England
Don Mills, Ontario • Sydney • Mexico City • Madrid • Amsterdam

Editor-in-Chief: Priscilla McGeehon

Development Editor: Joy Hilgendorf

Executive Marketing Manager: Sue Westmoreland

Supplements Editor: Joy Hilgendorf

Full Service Production Manager: Mark Naccarelli

Project Coordination and Text Design: Nesbitt Graphics, Inc.

Electronic Page Makeup: Nesbitt Graphics, Inc.

Cover Design Manager: Nancy Danahy

Cover Designer: Silvers Design

Cover: Detail of an embroidered silk banner of the Buddha Sakamuni preaching on Vulture Peak. China, Tang Dynasty, 618–906 A.D. Werner Forman/Stein Collection, British Museum/Art Resource, NY.

Art Studio: Mapping Specialists Limited

Photo Researcher: Photosearch, Inc.

Senior Print Buyer: Hugh Crawford

Printer and Binder: The Maple-Vail Book Manufacturing Group

Cover Printer: Coral Graphics

Library of Congress Cataloging-in-Publication Data

Stearns, Peter N.
    Documents in world history / Peter N. Stearns, Stephen S. Gosch,
Erwin P. Grieshaber, — 2nd ed.
      p. cm.
    Contents: v. 1. The great traditions, from ancient times to 1500 —
v. 2. Modern centuries, from 1500 to the present.
    ISBN 0-321-03856-8 (pbk. : v. 1). — ISBN 0-321-03857-6 (pbk. : v. 2)
    1. World history—Sources. I. Gosch, Stephen S. (Stephen
Spencer), 1941–   . II. Grieshaber, Erwin P. (Erwin Peter), 1943–
III. Title.
D5.D623 1999
909—DC21   99-25704
                                        CIP

Please visit our website at http://www.awlonline.com

ISBN 0-321-03856-8

345678910—MA—020100

Contents

Geographical Contents:
The Major Civilizations

Topical Contents

Women and the Family

Trade and Cities

Preface

When many people think of world history, they think of a textbook. World history does have a survey element that textbooks serve very well. But world history also stems from the lives of many people in a variety of environments. The flavor of the human aspect of world history can in no way be captured solely by a progression of names, dates, and main developments. These subtleties come through in a sampling of the expressions people have produced, in different societies at various periods. Learning to interpret a document from a distant place or time is a vital part of world history study, yielding skills of interpretation that go well beyond an introductory history course.

This book offers a range of documents to illustrate characteristic features of key civilizations during major stages of world history since the beginnings of written records to the start of the modern age around 1500 C.E. The documents were not written for posterity; some were not even intended for a wide audience when written. They are collected here to get beneath the survey level and raise issues of understanding and interpretation that can enliven and enrich the world history course.

The book covers several key facets of the human experience, again at various times and in a variety of places. It deals with the organization and functions of the state. It treats philosophy and religion and at points literature and science. It explores contacts among civilizations, such as the diverse impacts of Islam or early contacts between Europe and Asia, plus a number of relationships through trade. It also deals with families and women and with issues of social structure.

The book's organization facilitates relating it to a core textbook. Major civilizations are represented with several readings—East Asia, the West, India, the Middle East, Eastern Europe, Africa, and Latin America. Thus a course can trace elements of change and continuity within each civilization. A section in each period also focuses explicitly on contacts across civilizations. The readings are also divided by basic time periods: early civilization, the classical era to about 500 C.E., and the spread of civilization and major religions, to roughly 1500 C.E. This chronological coverage focuses on the establishment of the major civilization traditions and contact patterns still present in the world today.

Although comprehensive, the goal is not maximum coverage. All sorts of attractive and significant documents are left out, of necessity. This book is deliberately intended to be usefully brief and accessible (and at least comparatively afford-able). We chose readings that illustrate key facets of an area or period, that raise challenging problems of interpretation, or that—at least in many cases—express some charm and human drama. The readings also invite comparisons across cultures and over time. Chapter introductory notes not only identify the readings but also raise some issues that can be explored in class discussion or otherwise. Study Questions at the end of each chapter further enrich discussion of issues.

This book was prepared by three world history teachers at work in several kinds of institutions. It is meant, correspondingly, to serve the needs of different kinds of students. It is motivated by two common purposes: first, a strong belief that some perspective on the world is both desirable and possible as a key element in contemporary American education; and second, that understanding world history can be greatly enhanced not just by exposure to an overall factual and interpretive framework, but also by the kinds of challenges and insights raised by primary materials, not written by scholars but by people actually living out the diverse and changing patterns we are grappling to understand.

Dealing with primary sources is not an easy task. Precisely because the materials are not written with American college students in mind, they require some thought. They must be related to other elements we know about the particular society; they must be given meaning; and they must be evaluated more carefully than a secondary account or textbook designed deliberately to pinpoint what should be learned. By the same token, however, gaining some ease with the meaning of primary sources is a skill that carries well beyond a survey history course into all sorts of research endeavors. Gaining this skill in the context of the diverse civilizations that compose the world goes some distance toward understanding how our world has become what it is—which is, in essence, the central purpose of history. The study of primary sources also offers students something of a relief from the demands imposed by a standard world history textbook. This book is composed of a diverse mixture of writings, many of which can be fun to savor and ponder.

Thanks go to the reviewers of this edition. They are Professor Jolane Culhane, Western New Mexico University; Professor Susan Hult, Houston Community College Central; Professor Gary Land, Andrews University; Mary Lauranne Lifka, Lewis University; Professor William Rodner, Tidewater Community College; Professor Arthur Schmidt, Temple University; Professor Marvin Slind, Washington State University; and Professor Andrew Zimmerman, University of California–San Diego.

Peter N. Stearns

Introduction

The selections in this volume are designed to provide insight into major developments and characteristics in the history of leading civilizations and the formation of international connections. They also convey some of the major changes and processes in the field of world history. The selections are source materials that were written during significant periods in the past, but not as formal histories or studies. As documents rather than research pieces, they convey a direct sense of other times and places. They also demand some analysis and interpretation to relate them to more general themes and issues.

The need to study world history becomes increasingly apparent. Although the twentieth century was hailed as the "American century," it is obvious that even given the United States' claim to some world leadership, it must interact with various other societies and, in part, on their terms. As a power with worldwide military responsibilities or aspirations, the United States maintains increasingly close diplomatic contacts with all the inhabited continents. Economically, American reliance on exports and imports—once a minor footnote to this nation's industrial vigor—grows greater every year. Cultural influences from abroad are significant. Even though the United States remains a leading exporter of consumer fads and styles, we can see among the American people European cultural standards and popular fashion and musical imports from Great Britain joined by interest in various schools of Buddhism or a fascination with Japan's gifts at social coordination. Even the composition of the United States population reflects growing worldwide contacts. The United States is now experiencing its highest rates of immigration ever, with new arrivals from Latin America and various parts of Asia joining earlier immigrant groups from Europe and Africa.

Enmeshed in this world, shaping it but also shaped by it, United States citizens need to know something of how that world has been formed and what major historical forces created its diversities and contacts. We need to know, in sum, something about world history. Study of our own past—that is, United States history—or even the larger history of Western civilization from which many American institutions and values spring, risks now being unduly narrow, although worthy and interesting. This explains why the study of world history is receiving renewed attention.

The need to know leading themes in world history thus involves the need to understand why, because of their earlier traditions, Chinese and Japanese governments are today more effective in regulating personal behaviors, such as birthrates, than governments in other parts of Asia, such as India, are. East Asian traditions never posited the boundary line between state and society that other cultures (including our own in the United States) take for granted, and the contemporary version of this special tradition has produced fascinating results. Tradition combined with more recent changes, including bitter experience with Western intrusions, helps explain why many countries in the Islamic world are demonstrating strong opposition to lifestyles and economic forms that modern Westerners take for granted. Our world, obviously, is shaped by the past; we can best understand changes we are experiencing now when we compare them with past changes. Therefore, on a small interdependent globe, a grasp of world history becomes an intellectual necessity.

A danger exists, however, in stressing the need to study world history too piously. True, growing global interdependence and communication make knowledge of past world patterns increasingly useful as the basis for interpreting policy options open to the United States or American business—or simply for grasping the daily headlines in more than a superficial manner. The mission, though, of a world history course does not rest entirely on the desire to create a more informed and mature citizenry. It can also rest directly on the intrinsic interest and the analytical challenge world history offers.

World history presents the opportunity to examine and evaluate a fascinating range of human experience. For example, it delves into interactions between humanity and nature through study of disease patterns that influenced particular societies or periods in time and through other aspects of the natural environment as well, including animals available for domestication. The Chinese, for example, built a solid civilization using a wide range of beasts of burden but without a particularly useful horse. They encountered the most advanced forms of the horse only during the Han dynasty, when their borders pushed into Central Asia. Then, delighted with the find, they proceeded to make the horse a common figure in their art. Human interaction with nature went beyond the objective natural environment, of course. Some major cultures venerated particular aspects of nature, removing these from daily use. Thus India held the cow in respect, and Westerners and Middle Easterners—unlike East Asians—refused to eat dog meat. Even human emotions varied by culture and over time. India, though in formal respects a highly patriarchal society, modified the impact of male control in daily family life by strong emphasis on affection and sexual passion. West Europeans, long schooled to view husband-wife relations as an economic arrangement to which emotional attachments were secondary, came to see positive virtues in romance, with suggestions of a new esteem for love some 600 years ago.

Variety and change at the more visible levels of high culture and government are equally familiar themes in world history. Indian society, although successful in commerce and technology, developed an otherworldly emphasis—a concern for spiritual explanations and goals—normally foreign to the higher reaches of Chinese society. Japan built an intricate set of feudal relationships among warriors into a durable tradition of group loyalty, whereas a similar set of warrior relations in Western Europe led less to group cohesion than to institutions—parliaments—that would watch and regulate the doings of kings. Culture contact led sub-Saharan Africa to borrow significantly from Islam but not to merge with the Islamic world.

Historical events worldwide illustrate ways that different societies interacted and the range of evil and good acts of which humans have proved capable as well. World history, in sum, can be interesting, even enjoyable, unless the human panorama offers no appeal. It has grown unfashionable in American education to emphasize joy in learning, lest a subject seem frivolous or irrelevant to careers and earning power. But the fact is that world history, like many but not all other academic subjects, offers potential for pleasure as well as support for an informed citizenry.

World history is also challenging. Putting the case mildly, much has happened in the history of the world; and although some developments, particularly in early societies, remain unknown for want of records, the amount that we do know is astounding—and steadily expanding. No person can master the whole, and in presenting a manageable course in world history, selectivity is certainly essential. Fortunately, there is considerable agreement on certain developments that are significant to a study of world history. The student must gain, for example, some sense of the special political characteristics of Chinese civilization; or of the new world economy that Western Europe organized, to its benefit, after about 1500; or of the ways major technological changes developed, spread, and had an impact on leading societies at various points in time, including the Industrial Revolution and even the more recent innovations in information technology. This list of history basics, of course, is not uniform, and it can change with new interests and new data. The condition of women, for example, as it varied from one civilization to the next and changed over time, has become a staple of up to date world history teaching in ways that were unimaginable 20 years ago. Despite changes in the list, though, the idea of approaching world history in terms of basics—key civilizations, key points of change, key factors such as technology or family—begins the process of making the vast menu of information digestible.

In practice, however, the teaching of world history has sometimes obscured the focus on basics with a stream-of-narrative textbook approach. An abundance of important and interesting facts can produce a way of teaching world history so bent on leaving nothing out (though in fact, much must be omitted in even the most ponderous tome) that little besides frenzied memorization takes place. Yet world history, although it must convey knowledge, must also stimulate thought—about why different patterns developed in various key civilizations, about what impact new contacts between civilizations had, about how our present world relates to worlds past.

One way to stimulate thought—and to give a dash of the spice that particular currents or episodes in world history offer—is to provide access to original sources. The purpose of this volume is to facilitate world history teaching by supplementing a purely textbook-survey approach with the immediacy of contact that original source documents offer.

The readings are designed to illustrate several features of various civilizations during key periods in world history through direct evidence. Thus the readings convey some sense of what Buddhism is all about through writings by Buddha's early disciples or of how Confucianism helped shape China's political institutions and underlying stability, again through direct statements. They require, however, some effort of interpretation. Because the writers were not necessarily trying to persuade others of their beliefs or even reporting what they saw at the time, they did not focus on distilling the essence of a religion, a political movement, or a list of government functions for early-twenty-first century students of world history. The reader must generate this distillation, aided by the brief contexts, the chapter introductions, and the questions provided at the end of each chapter. Analytical thinking is also encouraged and challenged by recurrent comparisons across space and time. Thus documents dealing with social or family structure in China can be compared with documents on the same subject for the Mediterranean world, and a picture of China's bureaucracy 2000 years ago begs for juxtaposition with descriptions of later Chinese politics to see what changes and what persists. Chapter 32 explicitly organizes comparison around the theme of merchants and trade in documents that originate in the postclassical period.

The documents presented are not randomly chosen, and it will help in using them if the principles of organization are clear. The principles correspond to the selection-for-manageability essential in studying world history. The hope is, of course, that the documents reflect particularly interesting insights; we selected them in part because they are lively as well as significant. They were *not* selected to maximize factual coverage. This is a difficult goal even in a text, and it becomes almost impossible in a collection of readings. We made choices of materials in this book in order to present passages of some substance (rather than snippets) and depth (rather than just a law or two, a real discussion of how a government worked). By the same token, the materials leave out vastly more possibilities than they embrace, even in the realm of "famous" documents such as treaties or constitutions. The book is thus intended to stimulate, but it is decidedly not intended to pepper the carcass of world history with as much buckshot as possible.

Eschewing coverage as a goal, the selections do follow certain general principles around which one can organize an approach to world history. Quite simply, these principles involve place, time, and topic. By choosing readings—which may or may not be important documents in themselves—that illustrate important societies in distinctive periods of time and significant facets of the human experience, the book offers a collection of telling insights that usefully complement and challenge the survey approach. Knowing the principles of selection, in turn, facilitates relating the readings to each other and to a more general understanding of world history.

First is the principle of major civilizations in organizing choice of place. The readings focus on seven parts of the world that have produced durable civilizations that still exist, at least in part. They do not simply focus on the West in a world context. East Asia embraces China and a surrounding zone—most notably Japan—that came under partial Chinese influence. Indian civilization, which constitutes the second case, had considerable influence in other parts of southern Asia, although we do not offer readings on Southeast Asia directly. The Middle East and North Africa, where civilization was born, form a third society to be addressed at various points in time, both before and after the advent of its major religion, Islam. Europe, although ultimately sharing some common values through Christianity and a recollection of the glories of Greece and Rome, developed two partially distinct civilizations in the east (centered ultimately on Russia) and west. Both East and West European civilizations innovated as new religion, trade, and political organizations spread northward. Values and institutions from Western Europe would also help shape new settler societies in North America and in Australia and New Zealand. Sub-Saharan Africa, a vast region with great diversity, forms a sixth civilization area. Finally, civilization developed independently in the Americas. Here, as in Africa, signs of civilizations showed early, but a full statement—and elaborate records—developed rather late in time. The seven civilizations represented in the readings are not sacrosanct: They do not embrace all the world's cultures, past or present. They overlap at points, and they contain some marked internal divisions, such as the division between China and Japan in East Asia. These civilizations, however, do provide some geographic coherence for the study of world history, and they are all represented repeatedly in the selections that follow.

Separate civilizations, even when compared, are only one of the geographic and cultural bases for world history. The second basis is contact among different societies, as a result of migrations, invasions, trade, deliberate borrowing, or missionary intrusions. Here is a key, recurrent source of change, friction, and creativity. Documents on the nature and results of significant contacts complement those focused on the characteristics of major civilizations. For each period after the earliest, one or more sections on global contacts highlight key interchanges among societies in different parts of the world.

Time is the second organizing principle. Obviously, some of the civilizations currently important in the world did not exist 1500 years ago, so the factor of chronology is vital just to order the list of civilizations. Further, even ancient civilizations changed over time, and we need a sense of major periods to capture this evolution. Finally, the inhabited world as a whole has gone through various stages of interaction and diversification, and periods in world history reflect these patterns as well.

Because the selections that follow deal with written evidence, no treatment is included of the long, fascinating trajectory of the human species before civilization emerged, around 3500 B.C.E. Several selections represent the first phase of civilization in Asia and North Africa, when river-valley cultures developed formal political organizations, cities, written laws, and elaborate commerce. River-valley civilizations in the Middle East, Egypt, northwest India, and northern China flourished over a long period of time, gradually giving way to more extensive cultures that built on their technical and cultural achievements. Even during the early period of civilization, particularly in the Middle East, civilizations began to produce offshoots and variants that would have lasting impact; a crucial example is the monotheistic religion the Jews developed.

Between 1000 B.C.E. and about 500 C.E., larger civilizations took hold in China, India, and around the Mediterranean. This second, or classical, phase of civilization—though still limited in spatial terms—embraced wider areas than before. These three major classical civilizations also generated value systems (such as the Hindu religion in India and Confucianism in China) that not only described the classical period itself but would also have durable influence lasting into the twentieth century. They produced institutions, such as the Chinese bureaucracy and the Indian caste system, of long-range impact as well. The classical period thus describes the development of elaborate societies in key parts of Eurasia and North Africa that bequeathed core features, not just ruins and scattered traces, to later world history.

Attacked by nomadic invaders and undermined by diverse internal pressures, the classical civilizations declined or collapsed between 300 and 600 C.E. A thousand-year period followed in which a wider array of civilizations developed, some independently and some as offshoots from earlier centers. Christian missionaries from Mediterranean Europe brought cultural and political change to northwestern Europe and Russia—including writing and the other basic trappings of civilization. Civilizations that expanded in various parts of sub-Saharan Africa were, in some cases, soon influenced by the Islamic religion and Middle Eastern commercial and bureaucratic forms. It was during this period that Japan gained civilization by selectively copying China. Finally—but in complete isolation—civilization sprang up in Central America and the Andes. By 1400 C.E., some version of the seven civilizations still vigorous in our world had taken shape. In close relationship, major world religions spread or developed during the centuries following the classical age. Islam, the newest of the great faiths, formed around C.E. 600 and anchored Arab dynamism around the Mediterranean and Indian oceans for some centuries thereafter. Christianity took firm hold in Europe, based separately around the Roman papacy and the Eastern Orthodox faith of the Byzantine empire. Buddhism spread from India to Southeast Asia and to China and Japan. Thus new religions—or, as in the case of Buddhism, a new outreach—featuring elaborate doctrines and a new concern for an afterlife helped shape a distinctive period in world history. Even India, already embraced by Hinduism, saw religious change with greater popularization of the Hindu faith and the advent of a new Muslim minority.

Mongol invasions, which swept over much of Asia and Eastern Europe during the thirteenth and fourteenth centuries, helped bring the last traditional period of world civilizations to a close. By the fifteenth century, along with a host of major developments in particular civilizations, the emerging dominant themes of world history were: the spread of more advanced technologies, the development of more intricate economic contacts around the world; including the Americas as well as the old continents; and the rise of Western colonialism. Population growth in many societies and heightened levels of commercial exchange were offshoots of these processes. For several centuries, and to an extent into our own day, the West replaced the Islamic Middle East as the world's most dynamic civilization.

Much of the drama of world history, and its relevance in understanding present conditions and even future prospects, lies in playing the traditions of the major civilizations against the trends of more modern times. A second volume of documents, organized on lines similar to to the present volume, takes the story of world history into the modern centuries and allows a comparison of recent developments with their counterparts in the earlier history of civilizations as a means of measuring change and continuity.

The present volume, however, in covering the many centuries from civilization's first emergence to its spread almost literally worldwide, has its own significant themes, independent of what came later. It allows a grasp of the major features of civilization itself, from the development of formal governments to more systematic social inequalities.

Although the emphasis of this volume lies in the formation of basic traditions and traditional contacts, the theme of change must be traced as well. New religions and the rise and fall of political systems brought important shifts. Contacts among most of the world's civilizations increased, particularly rapidly after about 800 C.E. Tradition evolved further as it fed into more modern world history.

In summary, the readings in this book cluster around seven civilizations through three time periods: early civilization, classical, and the centuries of civilization's further spread. Without too much forcing, we can see the three periods as embracing the origin and elaboration of basic traditions in the key civilizations spiced by religious transformations and other innovations; they would be followed by several modern periods that focused on modifications in traditions through Western intrusions, population growth, higher levels of commercial interaction, and industrial technology. Traditional periods were not, of course, static, and the modern periods have hardly displaced all traditions. Nevertheless, world history gains a rough coherence through an understanding that early civilizations were built on the basis of agriculture, and that this basis was later challenged by new commercial and industrial forms. This central modern drama, in turn, continues to shape primary features of the world today, from China's attempt to develop a political regime suitable for modern economic growth to Islamic or Soviet attempts to build modern societies free from some of the trappings of Western consumerism or family instability.

The third organizing principle is topic. In dealing with major periods and civilizations, the readings in this book reflect an attempt to convey four features inherent in human society. First, every civilization must develop some government structure and political values. Second, it must generate a culture, that is, a system of beliefs and artistic expressions that help explain how the world works. Among these, religion is often a linchpin of a society's culture, but science and art play crucial roles as well. Many civilizations saw tensions pull among these various cultural expressions, which could be a source of creativity. Economic relationships—the nature of agriculture, the level of technology and openness to technological change, the position of merchants—form a third feature of a civilization. And fourth, social groupings, hierarchies, and family institutions—including gender relations—organize human relationships and provide for the training of children. Until recently, world history focused primarily on the political and cultural side of the major societies, with some bows to technology and trade. More recently, the explosion of social history—with its inquiry into popular as well as elite culture, families, and social structure—has broadened world history concerns. Readings in this book provide a sense of all four aspects of the leading civilizations—political, cultural, economic, and social—and a feeling for how they changed under the impact of new religions, the rise and fall of empires, or new contacts among civilizations themselves.

The effort to present lively documents that illuminate several time periods, differing cultural traditions, and the variety in features of the way societies function must, again, be evocative. This book is not intended to teach everything one should know about the evolution of Western families, Chinese ideas about nature, or such big processes as the development of the modern world economy. It aims, rather, at providing the flavor of such topics, a sense of how people at the time lived and perceived them, and some understanding of the issues involved in interpreting and comparing diverse documents from the past. The collection is meant to help readers themselves breathe life into world history and grasp some of the ways that both great and ordinary people have lived, suffered, and created in various parts of the world at various points in our rich human past.

Section One

Early Civilizations

River valley civilizations developed in several places between 3500 and 500 B.C.E. They set up more formal governments than had existed before and developed important religious and cultural principles. Both areas of achievement depended on the creation of writing, which in turn left more diverse and explicit records than was possible for preliterate societies.

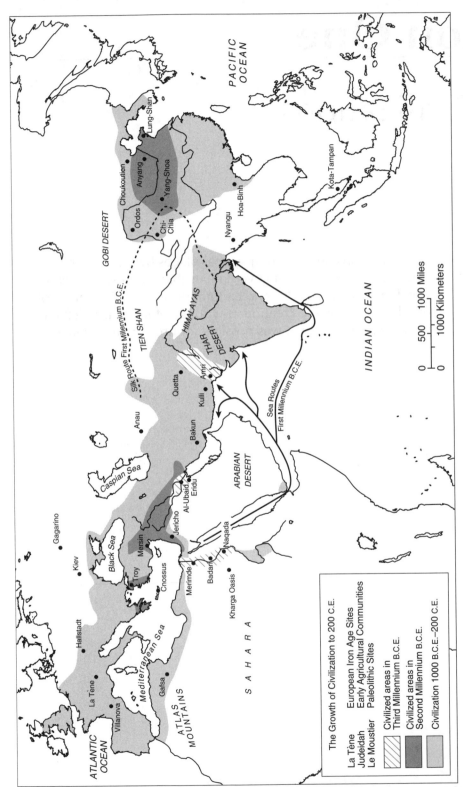

The Growth of Civilization to 200 C.E.

La Tène — European Iron Age Sites
Judeidah — Early Agricultural Communities
Le Moustier — Paleolithic Sites

Civilized areas in Third Millennium B.C.E.

Civilized areas in Second Millennium B.C.E.

Civilization 1000 B.C.E.–200 C.E.

PACIFIC OCEAN

GOBI DESERT

Lung-Shan
Choukoutien
Anyang
Yang-Shoa
Ordos
Chi-Chia
Nyangu
Hoa-Binh
Kota-Tampan

Silk Route First Millennium B.C.E.

TIEN SHAN

HIMALAYAS

THAR DESERT

Quetta
Amri
Kulli
Bakun
Anau

INDIAN OCEAN

Sea Routes First Millennium B.C.E.

Caspian Sea

ARABIAN DESERT

Al-Ubaid
Eridu
Mersin
Jericho
Naqada
Merimde
Badari
Kharga Oasis

Black Sea

Gagarino
Kiev
Troy
Crossus

Hallstadt

Mediterranean Sea

Gafsa

ATLAS MOUNTAINS

SAHARA

La Tène
Villanova

ATLANTIC OCEAN

0   500   1000 Miles
0   1000 Kilometers

Eurasia

10

1

Mesopotamian Values:
A Pessimistic View

Unlike the waters of the beneficent Nile, whose annual floods were predictable and controllable, those of the Tigris and Euphrates rivers proved erratic and often devastating. This factor, combined with the harshness of the physical terrain, the absence of protective natural barriers, and the steady intrusion of invaders who used the element of surprise, superb leadership, and technological advantage to gain temporary hegemony over the region, prompted a pessimistic outlook that found expression in the eclectic civilization that evolved in ancient Mesopotamia. The Sumerians, whose creative genius provided the cultural foundations of the region, perceived humans as lowly mortal servants to a pantheon of immortal gods and goddesses, and they viewed the miserable state of humanity as a consequence of human failure to obey divine commands. These views, frequently reiterated in the literature of the region, are best expressed in the great Babylonian heroic tale, *The Gilgamesh Epic*. This poem was preserved in 12 tablets that were recovered during nineteenth-century excavations of Ashurbanipal's (668–627 B.C.E.) palace library in Nineveh. It is the first known piece of written literature.

Heavily indebted to a variety of older oral stories, the epic describes the vain quest of its hero, Gilgamesh (ca. 2800 B.C.E.), fifth ruler of the first dynasty of Uruk, to secure immortality. By recounting the perilous ventures and hardships of Gilgamesh, the poem reaffirms that valiant personal efforts cannot prevent one's inevitable death and suggests that energy should instead be directed toward enjoying and making the most of life. During his quest, Gilgamesh sought and found Pernapishtim, the Babylonian Noah, who had secured immortality because of his piety. Tablet XI focuses on their meeting and provides Per-napishtim's account of the great deluge. A genetic relationship between his account and that of the Hebrews in Genesis is obvious, but the historical relationship between them is uncertain.

Epic literature developed in many early civilizations—not only that of Mesopotamia, but also in Hebrew, Greek, and Indian cultures. How would tales like *Gilgamesh* help shape and express a civilization's values? What purpose did these stories serve?

From *Assyrian and Babylonian Literature*, edited by Rossiter Johnson (New York: D. Appleton and Company, 1901), pp. 351–357.

[From the shore Per-napishtim, the favourite of the gods, now relates the story of the deluge to the hero, who, sitting in his ship, is listening to him.]

Per-napishtim then said unto Gilgamesh:
"I will reveal unto thee, O Gilgamesh, the mysterious story,
and the mystery of the gods I will tell thee.
The city of Shurippak, a city which, as thou knowest,
is situated on the bank of the river Euphrates.
That city was corrupt, so that the gods within it
decided to bring about a deluge, even the great gods,
as many as there were: their father, Anu;
their counsellor, the warrior Bel;
their leader, Ninib;
their champion, the god En-ui-gi.
But Ea, the lord of unfathomable wisdom, argued with them.
Their plan he told to a reed-hut, (saying):
'Reed-hut, reed-hut, clay-structure, clay-structure!
Reed-hut, hear; clay-structure, pay attention!
Thou man of Shurippak, son of Ubara-Tutu,
Build a house, construct a ship;
Forsake thy possessions, take heed for thy life!
Abandon thy goods, save (thy) life,
and bring living seed of every kind into the ship.
As for the ship, which thou shalt build,
let its proportions be well measured:
Its breadth and its length shall bear proportion each to each,
and into the sea then launch it.'
I took heed, and said to Ea, my lord:
'I will do, my lord, as thou hast commanded;
I will observe and will fulfil the command.
But what shall I answer to (the inquiries of) the city, the
people, and the elders?'
Ea opened his mouth and spoke,
and he said unto me, his servant:
'Man, as an answer say thus unto them:
"I know that Bel hates me.
No longer can I live in your city;
Nor on Bel's territory can I live securely any longer;
I will go down to the 'deep,' I will live with Ea, my lord.
Upon you he will (for a time?) pour down rich blessing.
He will grant you fowl [in plenty] and fish in abundance,
Herds of cattle and an abundant harvest.
Shamash has appointed a time when the rulers of darkness
at eventide will pour down upon you a destructive rain."'

All that was necessary I collected together.
On the fifth day I drew its design;

In its middle part its sides were ten gar high;
Ten gar also was the extent of its deck;
I added a front-roof to it and closed it in.
I built it in six stories,
thus making seven floors in all;
The interior of each I divided again into nine partitions.
Beaks for water within I cut out.
I selected a pole and added all that was necessary.
Three (variant, five) shar of pitch I smeared on its outside;
three shar of asphalt I used for the inside (so as to make it water-tight).
Three shar of oil the men carried, carrying it in vessels.
One shar of oil I kept out and used it for sacrifices,
while the other two shar the boatman stowed away.
For the temple of the gods (?) I slaughtered oxen;
I killed lambs (?) day by day.
Jugs of cider (?), of oil, and of sweet wine,
Large bowls (filled therewith?), like river water (i.e., freely) I poured out as
    libations.
I made a feast (to the gods) like that of the New-Year's Day.
To god Shamash my hands brought oil.
[* * *] the ship was completed.
[* * *] heavy was the work, and
I added tackling above and below, [and after all was finished,]
The ship sank into water two thirds of its height.
With all that I possessed I filled it;
with all the silver I had I filled it;
with all the gold I had I filled it;
with living creatures of every kind I filled it.
Then I embarked also all my family and my relatives,
cattle of the field, beasts of the field, and the uprighteous people—all them
    I embarked.
A time had Shamash appointed, (namely):
'When the rulers of darkness send at eventide a destructive rain,
then enter into the ship and shut its door.'
This very sign came to pass, and
The rulers of darkness sent a destructive rain at eventide.
I saw the approach of the storm,
and I was afraid to witness the storm;
I entered the ship and shut the door.
I intrusted the guidance of the ship to Purur-bel, the boatman,
the great house, and the contents thereof.
As soon as early dawn appeared,
there rose up from the horizon a black cloud,
within which the weather god (Adad) thundered,
and Nabu and the king of the gods (Marduk) went before.
The destroyers passed across mountain and dale (literally, country).
Dibbara, the great, tore loose the anchor-cable (?).

There went Ninib and he caused the banks to overflow;
the Anunnaki lifted on high (their) torches,
and with the brightness thereof they illuminated the universe.
The storm brought on by Adad swept even up to the heavens,
and all light was turned into darkness.
[   ] overflooded the land like * * *
It blew with violence and in one day (?) it rose above the mountains (??).
Like an onslaught in battle it rushed in on the people.
Not could brother look after brother.
Not were recognised the people from heaven.
The gods even were afraid of the storm;
they retreated and took refuge in the heaven of Anu.
There the gods crouched down like dogs, on the inclosure of heaven they
     sat cowering.
Then Ishtar cried out like a woman in travail,
and the lady of the gods lamented with a loud voice, (saying):
'The world of old has been turned back into clay,
because I assented to this evil in the assembly of the gods.
Alas! that when I assented to this evil in the council of the gods,
I was for the destruction of my own people.
What I have created, where is it?
Like the spawn of fish it fills the sea.'
The gods wailed with her over the Anunnaki.
The gods were bowed down, and sat there weeping.
Their lips were pressed together (in fear and in terror).
Six days and nights
The wind blew, and storm and tempest overwhelmed the country.
When the seventh day drew nigh the tempest, the storm, the battle
which they had waged like a great host began to moderate.

The sea quieted down; hurricane and storm ceased.
I looked out upon the sea and raised loud my voice,
But all mankind had turned back into clay.
Like the surrounding field had become the bed of the rivers.
I opened the air-hole and light fell upon my cheek.
Dumfounded I sank backward, and sat weeping,
while over my cheek flowed the tears.
I looked in every direction, and behold, all was sea.
Now, after twelve (days?) there rose (out of the water) a strip of land.
To Mount Nisir the ship drifted.
On Mount Nisir the boat stuck fast and it did not slip away.
The first day, the second day, Mount Nisir held the ship fast, and did not let
     it slip away.
The third day, the fourth day, Mount Nisir held the ship fast, and did not let
     it slip away.
The fifth day, the sixth day, Mount Nisir held the ship fast, and did not let it
     slip away.

When the seventh day drew nigh
I sent out a dove, and let her go.
The dove flew hither and thither,
but as there was no resting-place for her, she returned.
Then I sent out a swallow, and let her go.
The swallow flew hither and thither,
but as there was no resting-place for her she also returned.
Then I sent out a raven, and let her go.
The raven flew away and saw the abatement of the waters.
She settled down to feed, went away, and returned no more.
Then I let everything go out unto the four winds, and I offered a sacrifice.
I poured out a libation upon the peak of the mountain.
I placed the censers seven and seven,
and poured into them calamus, cedar-wood, and sweet-incense.
The gods smelt the savour;
yea, the gods smelt the sweet savour;
the gods gathered like flies around the sacrificer.

STUDY QUESTIONS

1. What are the main features of the flood story?
2. What does the story mean? What values was it meant to impress on the audience?
3. What religious beliefs does *The Gilgamesh Epic* express? What is the nature of divinity? Of evil? What is the relationship of humans to the gods?

2

Babylonian Law: How an Early State Regulated Its Subjects

Once he successfully reunited Mesopotamia by victories over Assyria and the neighboring Sumerian city-states, the Babylonian king Hammurabi (ca. 1850–1750 B.C.E.) played a dominant role in the Near East. In his 43-year reign, he earned a reputation for just and efficient administration, secured prosperity within his domain by strict control of Western trade routes and judicious regulation of trade, and encouraged the production of an extensive literature. Although his ephemeral empire gave way to Kassite tribes after his death, Hammurabi left for posterity the famous Code of Hammurabi, the earliest major collection of laws in history currently extant. Consisting of 282 case laws inscribed in the Akkadian (Semitic) language and presented in a series of horizontal bands on a massive diorite slab (discovered in 1901 at Susa, Iran, and now in the Louvre), the code represented no attempt by Hammurabi to produce a codification of existing statutes and/or common laws into a formal legal system. Rather, it was a formal collection of select decisions rendered by Hammurabi, the "just" judge, on a variety of isolated cases intended for public dissemination that represented recommended rules of justice. As amendments to the Babylonian common law, the code omitted many important areas in the law and virtually ignored procedural law and the judiciary. Extant legal documents and reports indicate that neither judges nor litigants viewed laws in the code as binding or enforceable in Babylonian courts.

Despite the fact that Hammurabi's compilation represents only a minor contribution to the advancement of law and jurisprudence, his laws offer historians important insights into Babylonian social structure, real and personal property, land tenure, trade and commerce, marriage and the family, agriculture, wages and prices, slaves, and the professions.

Writing down and maintaining formal law are among the chief functions of any organized government, but although certain acts are almost always defined as crimes, other definitions—and related punishments—have varied greatly from one culture to the next. Judging by the following passages, what kind of social and family relations was the Babylonian state trying to uphold? How did it define crime and punishment?

From J. M. Powis Smith, *The Origin and History of Hebrew Law* (Chicago: University of Chicago Press, 1931), pp. 181–183, 186, 190–193, 195, 199–200, 209–213.

When the lofty Anu, king of the Anunnaki, and Enlil, lord of heaven and earth, who determines the destinies of the land, committed the rule of all mankind to Markduk . . . when they pronounced the lofty name of Babylon, made it great among the quarters of the world and in its midst established for him an everlasting kingdom whose foundations were firm as heaven and earth—at that time Anu and Enlil named me, Hammurabi, the exalted prince, the worshiper of the gods, to cause righteousness to prevail in the land, to destroy the wicked and the evil, to prevent the strong from plundering the weak.

. . .

1

If a man accuse a man, and charge him with murder, but cannot convict him, the accuser shall be put to death.

2

If a man charge a man with sorcery, but cannot convict him, he who is charged with sorcery shall go to the sacred river, and he shall throw himself into the river; if the river overcome him, his prosecutor shall take to himself his house. If the river show that man to be innocent and he come forth unharmed, he that charged him with sorcery shall be put to death. He who threw himself into the river shall take to himself the house of his ancestor.

3

If a man, in a case (before the court), offer testimony concerning deeds of violence, and do not establish the testimony that he has given—if that case be a case involving life, that man shall be put to death.

4

If he offer testimony concerning grain or money, he shall himself bear the penalty imposed in that case.

5

If a judge pronounce a judgment, render a decision, deliver a sealed verdict, and afterward reverse his judgment, they shall convict that judge of varying his judgment and he shall pay twelve-fold the claim in that suit; then they shall remove him from his place on the bench of judges in the assembly, and he shall not (again) sit in judgment with the judges.

22

If a man practice brigandage and be captured, that man shall be put to death.

23

If the brigand be not captured, the man who has been robbed shall establish the amount of his loss before the god, and the city and the governor, in whose land or border the robbery was committed, shall compensate him for whatsoever was lost.

24

If there were loss of life, the city and governor shall pay one mana of silver to his heirs.

48

If a man owe a debt and Adad [a god] inundate the field or the flood carry the produce away, or, through lack of water, grain have not grown in the field, in that year he shall not make any return of grain to the creditor, he shall alter his contract-tablet and he need not pay the interest for that year.

49

If a man obtain money from a merchant and give (as security) to the merchant a field prepared for grain or sesame, and say to him, "Cultivate the field, and harvest and take to thyself the grain and sesame which is produced"; and the cultivator raise grain or sesame in the field, at the time of harvest the owner of the field shall receive the grain or sesame which is in the field and he shall give to the merchant grain for the loan which he had obtained from him and for the interest and for the expenses of the cultivation.

55

If a man open his canal for irrigation and neglect it and he let the water carry away an adjacent field, he shall measure out grain on the basis of the adjacent fields.

66

If a man borrow money from a merchant, and his merchant foreclose(?) on him, if he have no money for repayment, but give his orchard, after (it has been) pollinated, to the merchant, and say to him, "The dates, as many as there (are produced) in the orchard, take for your money," that merchant shall not agree. The dates, as many as there are in the orchard, the owner shall take (gather) and shall pay the merchant the money and its interest according to the wording of his tablet; and the remaining dates which are in the orchard the owner shall take (for himself).

87

If he put out money at interest, for one shekel of silver he shall receive one-fifth of a shekel (*lit.,* one-sixth of a shekel plus six SHE) as interest.

105

If the agent be careless and do not take a receipt for the money which he has given to the merchant, the money not receipted for shall not be placed to his account.

127

If a man point the finger at a nun or the wife of a man and cannot justify it, they shall drag that man before the judges and they shall cut the hair of his forehead.

128

If a man take a wife and do not draw up a contract with her, that woman is not a wife.

129

If the wife of a man be taken in lying with another man, they shall bind them and throw them into the water. If the husband of the woman spare the life of his wife, the king shall spare the life of his servant (i.e., subject).

130

If a man force the (betrothed) wife of a man, who has not known a male and is living in her father's house, and lie in her bosom, and they take him, that man shall be put to death and that woman shall go free.

131

If a man accuse his wife and she have not been taken in lying with another man, she shall take an oath in the name of God and she shall return to her house.

132

If the finger have been pointed at the wife of a man because of another man, and she have not been taken in lying with another man, for her husband('s sake) she shall throw herself into the sacred river (i.e., she shall submit to the ordeal).

133 (Partly Restored)

If a man be taken captive and there be something to eat in his house and his wife go out of her house and she do not protect her body and she enter into another house, because that woman did not protect her body and entered into another house they shall convict that woman and they shall throw her into the water.

134

If a man be taken captive and there be nothing to eat in his house and his wife enter into another house, that woman has no blame.

135

If a man be taken captive and there be nothing to eat in his house, and his wife enter into another house and bear children; if later her husband return and reach his city, that woman shall return to her husband; the children shall go to their father.

194

If a man give his son to a nurse and that son die in the hands of the nurse, and without (the knowledge of) his father and mother the nurse come to an agreement (with some other family to substitute) another son, they shall convict her, and because she has made an agreement (to substitute) another son without the consent of the father and mother, they shall cut off her breast.

195

If a man strike his father, they shall cut off his hand.

196

If a man destroy the eye of another man, they shall destroy his eye.

197

If he break a man's bone, they shall break his bone.

198

If he destroy the eye of a common man or break a bone of a common man, he shall pay one mana of silver.

199

If he destroy the eye of a man's slave or break a bone of a man's slave, he shall pay one-half his price.

200

If a man knock out a tooth of a man of his own rank, they shall knock out his tooth.

201

If he knock out a tooth of a common man, he shall pay one-third mana of silver.

202

If a man smite on the cheek a man who is his superior, he shall receive sixty strokes with an oxtail whip in public.

203

If the son of a gentleman smite the son of a gentleman of his own rank on the cheek, he shall pay one mana of silver.

204

If a common man smite a common man on the cheek, he shall pay ten shekels of silver.

205

If a man's slave smite the son of a gentleman on the cheek, they shall cut off his ear.

206

If a man strike (another) man in a quarrel and wound him, that man shall swear, "I did not strike him intentionally," and he shall be responsible for the physician.

207

If he die as the result of the blow, he shall swear (as above), and if it were the son of a gentleman, he shall pay one-half mana of silver.

208

If it were a common man, he shall pay one-third mana of silver.

209

If a man strike the daughter of a man and bring about a miscarriage, he shall pay ten shekels of silver for her miscarriage.

210

If that woman die, they shall put his daughter to death.

211

If through a blow he bring about a miscarriage to the daughter of a common man, he shall pay five shekels of silver.

212

If that woman die, he shall pay one-half mana of silver.

213

If he strike the maidservant of a man and bring about a miscarriage, he shall pay two shekels of silver.

214

If that maidservant die, he shall pay one-third mana of silver.

215

If a physician make a deep incision upon a man (i.e., perform a major operation) with his bronze lancet and save the man's life; or if he operate on the eye socket of a man with his bronze lancet and save that man's eye, he shall receive ten shekels of silver.

216

If it were a common man, he shall receive five shekels.

217

If it were a man's slave, the owner of the slave shall give two shekels of silver to the physician.

218

If a physician make a deep incision upon a man with his bronze lancet and cause the man's death, or operate on the eye socket of a man with his bronze lancet and destroy the man's eye, they shall cut off his hand.

219

If a physician make a deep incision upon a slave of a common man with his bronze lancet and cause his death, he shall substitute a slave of equal value.

226

If a barber without (the consent of) the owner of the slave cut the hair of the forehead of a slave (making him) unrecognizable, they shall cut off the hand of that barber.

235

If a shipbuilder construct a boat for a man and he do not make its construction trustworthy, and that boat develop structural weakness the same year (and) have an accident, the shipbuilder shall dismantle that boat and he shall strengthen it at his own expense and he shall give the strengthened boat to the owner of the boat.

STUDY QUESTIONS

1. Is it apparent that the Hammurabic Code is clearly the product of a civilization, rather than some other kind of early society? Does the code illustrate key elements of what a civilization is?
2. How many social classes did Babylonia have? Does the code suggest wide gaps among them?
3. What protections did women have in Babylonian law? Why is it clear that this was a patriarchal society?
4. Did Babylonia have a powerful state with a large bureaucracy? What state services, now taken for granted in dealing with crimes, were absent in this society? Why was so much attention given to issues of false accusation?
5. What religious beliefs did the code reflect?
6. What kind of economy did Babylonia have? What were some common problems relating to economic activity that the Code addressed? What principles were used to deal with such problems? How do they compare with principles used in more modern societies?

3

Egypt: Religious Culture and the Afterlife

Egyptian civilization was the second great river-valley center in the ancient Mediterranean, but this one was in Africa rather than the Middle East. Egyptian kingdoms, developing from about 3000 B.C.E. onward, had frequent contact with Mesopotamia, particularly in trade but periodically in wars of defense and conquest. Although there was also some cultural interaction, Egyptian religion and art emerged along very distinctive lines. Strong emphasis was placed on the power of the gods, starting with the god of the sun, Re. A host of other gods served other specific purposes and warranted careful propitiation by humans; Osiris, particularly, had power over the passage after death. The strong Egyptian state was headed by a king, or pharaoh, who himself claimed divine status, while working in tandem with the powerful priests. Egypt enjoyed political stability over long stretches of time, and this, plus the reliability of irrigation from the river Nile, may have given Egyptians an optimistic sense of control.

Concern about the afterlife was a hallmark of Egyptian civilization, motivating elaborate art for shrines and an active trade in mummification to preserve the body from decay. The following selection deals with Egyptian religious beliefs and their relationship to ethics and to preparations for the afterlife. These preparations not only included awareness of an awesome judgment day in which one's deeds would be tallied but also protection by evocation of magical powers through spells that could help ensure benign treatment in the Netherworld after death. Concern for protection, in other words, did not end with death.

The material is taken from what is now called the *Book of the Dead*, which is a sheet of papyrus (the Egyptian writing material) covered with magical texts and illustrations that Egyptians placed with their dead to help them pass through the dangers of the Underworld and attain a blissful afterlife in the Field of Reeds, the Egyptian heaven. Even ordinary people frequently ordered texts of this sort, and the rich commissioned elaborate statements. The material dates up to the mid–fifteenth century B.C.E.

From *The Ancient Egyptian Book of the Dead,* edited by Carol Andrews and translated by Raymond O. Faulkner, published for the Trustees of the British Museum (London: British Museum Publications, 1985), pp. 27–28, 29, 31, 36, 153–154. © the British Museum, British Museum Press.

INTRODUCTORY HYMN TO THE SUN-GOD RE

Worship of Re when he rises in the eastern horizon of the sky by N

He says: Hail to you, you having come as Khepri, even Khepri who is the creator of the gods. You rise and shine on the back of your mother (the sky), having appeared in glory as King of the gods. Your mother Nut shall use her arms on your behalf in making greeting. The Manu-mountain receives you in peace, Maat embraces you at all seasons. May you give power and might in vindication—and a coming forth as a living soul to see Horakhty—to the ka of N.

He says: O all you gods of the Soul-mansion who judge sky and earth in the balance, who give food and provisions; O Tatenen, Unique One, creator of mankind; O Southern, Northern, Western and Eastern Enneads, give praise to Re, Lord of the Sky, the Sovereign who made the gods. Worship him in his goodly shape when he appears in the Day-bark. May those who are above worship you, may those who are below worship you, may Thoth and Maat write to you daily; your serpent-foe has been given over to the fire and the rebel-serpent is fallen, his arms are bound, Re has taken away his movements, and the Children of Impotence are nonexistent. The Mansion of the Prince is in festival, the noise of shouting is in the Great Place, the gods are in joy, when they see Re in his appearing, his rays flooding the lands. The Majesty of this noble god proceeds, he has entered the land of Manu, the land is bright at his daily birth, and he has attained his state of yesterday. May you be gracious to me when I see your beauty, having departed from upon earth. May I smite the Ass, may I drive off the rebel-serpent, may I destroy Apep when he acts, for I have seen the abdju-fish in its moment of being and the bulti-fish piloting the canoe on its waterway. I have seen Horus as helmsman, with Thoth and Maat beside him, I have taken hold of the bow-warp of the Night-bark and the stern-warp of the Day-bark. May he grant that I see the sun-disc and behold the moon unceasingly every day; may my soul go forth to travel to every place which it desires; may my name be called out, may it be found at the board of offerings; may there be given to me loaves in the Presence like the Followers of Horus, may a place be made for me in the solar bark on the day when the god ferries across, and may I be received into the presence of Osiris in the Land of Vindication.

For the ka of N.

INTRODUCTORY HYMN TO OSIRIS

Worship of Osiris Wennefer, the Great God who dwells in the Thinite nome, King of Eternity, Lord of Everlasting, who passes millions of years in his lifetime, first-born son of Nut, begotten of Geb, Heir, Lord of the Wereret-crown, whose White Crown is tall, Sovereign of gods and men. He has taken the crook and the flail and the office of his forefathers. May your heart which is in the desert land be glad, for your son Horus is firm on your throne, while you have appeared as Lord of Busiris, as the Ruler who is in Abydos. The Two Lands flourish in vindication because of you in the presence of the Lord of All. All that exists is ushered in to him in his name of 'Face to whom men are ushered'; the Two Lands are marshalled for him as leader in this his name of Sokar; his might is far-reaching, one greatly feared in this his name of Osiris; he passes over the length of eternity in his name of Wennefer.

Hail to you, King of Kings, Lord of Lords, Ruler of Rulers, who took possession of the Two Lands even in the womb of Nut; he rules the plains of the Silent Land, even he the golden of body, blue of head, on whose arms is turquoise. O Pillar of Myriads, broad of breast, kindly of countenance, who is in the Sacred Land: May you grant power in the sky, might on earth and vindication in the realm of the dead, a journeying downstream to Busiris as a living soul and a journeying upstream to Abydos as a heron; to go in and out without hindrance at all the gates of the Netherworld. May there be given to me bread from the House of Cool Water and a table of offerings from Heliopolis, my toes being firm-planted in the Field of Rushes. May the barley and emmer which are in it belong to the ka of the Osiris N.

THE JUDGEMENT OF THE DEAD

The Heart of the Dead Man Is Weighed in the Scales of the Balance
Against the Feather of Righteousness

Spell 2
Spell for going out into the day and living after death
O you Sole One who shine in the moon, O you Sole One who glow in the sun, may N go forth from among those multitudes of yours who are outside, may those who are in the sunshine release him, may the Netherworld be opened to him when N goes out into the day in order to do what he wishes on earth among the living. . . .

Spell 6
Spell for causing a shabti to do work for a man in the realm of the dead
O shabti, allotted to me, if I be summoned or if I be detailed to do any work which has to be done in the realm of the dead; if indeed obstacles are implanted for you therewith as a man at his duties, you shall detail yourself for me on every occasion of making arable the fields, of flooding the banks or of conveying sand from east to west; 'Here am I,' you shall say.

Spell 30b
O my heart which I had from my mother! O my heart which I had from my mother! O my heart of my different ages! Do not stand up as a witness against me, do not be opposed to me in the tribunal, do not be hostile to me in the presence of the Keeper of the Balance, for you are my ka which was in my body, the protector who made my members hale. Go forth to the happy place whereto we speed; do not make my name stink to the Entourage who make men. Do not tell lies about me in the presence of the god; it is indeed well that you should hear!
Thus says Thoth, judge of truth, to the Great Ennead which is in the presence of Osiris; Hear this word of very truth. I have judged the heart of the deceased, and his soul stands as a witness for him. His deeds are righteous in the great balance, and no sin has been found in him. He did not diminish the offerings in the temples, he did not destroy what had been made, he did not go about with deceitful speech while he was on earth.
Thus says the Great Ennead to Thoth who is in Hermopolis: This utterance of yours is true. The vindicated Osiris N is straightforward, he has no sin, there is no

Egyptian Artifacts for the Dead. Boat for (symbolically) transporting the dead, twelfth dynasty, ca. 3000 B.C.E., housed in the Museum of Antiquities, Turin, Italy. *What ideas are suggested by the idea of a boat from this life to afterlife?* (Alinari/Art Resource, NY.)

accusation against him before us, Ammit shall not be permitted to have power over him. Let there be given to him the offerings which are issued in the presence of Osiris, and may a grant of land be established in the Field of Offerings as for the Followers of Horus.

Thus says Horus son of Isis: I have come to you, O Wennefer, and I bring N to you. His heart is true, having gone forth from the balance, and he has not sinned against any god or any goddess. Thoth has judged him in writing which has been told to the Ennead, and Maat the great has witnessed. Let there be given to him bread and beer which have been issued in the presence of Osiris, and he will be for ever like the Followers of Horus.

Thus says N: Here I am in your presence, O Lord of the West. There is no wrong-doing in my body, I have not wittingly told lies, there has been no second fault. Grant that I may be like the favoured ones who are in your suite, O Osiris, one greatly favoured by the good god, one loved of the Lord of the Two Lands, N, vindicated before Osiris.

. . . Hail to you, great god, Lord of Justice! I have come to you, my lord, that you may bring me so that I may see your beauty, for I know you and I know your name, and I know the names of the forty-two gods of those who are with you in this Hall of Justice, who live on those who cherish evil and who gulp down their blood on that day of the reckoning of characters in the presence of Wennefer. Behold the double son of the Songstresses; Lord of Truth is your name. Behold, I have come to you, I have brought you truth, I have repelled falsehood for you. I have not done falsehood against men, I have not impoverished my associates, I have done no wrong in the

Place of Truth, I have not learnt that which is not, I have done no evil, I have not daily made labour in excess of what was due to be done for me, my name has not reached the offices of those who control slaves, I have not deprived the orphan of his property, I have not done what the gods detest, I have not calumniated a servant to his master, I have not caused pain, I have not made hungry, I have not made to weep, I have not killed, I have not commanded to kill, I have not made suffering for anyone, I have not lessened the food-offerings in the temples, I have not destroyed the loaves of the gods, I have not taken away the food of the spirits, I have not copulated, I have not misbehaved, I have not lessened food-supplies, I have not diminished the aroura, I have not encroached upon fields, I have not laid anything upon the weights of the hand-balance, I have not taken anything from the plummet of the standing scales, I have not taken the milk from the mouths of children, I have not deprived the herds of their pastures, I have not trapped the birds from the preserves of the gods, I have not caught the fish of their marshlands, I have not diverted water at its season, I have not built a dam on flowing water, I have not quenched the fire when it is burning, I have not neglected the dates for offering choice meats, I have not withheld cattle from the god's-offerings, I have not opposed a god in his procession.

I am pure, pure, pure, pure! My purity is the purity of that great phoenix which is in Heracleopolis, because I am indeed the nose of the Lord of Wind who made all men live on that day of completing the Sacred Eye in Heliopolis *in the 2nd month of winter last day*, in the presence of the lord of this land. I am he who saw the completion of the Sacred Eye in Heliopolis, and nothing evil shall come into being against me in this land in this Hall of Justice, because I know the names of these gods who are in it. . . .

Spell 154
Spell for not letting the corpse perish

Hail to you, my father Osiris! I have come to you to the intent that you may heal my flesh; I am complete like my father Khepri, who is the like of one who does not perish. Come, that my breath may be stronger than yours, O Lord of Breath; where are the likes of him? May I endure longer than you, for I am fashioned as the possessor of a burial; may you permit me to go down into the earth for ever like that one who serves you and your father Atum, and his corpse will not perish; such is he who will not be destroyed. I have not done what you dislike; may your ka love me and not thrust me aside; take me after you. May I not become corrupt, being like that one who served you better than any god or any goddess, than any herds or any snakes who shall perish. May my soul ascend aloft after death; may it descend only after it has perished. Such is he who is decayed; all his bones are corrupt, his flesh is slain, his bones are softened, his flesh is made into foul water, his corruption stinks and he turns into many worms. . .

Now every mortal is thus, one who will die whether (men), herds, fowl, fish, snakes or worms; those who live will die. May no worm at all pass by; may they not come against me in their various shapes; you shall not give me over to that slayer who is in his . . . , who kills the body, who rots the hidden one, who destroys a multitude of corpses, who lives by killing the living, who carries out his business and who does what has been commanded to him. You shall not give me over to his fingers, he shall not have power over me, for I am at your command, O Lord of the Gods.

Hail to you, my father Osiris! You shall possess your body; you shall not become corrupt, you shall not have worms, you shall not be distended, you shall not stink, you shall not become putrid, you shall not become worms. I am Khepri; I will possess my body for ever, for I will not become corrupt, I will not decay, I will not be putrid, I will not become worms. . .

STUDY QUESTIONS

1. What were some of the main features of the Egyptian religion? What kinds of gods did the Egyptians believe in? What was the relationship between people and gods?
2. What did Egyptians expect concerning judgment after death? How might these expectations affect behavior?
3. What was the Egyptian concept of the afterlife? How did it compare with views of heaven in other religions later on? What powers might people have in the afterlife? What was the purpose of special spells and incantations?
4. How did Egyptian views of religion and relationships of humans with the gods compare with those in Mesopotamia, suggested in *The Gilgamesh Epic*?

4

The Hebrew Bible

The Jewish people settled near the eastern Mediterranean around 1200 B.C.E.—the first fully reliable record of their existence comes from the 1100s, although the Jewish religion urged an earlier history including enslavement in Egypt. Jews formed a regional state in the period when the larger river-valley empires in Egypt and Mesopotamia were weakening. Jewish political independence did not last long (the prime period of the Israelite state was 1000 to 922 B.C.E.), but the religion the Jewish leaders had formulated was another story.

The principal gift of the ancient Hebrews to the world cultural bank was their monotheistic religion, which today thrives as a major religion and in the past served as an essential ingredient for the successor religions of Christianity and Islam. Stressing complete submission to the laws and commands of their omnipotent and omnipresent God, a deity whom Hebrews perceived as outside of nature and comprehensible in intellectual and abstract terms, the religion focused on God's covenant with the Hebrews and the history of their special relationship. As lawgiver and universal upholder of moral order, God is depicted in the Holy Writ of Israel as beneficent and loving but also as a stern and vengeful overseer who unhesitatingly punishes those who refuse to comply. Both the evolution of their unique covenant theology and their laws receive prominent treatment in this canonical text, which offers a history of the ancient Hebrews and serves as a remarkable literary masterpiece as well.

Priests and prophets began spelling out the tenets of the Hebrew religion in oral form, emphasizing not only God's power but a series of laws and ethical obligations that also endowed the religion with distinctive qualities. Elements of the Hebrew Bible began to be written down from the eighth century B.C.E. onward, and were gradually collected into a coherent larger holy text.

The first selection emphasizes two aspects of the religion: first, the definition of a single God and then God's relationship to the Jewish people. The second selection deals more with laws and ethical codes; here, Hebrew writings emphasized that

From *The Oxford Study Bible: Revised English Bible with the Aprocrypha,* edited by M. Jack Suggs, Katharine Dobb Skenfeld, and James R. Mueller (New York: Oxford University Press, 1992). *Revised English Bible* © Oxford University Press and Cambridge University Press, 1989. Selection 1, Isaiah: pp. 747–748, 40:1–31; 41:1–24. Selection 1, Psalms: p. 615, 93:1–5; 94:1–20. Selection 2, Exodus: pp. 81–66, 19:1–6; 20:1–17; 21:1–7, 33–36; 22:1–5, 16, 21–27; 23:1–8, 13–32.

God gave a series of laws to Moses after the flight from enslavement in Egypt. These laws included the Ten Commandments but also a subsequent series of rules and ethical prescriptions.

1. THE NATURE OF GOD: ISAIAH AND PSALMS

Isaiah

Comfort my people; bring comfort to them,
says your God;
speak kindly to Jerusalem
and proclaim to her
that her term of bondage is served,
her penalty is paid;
for she has received at the LORD's hand
double measure for all her sins.

A voice cries:
'Clear a road through the wilderness for the LORD,
prepare a highway across the desert for our God.
Let every valley be raised,
every mountain and hill be brought low,
uneven ground be made smooth,
and steep places become level.
Then will the glory of the LORD be revealed
and all mankind together will see it.
The LORD himself has spoken.'

A voice says, 'Proclaim!'
and I asked, 'What shall I proclaim?'
'All mortals are grass,
they last no longer than a wild flower of the field.
The grass withers, the flower fades,
when the blast of the LORD blows on them.
Surely the people are grass!
The grass may wither, the flower fade,
but the word of our God will endure for ever.'

Climb to a mountaintop,
you that bring good news to Zion;
raise your voice and shout aloud,
you that carry good news to Jerusalem,
raise it fearlessly;
say to the cities of Judah, 'Your God is here!'
Here is the LORD GOD; he is coming in might,
coming to rule with powerful arm.
His reward is with him,
like recompense before him.
Like a shepherd he will tend his flock

and with his arm keep them together;
he will carry the lambs in his bosom
and lead the ewes to water.

WHO has measured the waters of the sea in the hollow of his hand,
or with its span gauged the heavens?
Who has held all the soil of the earth in a bushel,
or weighed the mountains on a balance,
the hills on a pair of scales?
Who has directed the spirit of the LORD?

What counsellor stood at his side to instruct him?
With whom did he confer to gain discernment?
Who taught him this path of justice,
or taught him knowledge,
or showed him the way of wisdom?
To him nations are but drops from a bucket,
no more than moisture on the scales;
to him coasts and islands weigh as light as specks of dust!
Lebanon does not yield wood enough for fuel,
beasts enough for a whole-offering.
All the nations are as naught in his sight;
he reckons them as less than nothing.

What likeness, then, will you find for GOD
or what form to resemble his?
An image which a craftsman makes,
and a goldsmith overlays with gold
and fits with studs of silver?
Or should someone choose mulberry-wood,
a wood that does not rot,
and seek out a skilful craftsman for the task
of setting up an image and making it secure? . . .
Do you not know, have you not heard,
were you not told long ago,
have you not perceived ever since the world was founded,
that God sits enthroned on the vaulted roof of the world,
and its inhabitants appear as grasshoppers?

He stretches out the skies like a curtain,
spreads them out like a tent to live in;
he reduces the great to naught
and makes earthly rulers as nothing.
Scarcely are they planted, scarcely sown,
scarcely have they taken root in the ground,
before he blows on them and they wither,
and a whirlwind carries them off like chaff.
To whom, then, will you liken me,
whom set up as my equal?

asks the HOLY ONE.
Lift up your eyes to the heavens;
consider who created these,
led out their host one by one,
and summoned each by name.
Through his great might, his strength and power,
not one is missing.

Jacob, why do you complain,
and you, Israel, why do you say,
'My lot is hidden from the LORD,
my cause goes unheeded by my God'?
Do you not know, have you not heard?
The LORD, the eternal God,
creator of earth's farthest bounds,
does not weary or grow faint;
his understanding cannot be fathomed.
He gives vigour to the weary,
new strength to the exhausted.
Young men may grow weary and faint,
even the fittest may stumble and fall;
but those who look to the LORD will win new strength,
they will soar as on eagles' wings;
they will run and not feel faint,
march on and not grow weary.

Listen in silence to me, all you coasts and islands;
let the peoples come to meet me.
Let them draw near, then let them speak up;
together we shall go to the place of judgement.

Who has raised up from the east
one greeted by victory wherever he goes,
making nations his subjects
and overthrowing their kings?
He scatters them with his sword like dust
and with his bow like chaff driven before the wind;
he puts them to flight and passes on unscathed,
swifter than any traveller on foot.
Whose work is this, who has brought it to pass?
Who has summoned the generations from the beginning?
I, the LORD, was with the first of them,
and I am with those who come after . . .

But you, Israel my servant,
Jacob whom I have chosen,
descendants of my friend Abraham,
I have taken you from the ends of the earth,
and summoned you from its farthest corners;

I have called you my servant,
have chosen you and no rejected you:
have no fear, for I am with you;
be not afraid, for I am your God.
I shall strengthen you and give you help
and uphold you with my victorious right hand.

Now all who defy you
will be confounded and put to shame;
all who set themselves against you
will be as nothing and will vanish.
You will look for your assailants
but you will not find them;
those who take up arms against you
will be reduced to nothing.
For I, the LORD your God,
take you by the right hand
and say to you, Have no fear;
it is I who help you.

Have no fear, Jacob you worm and Israel you maggot.
It is I who help you, declares the LORD;
your redeemer is the Holy One of Israel.
See, I shall make of you a sharp threshing-sledge,
new and studded with teeth;
you will thresh mountains and crush them to dust
and reduce the hills to chaff;
you will winnow them; the wind will carry them away
and a gale will scatter them.
Then you will rejoice in the LORD
and glory in the Holy One of Israel.

The poor and the needy look for water and find none;
their tongues are parched with thirst.
But I the LORD shall provide for their wants;
I, the God of Israel, shall not forsake them.
I shall open rivers on the arid heights,
and wells in the valleys;
I shall turn the desert into pools
and dry land into springs of water;
I shall plant cedars in the wilderness,
acacias, myrtles, and wild olives;
I shall grow pines on the barren heath
side by side with fir and box tree,
that everyone may see and know,
may once for all observe and understand
that the LORD himself has done this:
it is the creation of the Holy One of Israel.

Come, open your plea, says the LORD,
present your case, says Jacob's King;
let these idols come forward
and foretell the future for us.
Let them declare the meaning of these past events
that we may reflect on it;
let them predict the future to us
that we may know what it holds.

Declare what is yet to happen;
then we shall know you are gods.
Do something, whether good or bad,
anything that will strike us with dismay and fear.
You cannot! You are sprung from nothing,
your works are non-existent.
To choose you is outrageous! . . .

Psalms

The LORD has become King, clothed with majesty;
the LORD is robed, girded with might.

The earth is established immovably;
your throne is established from of old;
from all eternity you are God.
LORD, the great deep lifts up,
the deep lifts up its voice;
the deep lifts up its crashing waves.
Mightier than the sound of great waters,
mightier than the breakers of the sea,
mighty on high is the LORD.

Your decrees stand firm,
and holiness befits your house,
LORD, throughout the ages.

GOD of vengeance, LORD,
GOD of vengeance, show yourself!
Rise, judge of the earth;
repay the arrogant as they deserve.
LORD, how long will the wicked,
how long will the wicked exult?
Evildoers are all full of bluster,
boasting and bragging.

They crush your people, LORD,
and oppress your chosen nation;
they murder the widow and the stranger
and put the fatherless to death.
They say, 'The LORD does not see,
the God of Jacob pays no heed.'

Take heed yourselves, most stupid of people;
you fools, when will you be wise?
Can he who implanted the ear not hear,
he who fashioned the eye not see?
Will he who instructs the nations not correct them?
The teacher of mankind, has he no knowledge?
The LORD knows that the thoughts of everyone
are but a puff of wind.

Happy the one whom you, LORD, instruct
and teach from your law,
giving him respite from misfortune
until a pit is dug for the wicked.
The LORD will not abandon his people
or forsake his chosen nation;
for justice will again be joined to right,
and all who are upright in heart will follow it.

Who is on my side against the wicked?
Who will stand up for me against the evildoers?
Had the LORD not been my helper,
I should soon have dwelt in the silent grave
If I said that my foot was slipping,
your love, LORD, continued to hold me up.
When anxious thoughts filled my heart,
your comfort brought me joy.
Will corrupt justice win you as an ally,
contriving mischief under cover of law? . . .

2. HEBREW LAW

Exodus

In the third month after Israel had left Egypt, they came to the wilderness of Sinai.
They set out from Rephidim and, entering the wilderness of Sinai, they encamped
there, pitching their tents in front of the mountain. Moses went up to God, and the
LORD called to him from the mountain and said, 'This is what you are to say to the
house of Jacob and tell the sons of Israel:

You yourselves have seen what I did to Egypt, and how I have carried you on
eagles' wings and brought you here to me. If only you will now listen to me and
keep my covenant, then out of all peoples you will become my special possession;
for the whole earth is mine. You will be to me a kingdom of priests, my holy nation.
Those are the words you are to speak to the Israelites.' . . .

God spoke all these words:
I am the LORD your God who brought you out of Egypt, out of the land of slavery.
You must have no other god besides me.
You must not make a carved image for yourself, nor the likeness of anything
in the heavens above, or on the earth below, or in the waters under the earth.

You must not bow down to them in worship; for I, the LORD your God, am a jealous God, punishing the children for the sins of the parents to the third and fourth generation of those who reject me. But I keep faith with thousands, those who love me and keep my commandments.

You must not make wrong use of the name of the LORD your God; the LORD will not leave unpunished anyone who misuses his name.

Remember to keep the sabbath day holy. You have six days to labour and do all your work; but the seventh day is a sabbath of the LORD your God; that day you must not do any work, neither you, nor your son or your daughter, your slave or your slave-girl, your cattle, or the alien residing among you; for in six days the LORD made the heavens and the earth, the sea, and all that is in them, and on the seventh day he rested. Therefore the LORD blessed the sabbath day and declared it holy.

Honour your father and your mother, so that you may enjoy long life in the land which the LORD your God is giving you.

Do not commit murder.

Do not commit adultery.

Do not steal.

Do not give false evidence against your neighbour.

Do no covet your neighbour's household: you must not covet your neighbour's wife, his slave, his salve-girl, his ox, his donkey, or anything that belongs to him. . . .

These are the laws you are to set before them:

When you purchase a Hebrew as a slave, he will be your slave for six years; in the seventh year he is to go free without paying anything.

If he comes to you alone, he is to go away alone; but if he is already a married man, his wife is to go away with him.

If his master gives him a wife, and she bears him sons or daughters, the woman with her children belongs to her master, and the man must go away alone. But if the slave should say, 'I am devoted to my master and my wife and children; I do not wish to go free,' then his master must bring him to God: he is to be brought to the door or the doorpost, and his master will pierce his ear with an awl; the man will then be his slave for life.

When a man sells his daughter into slavery, she is not to go free as male slaves may.

If she proves unpleasing to her master who had designed her for himself, he must let her be redeemed; he has treated her unfairly, and therefore he has no right to sell her to foreigners. If he assigns her to his son, he must allow her the rights of a daughter. If he takes another woman, he must not deprive the first of meat, clothes, and conjugal rights; if he does not provide her with these three things, she is to go free without payment. . . .

When a man removes the cover of a cistern or digs a cistern and leaves it uncovered, then if an ox or a donkey falls into it, the owner of the cistern must make good the loss; he must pay the owner the price of the animal, and the dead beast will be his.

When one man's ox butts another's and kills it, they must sell the live ox, share the price, and also share the dead beast. But if it is known that the ox has for some time past been vicious and the owner has not kept it under control, he must make good the loss, ox for ox, but the dead beast is his.

When a man steals an ox or a sheep and slaughters or sells it, he must repay five beasts for the ox and four sheep for the sheep. He must pay in full; if he has no means, he is to be sold to pay for the theft. But if the animal is found alive in his possession, be it ox, donkey, or sheep, he must repay two for each one stolen.

If a burglar is caught in the act and receives a fatal injury, it is not murder; but if he breaks in after sunrise and receives a fatal injury, then it is murder.

When a man burns off a field or a vineyard and lets the fire spread so that it burns another man's field, he must make restitution from his own field according to the yield expected; and if the whole field is laid waste, he must make restitution from the best part of his own field or vineyard. . . .

When a man seduces a virgin who is not yet betrothed, he must pay the bride-price for her to be his wife. If her father refuses to give her to him, the seducer must pay in silver a sum equal to the bride-price for virgins. . . .

You must not wrong or oppress an alien; you were yourselves aliens in Egypt.

You must not wrong a widow or a fatherless child. If you do, and they appeal to me, be sure that I shall listen; my anger will be roused and I shall kill you with the sword; your own wives will become widows and your children fatherless.

If you advance money to any poor man amongst my people, you are not to act like a moneylender; you must not exact interest from him.

If you take your neighbour's cloak in pawn, return it to him by sunset, because it is his only covering. It is the cloak in which he wraps his body; in what else can he sleep? If he appeals to me, I shall listen, for I am full of compassion. . . .

You must not be led into wrongdoing by the majority, nor, when you give evidence in a lawsuit, should you side with the majority to pervert justice; nor should you show favouritism to a poor person in his lawsuit.

Should you come upon your enemy's ox or donkey straying, you must take it back to him. Should you see the donkey of someone who hates you lying helpless under its load, however unwilling you may be to help, you must lend a hand with it.

You must not deprive the poor man of justice in his lawsuit. Avoid all lies, and do not cause the death of the innocent and guiltless; for I the LORD will never acquit the guilty. Do not accept a bribe, for bribery makes the discerning person blind and the just person give a crooked answer. . . .

Be attentive to every word of mine. You must not invoke other gods: their names are not to cross your lips.

Three times a year you are to keep a pilgrim-feast to me. You are to celebrate the pilgrim-feast of Unleavened Bread: for seven days, as I have commanded you, you are to eat unleavened bread at the appointed time in the month of Abib, for in that month you came out of Egypt; and no one is to come into my presence without an offering. You are to celebrate the pilgrim-feast of Harvest, with the firstfruits of your work in sowing the land, and the pilgrim-feast of Ingathering at the end of the year, when you gather the fruits of your work in from the land. Those three times a year all your males are to come into the presence of the LORD GOD.

Do not offer the blood of my sacrifice at the same time as anything leavened.

The fat of my festal offering is not to remain overnight till morning.

You must bring the choicest firstfruits of your soil to the house of the LORD your God.

Do not boil a kid in its mother's milk.

And now I am sending an angel before you to guard you on your way and to bring you to the place I have prepared. Heed him and listen to his voice. Do not defy him; he will not pardon your rebelliousness, for my authority rests in him. If you will only listen to his voice and do all I tell you, then I shall be an enemy to your enemies, and I shall harass those who harass you. My angel will go before you and bring you to the Amorites, the Hittites, the Perizzites, the Canaanites, the Hivites, and the Jebusites, and I will make an end of them. You are not to bow down to their gods; you are not to worship them or observe their rites. Rather, you must tear down all their images and smash their sacred pillars. You are to worship the LORD your God, and he will bless your bread and your water. I shall take away all sickness out of your midst. No woman will miscarry or be barren in your land. I shall grant you a full span of life.

I shall send terror of me ahead of you and throw into panic every people you find in your path. I shall make all your enemies turn their backs towards you. I shall spread panic before you to drive out the Hivites, the Canaanites, and the Hittites in front of you.

I shall not drive them out all in one year, or the land would become waste and the wild beasts too many for you, but I shall drive them out little by little until you have grown numerous enough to take possession of the country. I shall establish your frontiers from the Red Sea to the sea of the Philistines, and from the wilderness to the river Ephrates. I shall give the inhabitants of the land into your power, and you will drive them out before you. You are not to make any alliance with them and their gods. They must not stay in your land, for fear they make you sin against me by ensnaring you into the worship of their gods. . . .

STUDY QUESTIONS

1. What were the qualities of the Hebrew God? What were the obligations to God?
2. Why were Hebrews called the chosen people? Does their relationship with God help explain why Judaism did not become an active missionary religion? Does it help explain the durability of Jewish religion in adverse circumstances?
3. Why is the Hebrew insistence on monotheism an important turning point in the history of Mediterranean religions?
4. How did Hebrew law compare with the Hammurabic Code? Did it reflect the same social and gender structure and prescriptions, or were there subtle differences in the treatment of lower social groups and of women?
5. The Hammurabic Code was a royal compilation, though sanctioned by a god; Hebrew law was held to emanate from God. How does this difference emerge in the laws offered—what behaviors they cover, how they are sanctioned? Is a clearer set of ethical obligations involved in Hebrew law?
6. How did the Hebrew approach to God and to divine sanctions for good behavior compare with Egyptian religion? What were the main similarities and differences?

Section Two

The Classical Period, 1000 B.C.E. to 500 C.E.

Basic political, cultural, and social traditions developed in China, India, and the Mediterranean world during these centuries. The key features of classical civilizations were *expansion* and *integration.* Each civilization expanded in territory and population, using the advantages of iron weaponry and tools. Expansion required new systems to hold larger territories together, including cultures (both religious and political beliefs) that could be widely shared at least among elites. Political capacities expanded, allowing great empires. So did systems of internal trade. Nonetheless, each classical civilization defined its own distinctive beliefs and institutions, setting up enduring cultural and political differences that would affect later periods as well. But there was also new contact, particularly trade along the "Silk Road." Contacts brought opportunities for exchanges ranging from ideas to diseases, and this development had its own rich implications for the classical period and beyond.

5

Key Chinese Values: Confucianism

Many Chinese beliefs were formed early, as civilization emerged along the Yellow river before 1000 B.C.L. One such belief stressed the importance of harmony in and with nature around the concept of the Way. More formal systems of thought developed later, in the sixth and fifth centuries B.C.E., during a divided and troubled period of Chinese politics. Various thinkers sought means to shore up a strong political system or live without one. Of the resulting philosophies or religions, Confucianism proved the most durable and significant.

Deemed by students a "Divine Sage," Confucius (K'ung Fu-tzu) (ca. 551–479 B.C.E.) was founder of a humanistic school of philosophy that offered Zhou China a social and political ethos derived from idealized values of the past. As a remedy for the political chaos of his age, the famous teacher abandoned the decadent aristocratic code and offered in its place an ethical system focused on individual moral conduct, propriety, ritual, and benevolence. Arguing that the foundations of good government and the well-being of society rested on individual ethical behavior, Confucius urged the emperor and his assistants, the *chun-tzu* (gentlemen), to provide moral examples for society at large. Confucius believed the appointment of modest, wise, polite, and virtuous gentlemen scholars was essential for good government and that this was the best means for eliminating the immorality and amorality that undermined law and order. Idealistic gentlemen could restore the conditions prevailing under the early Zhou dynasty, whose government Confucius viewed as a perfect form. In the selection from the *Analects*, which is collection of sayings attributed to the "Master" and set down long after his death, one finds his views of gentlemen. Because scholars doubt that Confucius put his ideas into writing, it is impossible to determine whether these views are authentically his own or those of later Confucianists.

Confucian theories of government were adopted as state ideology during the Han dynasty, and many of his concepts proved fundamental to Chinese philosophy more

From Confucians, *The Analects of Confucius,* translated and annotated by Arthur Waley (London: George Allen and Unwin, Ltd., 1938), pp. 85, 90–91, 104, 105, 106, 121, 131, 152, 163, 167, 177, 178, 181, 187, 188, 197, 199, 200, 205–207, 233. Permission granted by the Arthur Waley Estate.

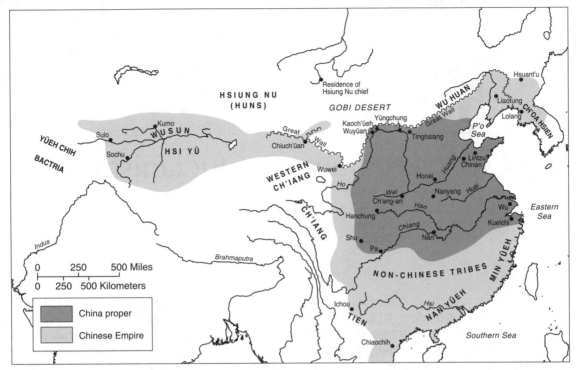

China Under Emperor Wu, About 100 B.C.E. Confucianism, launched earlier, was spreading widely by this point, with government backing.

generally. From the following passages, consider what the main interests and values of Confucianism were. Compare these with leading value systems—typically religious systems—in other ancient and classical civilizations. How do they compare with Judaism or with Hindu or Buddhist concepts developing during the same time period in India?

The Master said, If a gentleman is frivolous, he will lose the respect of his inferiors and lack firm ground upon which to build up his education. First and foremost he must learn to be faithful to his superiors, to keep promises, to refuse the friendship of all who are not like him. And if he finds he has made a mistake, then he must not be afraid of admitting the fact and amending his ways.

Tzu-kung asked about the true gentleman. The Master said, He does not preach what he practises till he has practised what he preaches.

The Master said, A gentleman can see a question from all sides without bias. The small man is biased and can see a question only from one side.

The Master said, A gentleman in his dealings with the world has neither enmities nor affections; but wherever he sees Right he ranges himself beside it.

The Master said, A gentleman takes as much trouble to discover what is right as lesser men take to discover what will pay.

The Master said, A gentleman covets the reputation of being slow in word but prompt in deed.

The Master said, A gentleman who is widely versed in letters and at the same time knows how to submit his learning to the restraints of ritual is not likely, I think, to go far wrong.

The Master said, A true gentleman is calm and at ease; the Small Man is fretful and ill at ease.

At home in his native village his manner is simple and unassuming, as though he did not trust himself to speak. But in the ancestral temple and at Court he speaks readily, though always choosing his words with care.

At Court when conversing with the Under Ministers his attitude is friendly and affable; when conversing with the Upper Ministers, it is restrained and formal. When the ruler is present it is wary, but not cramped.

When the ruler summons him to receive a guest, a look of confusion comes over his face and his legs seem to give beneath his weight. When saluting his colleagues he passes his right hand to the left, letting his robe hang down in front and behind; and as he advances with quickened step, his attitude is one of majestic dignity.

When the guest has gone, he reports the close of the visit, saying, "The guest is no longer looking back."

On entering the Palace Gate he seems to shrink into himself, as though there were not room. If he halts, it must never be in the middle of the gate, nor in going through does he ever tread on the threshold. As he passes the Stance a look of confusion comes over his face, his legs seem to give way under him and words seem to fail him. While, holding up the hem of his skirt, he ascends the Audience Hall, he seems to double up and keeps in his breath, so that you would think he was not breathing at all. On coming out, after descending the first step his expression relaxes into one of satisfaction and relief. At the bottom of the steps he quickens his pace, advancing with an air of majestic dignity. On regaining his place he resumes his attitude of wariness and hesitation.

When carrying the tablet of jade, he seems to double up, as though borne down by its weight. He holds it at the highest as though he were making a bow, at the lowest, as though he were proffering a gift. His expression, too, changes to one of dread and his feet seem to recoil, as though he were avoiding something. When presenting ritual-presents, his expression is placid. At the private audience his attitude is gay and animated.

A gentleman does not wear facings of purple or mauve, nor in undress does he use pink or roan. In hot weather he wears an unlined gown of fine thread loosely woven, but puts on an outside garment before going out-of-doors. With a black robe he wears black lambskin; with a robe of undyed silk, fawn. With a yellow robe, fox fur. On his undress robe the fur cuffs are long; but the right is shorter than the left. His bedclothes must be half as long again as a man's height. The thicker kinds of fox and badger are for home wear. Except when in mourning, he wears all his girdle-ornaments. Apart from his Court apron, all his skirts are wider at the bottom than at the waist. Lambskin dyed black and a hat of dark-dyed silk must not be worn when making visits of condolence. At the Announcement of the New Moon he must go to Court in full Court dress.

When preparing himself for sacrifice he must wear the Bright Robe, and it must be of linen. He must change his food and also the place where he commonly sits. But there is no objection to his rice being of the finest quality, nor to his meat being finely minced. Rice affected by the weather or turned he must not eat, nor fish that is not sound, nor meat that is high. He must not eat anything discoloured or that smells bad. He must not eat what is overcooked nor what is undercooked, nor anything that is out of season. He must not eat what has been crookedly cut, nor any dish that lacks its proper seasoning. The meat that he eats must at the very most not be enough to make his breath smell of meat rather than of rice. As regards wine, no limit is laid down; but he must not be disorderly. He may not drink wine bought at a shop or eat dried meat from the market. He need not refrain from such articles of food as have ginger sprinkled over them; but he must not eat much of such dishes.

After a sacrifice in the ducal palace, the flesh must not be kept overnight. No sacrificial flesh may be kept beyond the third day. If it is kept beyond the third day, it may no longer be eaten. While it is being eaten, there must be no conversation, nor any word spoken while lying down after the repast. Any article of food, whether coarse rice, vegetables, broth or melon, that has been used as an offering must be handled with due solemnity.

He must not sit on a mat that is not straight.

When the men of his village are drinking wine he leaves the feast directly the village-elders have left. When the men of his village hold their Expulsion Rite, he puts on his Court dress and stands on the eastern steps.

When sending a messenger to enquire after someone in another country, he prostrates himself twice while speeding the messenger on his way. When K'ang-tzu sent him some medicine he prostrated himself and accepted it; but said, As I am not acquainted with its properties, I cannot venture to taste it.

When the stables were burnt down, on returning from Court, he said, Was anyone hurt? He did not ask about the horses.

When his prince sends him a present of food, he must straighten his mat and be the first to taste what has been sent. When what his prince sends is a present of uncooked meat, he must cook it and make a sacrificial offering. When his prince sends a live animal, he must rear it. When he is waiting upon his prince at meal-times, while his prince is making the sacrificial offering, he (the gentleman) tastes the dishes. If he is ill and his prince comes to see him, he has himself laid with his head to the East with his Court robes thrown over him and his sash drawn across the bed. When the prince commands his presence he goes straight to the palace without waiting for his carriage to be yoked.

On entering the Ancestral Temple, he asks about every detail.

If a friend dies and there are no relatives to fall back on, he says, "The funeral is my affair." On receiving a present from a friend, even a carriage and horses, he does not prostrate himself. He does so only in the case of sacrificial meat being sent.

In bed he avoids lying in the posture of a corpse. When at home he does not use ritual attitudes. When appearing before anyone in mourning, however well he knows him, he must put on an altered expression, and when appearing before any-one in sacrificial garb, or a blind man, even informally, he must be sure to adopt the appropriate attitude. On meeting anyone in deep mourning he must bow across the bar of his chariot; he also bows to people carrying planks. When confronted with a particularly choice dainty at a banquet, his countenance should change and he should rise to his feet. Upon hearing a sudden clap of thunder or a violent gust of wind, he must change countenance.

When mounting a carriage, he must stand facing it squarely and holding the mounting-cord. When riding he confines his gaze, does not speak rapidly or point with his hands.

(The gentleman) rises and goes at the first sign, and does not "settle till he has hovered." (A song) says:

The hen-pheasant of the hill-bridge,
Knows how to bide its time, to bide its time!
When Tzu-lu made it an offering,
It sniffed three times before it rose.

Ssu-ma Niu asked about the meaning of the term Gentleman. The Master said, The Gentleman neither grieves nor fears. Ssu-ma Niu said, So that is what is meant by being a gentleman—neither to grieve nor to fear? The Master said, On looking within himself he finds no taint; so why should he either grieve or fear?

The Master said, The gentleman calls attention to the good points in others; he does not call attention to their defects. The small man does just the reverse of this.

The Master said, The true gentleman is conciliatory but not accommodating. Common people are accommodating but not conciliatory.

The Master said, The true gentleman is easy to serve, yet difficult to please. For if you try to please him in any manner inconsistent with the Way, he refuses to be pleased; but in using the services of others he only expects of them what they are capable of performing. Common people are difficult to serve, but easy to please. Even though you try to please them in a manner inconsistent with the Way, they will still be pleased; but in using the services of others they expect them (irrespective of their capacities) to do any work that comes along.

The Master said, The gentleman is dignified, but never haughty; common people are haughty, but never dignified.

The Master said, It is possible to be a true gentleman and yet lack Goodness. But there has never yet existed a Good man who was not a gentleman.

When the Master said, He who holds no rank in a State does not discuss its policies, Master Tsêng said, "A true gentleman, even in his thoughts, never departs from what is suitable to his rank."

The Master said, A gentleman is ashamed to let his words outrun his deeds.

The Master said, The Ways of the true gentleman are three. I myself have met with success in none of them. For he that is really Good is never unhappy, he that is really wise is never perplexed, he that is really brave is never afraid. Tzu-kung said, That, Master, is your own Way!

The Master said, (A gentleman) does not grieve that people do not recognize his merits; he grieves at his own incapacities.

The Master said, The gentleman who takes the right as his material to work upon and ritual as the guide in putting what is right into practice, who is modest in setting out his projects and faithful in carrying them to their conclusion, he indeed is a true gentleman.

The Master said, A gentleman is distressed by his own lack of capacity; he is never distressed at the failure of others to recognize his merits.

The Master said, A gentleman has reason to be distressed if he ends his days without making a reputation for himself.

The Master said, "The demands that a gentleman makes are upon himself; those that a small man makes are upon others."

The Master said, A gentleman is proud, but not quarrelsome, allies himself with individuals, but not with parties.

The Master said, A gentleman does not accept men because of what they say, nor reject sayings, because the speaker is what he is.

The Master said, A gentleman, in his plans, thinks of the Way; he does not think how he is going to make a living. Even farming sometimes entails times of shortage; and even learning may incidentally lead to high pay. But a gentleman's anxieties concern the progress of the Way; he has no anxiety concerning poverty.

The Master said, It is wrong for a gentleman to have knowledge of menial matters and proper that he should be entrusted with great responsibilities. It is wrong for a small man to be entrusted with great responsibilities, but proper that he should have a knowledge of menial matters

The Master said, from a gentleman consistency is expected, but not blind fidelity.

Master K'ung said, There are three things against which a gentleman is on his guard. In his youth, before his blood and vital humours have settled down, he is on his guard against lust. Having reached his prime, when the blood and vital humours have finally hardened, he is on his guard against strife. Having reached old age, when the blood and vital humours are already decaying, he is on his guard against avarice.

Master K'ung said, There are three things that a gentleman fears: he fears the will of Heaven, he fears great men, he fears the words of the Divine Sages. The small man does not know the will of Heaven and so does not fear it. He treats great men with contempt, and scoffs at the words of the Divine Sages.

Master K'ung said, The gentleman has nine cares. In seeing he is careful to see clearly, in hearing he is careful to hear distinctly, in his looks he is careful to be kindly; in his manner to be respectful, in his words to be loyal, in his work to be diligent. When in doubt he is careful to ask for information; when angry he has a care for the consequences, and when he sees a chance of gain, he thinks carefully whether the pursuit of it would be consonant with the Right.

The Master said, He who does not understand the will of Heaven cannot be regarded as a gentleman. He who does not know the rites cannot take his stand. He who does not understand words, cannot understand people.

STUDY QUESTIONS

1. What were the proper goals of life according to Confucius?
2. What was the Confucian definition of a gentleman? Why did Confucianism place so much emphasis on manners and ceremony?
3. Did Confucius judge human nature to be good or bad? What was his attitude toward human emotions?
4. What social structure did Confucianism imply? What were the key social classes, and how did they differ?
5. In what ways was Confucianism not a religion?
6. Why did Confucianism have such a deep impact on Chinese and East Asian history? What groups and institutions could benefit from it?

6

Legalism: An Alternative System

A student of the Confucian Xun Zi, Han Fei-Tzu (d. 233 B.C.E.) was the principal the-oretician of Legalism, a school of philosophy adopted by the Ch'in after unifying China in 256 B.C.E. This former Confucian adopted the pragmatic view that the Chinese, perceived as antisocial and inherently evil, must be firmly controlled by an authoritative central government through strictly applied punitive laws. This harsh but effective solution for resolving the chaotic conditions that plagued the Zhou dynasty included the introduction of new managerial techniques, an improved bureaucracy, enhanced communications, land reforms, and standardization of weights, measures, and coinage. Han Fei-Tzu, who served as an official for the powerful but short-lived Ch'in dynasty (that gave China its name), died from poison at the hands of Li Ssu, a jealous Legalist rival. Han Fei-Tzu wrote 20 books and was honored by the grand historian, Ssu-ma Ch'ien, with a biographical sketch.

How did Legalism differ from Confucianism in its view of human nature and the proper organization of the state? Officially, Legalism died with the demise of the Ch'in and the renewed interest in Confucian values. In fact, though, the Chinese state continued to combine Confucian ideals with the harsher policelike approach urged by Legalists—so this division of political approach was of more than passing importance. Both Legalism and Confucianism, somewhat ironically, promoted a strong state.

If orders are made trim, laws never deviate; if laws are equable, there will be no culprit among the officials. Once the law is fixed, nobody can damage it by means of virtuous words. If men of merit are appointed to office, the people will have little to say; if men of virtue are appointed to office the people will have much to talk about. The enforcement of laws depends upon the method of judicial administration. Who administers judicial affairs with ease . . . attains supremacy. . . . Whoever procrastinates in creating order, will see his state dismembered.

Govern by penalties; wage war by rewards; and enlarge the bounties so as to put the principles of statecraft into practice. If so, there will be no wicked people in

From Han Fei-Tzu, *The Complete Works*, 2 vols., translated by W. K. Liao (London: Arthur Probsthain, 1959), Vol. II, pp. 322–333. Copyright © 1959 by Arthur Probsthain. Reprinted by permission.

the state nor will there by any wicked trade at the market. If things are many and trifles are numerous, and if farming is relaxed and villainy prevails, the state will certainly be dismembered.

If the people have a surplus of food, make them receive rank by giving grain to the state. If only through their own effort they can receive rank, then farmers will not idle.

If a tube three inches long has no bottom, it can never be filled. Conferring office and rank or granting profit and bounty without reference to merit, is like a tube having no bottom.

If the state confers office and bestows rank, it can be said to devise plans with complete wisdom and wage war with complete courage. Such a state will find a rival. Again, if the state confers office and bestows rank according to merit, then rules will be simplified and opponents barred; this can be said to abolish government by means of government, abolish words by means of words, and bestow rank according to merit. Therefore the state will have much strength and none else in All-under-Heaven will dare to invade it. When its soldiers march out, they will take the objective and, having taken it, will certainly be able to hold it. When it keeps its soldiers in reserve and does not attack, it will certainly become rich.

The affairs of the government, however small, should never be abandoned. For instance, office and rank are always obtained according to the acquired merit; though there may be flattering words, it will be impossible thereby to make any interference in the state affairs. This is said to be "government by figures." For instance, in attacking with force, ten points are taken for every point given out; but in attacking with words, one hundred are lost for every one marched out. If a state is fond of force, it is called hard to attack; if a state is fond of words, it is called easy to attack.

If the ability of the official is equal to his post, if his duty is lightened and he never reserves any surplus energy in mind, and if he does not shift any responsibility of additional offices back to the ruler, then there will be no hidden grudge inside. If the intelligent ruler makes the state affairs never mutually interfere, there will be no dispute; if he allows no official to hold any kind of additional post, everybody will develop his talent or skill; and if he allows no two persons to share the same meritorious achievement, there will be no quarrel.

If penalties are heavy and rewards are few, it means that the superior loves the people, wherefore the people will die for rewards. If rewards are many and penalties are light, it means that the superior does not love the people, wherefore the people will never die for rewards.

If the profit issues from one outlet only, the state will have no rival; if it issues from two outlets, its soldiers will be half useful; and if the profit comes from ten outlets, the people will not observe the law. If heavy penalties are clear and if the people are always well disciplined and then if men are engaged in case of emergency, the superior will have all the advantage.

In inflicting penalties light offences should be punished severely; if light offences do not appear, heavy offences will not come. This is said to abolish penalties by means of penalties. And the state will certainly become strong. If crimes are serious but penalties are light, light penalties breed further troubles. This is said to create penalties through penalties, and such a state will infallibly be dismembered.

The sage in governing the people considers their springs of action, never tolerates their wicked desires, but seeks only for the people's benefit. Therefore, the penalty he inflicts is not due to any hatred for the people but to his motive of loving the people. If penalty triumphs, the people are quiet; if reward overflows, culprits appear. Therefore the triumph of penalty is the beginning of order; the overflow of reward, the origin of chaos.

Indeed, it is the people's nature to delight in disorder and detach themselves from legal restraints. Therefore, when the intelligent sovereign governs the state, if he makes rewards clear, the people will be encouraged to render meritorious services; if he makes penalties severe, the people will attach themselves to the law. If they are encouraged to render meritorious services, public affairs will not be obstructed; if they attach themselves to the law, culprits will not appear. Therefore, he who governs the people should nip the evil in the bud; he who commands troops, should inculcate warfare in the people's mind. If prohibitions can uproot causes of villainy, there will always be order; if soldiers can imagine warfare in mind, there will always be victory. When the sage is governing the people, he attains order first, wherefore he is strong; he prepares for war first, wherefore he wins.

Indeed, the administration of the state affairs requires the attention to the causes of human action so as to unify the people's mental trends; the exclusive elevation of public welfare so as to stop self-seeking elements; the reward for denunciation of crime so as to suppress culprits; and finally the clarification of laws so as to facilitate governmental procedures. Whoever is able to apply these four measures, will become strong; whoever is unable to apply these four measures, will become weak. Indeed, the strength of the state is due to the administration of its political affairs; the honour of the sovereign is due to his supreme power. Now, the enlightened ruler possesses the supreme power and the administrative organs; the ignoble ruler possesses both the supreme power and the administrative organs, too. Yet the results are not the same, because their standpoints are different. Thus, as the enlightened ruler has the supreme power in his grip, the superior is held in high esteem; as he unifies the administrative organs, the state is in order. Hence law is the origin of supremacy and penalty is the beginning of love.

Indeed, it is the people's nature to abhor toil and enjoy ease. However, if they pursue ease, the land will waste; if the land wastes, the state will not be in order. If the state is not orderly, it will become chaotic. If reward and penalty take no effect among the inferiors, government will come to a deadlock. Therefore, he who wants to accomplish a great achievement but hesitates to apply his full strength, can not hope for the accomplishment of the achievement; he who wants to settle the people's disorder but hesitates to change their traditions, can not hope to banish the people's disorder. Hence there is no constant method for the government of men. The law alone leads to political order. If laws are adjusted to the time, there is good government. If government fits the age, there will be great accomplishment. Therefore, when the people are naive, if you regulate them with fame, there will be good government; when everybody in the world is intelligent, if you discipline them with penalties, they will obey. While time is moving on, if laws do not shift accordingly, there will be misrule; while abilities are diverse, if prohibitions are not changed, the state will be dismembered. Therefore, the sage in governing the people makes laws move with time and prohibitions change with abilities. Who can exert his forces to land-utilization, will become rich; who can rush his forces at enemies, will become strong. The strong man not obstructed in his way will attain supremacy.

Therefore, the way to supremacy lies in the way of shutting culprits off and the way of blocking up wicked men. Who is able to block up wicked men, will eventually attain supremacy. The policy of attaining supremacy relies not on foreign states' abstention from disturbing your state, but on their inability to disturb your state. Who has to rely on foreign powers' abstention from disturbing his state before he can maintain his own independence, will see his state dismembered; who relies on their inability to disturb his state and willingly enacts the law, will prosper.

Therefore, the worthy ruler in governing the state follows the statecraft of invulnerability. When rank is esteemed, the superior will increase his dignity. He will accordingly bestow rewards on men of merit, confer ranks upon holders of posts, and appoint wicked men to no office. Who devotes himself to practical forces, gets a high rank. If the rank is esteemed, the superior will be honoured. The superior, if honoured, will attain supremacy. On the contrary, if the state does not strive after practical forces but counts on private studies, its rank will be lowered. If the rank is lowered, the superior will be humbled. If the superior is humbled, the state will be dismembered. Therefore, if the way of founding the state and using the people can shut off foreign invaders and block up self-seeking subjects, and if the superior relies on himself, supremacy will be attained. . . .

In general, wherever the state is extensive and the ruler is honourable, there laws are so strict that whatever is ordered works and whatever is prohibited stops. Therefore, the ruler of men who distinguishes between ranks and regulates bounties, makes laws severe and thereby makes the distinction strict.

Indeed, if the state is orderly, the people are safe; if affairs are confused, the country falls into peril. Who makes laws strict, hits on the true nature of mankind; who makes prohibitions lenient, misses the apparent fact. Moreover, everybody is, indeed, gifted with desperate courage. To exert desperate courage to get what one wants, is human nature. Yet everybody's likes and dislikes should be regulated by the superior. Now the people like to have profit and bounty and hate to be punished; if the superior catches their likes and dislikes and thereby holds their desperate courage under control, he will not miss the realities of affairs.

However, if prohibitions are lenient and facts are missed, reward and penalty will be misused. Again, when governing the people, if you do not regard conformity to law as right, you will eventually observe no law. Therefore, the science and philosophy of politics should by all means emphasize the distinction between degrees of penalty and of reward.

Who governs the state, should always uphold the law. In life there are ups and downs. If any ruler goes down, it is because in regulating rewards and penalties he makes no distinction between different degrees. Who governs the state, always distinguishes between reward and punishment. Therefore, some people might regard the distinction between reward and punishment as distinction, which should not be called distinction in the strict sense.

As regards the distinction made by the clear-sighted ruler, it is the distinction between different grades of reward and of punishment. Therefore, his subjects respect laws and fear prohibitions. They try to avoid crime rather than dare to expect any reward. Hence the saying: "Without expecting penalty and reward the people attend to public affairs."

For this reason, the state at the height of order is able to take the suppression of villainy for its duty. Why? Because its law comprehends human nature and accords with the principles of government.

If so, how to get rid of delicate villainy? By making the people watch one another in their hidden affairs. Then how to make them watch one another? By implicating the people of the same hamlet in one another's crime. When everyone knows that the penalty or reward will directly affect him, if the people of the same hamlet fail to watch one another, they will fear they may not be able to escape the implication, and those who are evil-minded, will not be allowed to forget so many people watching them. Were such the law, everybody would mind his own doings, watch everybody else, and disclose the secrets of any culprit. For, whosoever denounces a criminal offence, is not held guilty but is given a reward; whosoever misses any culprit, is definitely censured and given the same penalty as the culprit. Were such the law, all types of culprits would be detected. If the minutest villainy is not tolerated, it is due to the system of personal denunciation and mutual implication.

Indeed, the most enlightened method of governing a state is to trust measures and not men. For this reason, the tactful state is never mistaken if it does not trust the empty fame of men. If the land within the boundary is always in order it is because measures are employed. If any falling state lets foreign soldiers walk all over its territory and can neither resist nor prevent them, it is because that state trusts men and uses no measures. Men may jeopardize their own country, but measures can invade others' countries. Therefore, the tactful state spurns words and trusts laws.

Broadly speaking, it is hard to uncover a crooked merit that appears to fulfil the promise; it is hard to disclose the feature of the fault that is ornamented with beautiful words. Therefore, penalty and reward are often misled by double-dealers. What is alleged to be fulfilling the promise but is hard to uncover, is a villainous merit. Any minister's fault is hard to disclose, because its motive is missed. However, if by following reason you can not disclose the false merit and by analyzing feelings you are still deceived by the villainous motive, then can both reward and punishment have no mistake respectively?

For such reasons, false scholars establish names inside, while itinerants devise plans outside, till the stupid and the coward mix themselves with the brave and the clever. Inasmuch as the false path is customary, they are tolerated by their age. Therefore, their law does not work and their penalty affects nobody. If so, both reward and penalty have to be double-dealings.

Therefore, concrete facts have their limits of extension, but abstract principles involve no accurate measures. The absence of such measures is due not to the law but to the abandonment of law and the dependence on cleverness. If the law is abandoned and cleverness is employed, how can the appointee to office perform his duty? If duty and office are not equivalent to each other, then how can the law evade mistakes and how can penalty evade troubles? For this reason reward and punishment will be thrown into confusion and disorder, and the state policy will deviate and err, because neither penalty nor reward has any clear distinction of degree as in the difference between black and white.

STUDY QUESTIONS

1. What was the purpose of government, according to the Legalists? How did these views compare with Confucianism?
2. Did Legalists judge human nature to be good or bad?
3. Could Confucianists and Legalists agree on any major points? How might their views and recommendations be combined?
4. Can Legalism and Confucianism be explained by the different political contexts in which they arose?
5. Why was Legalism ultimately less successful than Confucianism in East Asian history?

7

Daoism

Along with Confucianism, the religious philosophy of Daoism was a product of the chaotic period of the later Zhou dynasty. It, took, too deep roots in Chinese culture. It, too, probably reflected earlier Chinese beliefs including the references to a balanced Tao, or "Way," to which the religion gave a particular definition. Daoism attracted many in the upper classes, who found its spirituality appealing; later, particularly as it additionally embraced beliefs in magical healing, it spread widely to the peasantry. After Buddhism began to reach China in the later Han dynasty, Daoists responded by more vigorous proselytizing efforts. Confucian officials recurrently attacked Daoism, but they never tried to proscribe it as they ultimately did with Buddhism, for although Daoism had different goals most Daoist leaders professed obedience to the emperor, which made the religion seem safe. Unlike most major religions, however, and unlike Confucianism itself, Daoism never spread significantly beyond its culture of origins, even to other parts of East Asia.

Daoism was attributed to Lao-zi, who probably lived in the fifth century B.C.E.—though his actual existence cannot be confirmed. Daoism stressed the divine impulse that directs all life, while urging a set of habits that would bring peace and harmony. The following passage is from the principal Daoist work, the *Tao Te Ching*, attributed to Lao-zi but which was probably compiled by Chuang Tzu in the fourth or third centuries B.C.E.

Assessing Daoist principles obviously invites comparison both with Confucianism (and Legalism) and with other major religions such as Hinduism and Buddhism. How could such a different set of ideas coexist with Chinese political philosophies without creating cultural disruption? How could some individuals be Confucianist and Daoist at the same time?

The tao that can be told
is not the eternal Tao.
The name that can be named
is not the eternal Name.

The unnamable is the eternally real.
Naming is the origin
of all particular things.

From *Tae Te Ching*, by Lao Tzu, *A New English Version with Forward and Notes* by Stephen Mitchell. Translation copyright © 1988 by Stephen Mitchell (New York: HarperCollins Publishers, Inc., 1988), pp. 1–4, 6–7, 20, 24, 30–31, 56–57. Reprinted by permission of HarperCollins, Inc..

Free from desire, you realize the mystery.
Caught in desire, you see only the manifestations.

Yet mystery and manifestations
arise from the same source.
This source is called darkness.

Darkness within darkness.
The gateway to all understanding.

When people see some things as beautiful,
other things become ugly.
When people see some things as good,
other things become bad.

Being and non-being create each other.
Difficult and easy support each other.
Long and short define each other.
High and low depend on each other.
Before and after follow each other.

Therefore the Master
acts without doing anything
and teaches without saying anything.
Things arise and she lets them come;
things disappear and she lets them go.
She has but doesn't possess,
acts but doesn't expect.
When her work is done, she forgets it.
That is why it lasts forever.

If you overesteem great men,
people become powerless.
If you overvalue possessions,
people begin to steal.

The Master leads
by emptying people's minds
and filling their cores,
by weakening their ambition
and toughening their resolve.
He helps people lose everything
they know, everything they desire,
and creates confusion
in those who think that they know.

Practice not-doing,
and everything will fall into place.

The Tao is like a well:
used but never used up.

It is like the eternal void:
filled with infinite possibilities.

It is hidden but always present.
I don't know who gave birth to it.
It is older than God. . . .

The Tao is called the Great Mother:
empty yet inexhaustible,
it gives birth to infinite worlds.

It is always present within you.
You can use it any way you want.

The Tao is infinite, eternal.
Why is it eternal?
It was never born;
thus it can never die.
Why is it infinite?
It has no desires for itself;
thus it is present for all beings.

The Master stays behind;
that is why she is ahead.
She is detached from all things;
that is why she is one with them.
Because she has let go of herself,
she is perfectly fulfilled. . . .

Stop thinking, and end your problems.
What difference between yes and no?
What difference between success and failure?
Must you value what others value,
avoid what others avoid?
How ridiculous!

Other people are excited,
as though they were at a parade.
I alone don't care,
I alone am expressionless,
like an infant before it can smile. . . .

If you want to accord with the Tao,
just do your job, then let go. . . .

Whoever relies on the Tao in governing men
doesn't try to force issues
or defeat enemies by force of arms.
For every force there is a counterforce.
Violence, even well intentioned,
always rebounds upon oneself.

The Master does his job
and then stops.
He understands that the universe
is forever out of control,
and that trying to dominate events
goes against the current of the Tao.
Because he believes in himself,
he doesn't try to convince others.
Because he is content with himself,
he doesn't need others' approval.
Because he accepts himself,
the whole world accepts him.
Weapons are the tools of violence;
all decent men detest them.

Weapons are the tools of fear;
a decent man will avoid them
except in the direst necessity
and, if compelled, will use them
only with the utmost restraint.
Peace is his highest value.
If the peace has been shattered,
how can he be content?
His enemies are not demons,
but human beings like himself.
He doesn't wish them personal harm.
Nor does he rejoice in victory.
How could he rejoice in victory
and delight in the slaughter of men?

He enters a battle gravely,
with sorrow and with great compassion,
as if he were attending a funeral. . . .

Those who know don't talk.
Those who talk don't know.

Close your mouth,
block off your senses,
blunt your sharpness,
untie your knots,
soften your glare,
settle your dust.
This is the primal identity.

Be like the Tao.
It can't be approached or withdrawn from,
benefited or harmed,
honored or brought into disgrace.

It gives itself up continually.
That is why it endures.
If you want to be a great leader,
you must learn to follow the Tao.
Stop trying to control.
Let go of fixed plans and concepts,
and the world will govern itself.

The more prohibitions you have,
the less virtuous people will be.
The more weapons you have,
the less secure people will be.
The more subsidies you have,
the less self-reliant people will be.

Therefore the Master says:
I let go of the law,
and people become honest.
I let go of economics,
and people become prosperous.
I let go of religion,
and people become serene.
I let go of all desire for the common good,
and the good becomes common as grass.

STUDY QUESTIONS

1. How is the Tao defined? How does it compare with a god or gods in other religions?
2. What kind of life should a Daoist lead, and why?
3. What might a Confucianist and a Daoist agree about? Where would they disagree? How would the two belief systems react to military activity?
4. Does the passage help explain why Daoism did not spread widely outside China?
5. How might Daoism affect other aspects of Chinese culture, such as artistic styles? Or science and medicine?

8

Women in Classical China: Pan Chao

Pan Chao (ca. 45–120 C.E.), China's "foremost woman scholar," served unofficially as imperial historian to Emperor Ho (89–105 C.E.) while acting as an instructor in history, classical writing, astronomy, and mathematics to the Empress Teng and her ladies-in-waiting. Summoned to complete the historical books (*Han Shu*) of her deceased brother, Ku, the scholarly and talented widow is the only woman in China to have served in that capacity. Her success in overcoming contemporary restraints on women was due to an exceptional education, which she attributed to her scholarly parents. As a historian, moralist, and royal servant, Pan Chao wrote numerous literary works, including narrative poems, commemorative verses, eulogies, and her famous *Lessons for Women.* This brief educational treatise, written expressly for women and the first of its kind in world history, offers interesting insights into the Chinese perceptions of the ideal woman as well as first-century Chinese customs. It contains advice in matters of customs and manners for girls in her family so that they might not "humiliate both your ancestors and your clan."

Pan Chao's manual was the most successful and durable advice book for women in Chinese history, helping to support a firmly patriarchal gender system. The book was reprinted and widely used through the nineteenth century.

How does Pan Chao define womanhood and women's roles? How do these definitions relate to other aspects of Chinese society such as Confucianism?

Introduction

I, the unworthy writer, am unsophisticated, unenlightened, and by nature unintelligent, but I am fortunate both to have received not a little favor from my scholarly father, and to have had a (cultured) mother and instructresses upon whom to rely for a literary education as well as for training in good manners. More than forty years have passed since at the age of fourteen I took up the dustpan and the broom in the Ts'ao family. During this time with trembling heart I feared constantly that I might disgrace my parents, and that I might multiply difficulties for both the women and the men (of my husband's family). Day and night I was distressed in heart, (but) I labored without confessing weariness. Now and hereafter, however, I know how to escape (from such fears).

From Nancy Lee Swann, Pan Chao, "Lessons for Women," in *Pan Chao: Foremost Woman Scholar of China* (New York: The Century Co., 1932), pp. 82–87. Reprint permission granted by the American Historical Association.

曹大家班惠班昭

惠班名昭一名姬博學高才逮曹世叔兄固著漢書未及竟而卒和帝詔昭踵而成之數召入宮令皇后諸貴人師事馬號曰大家

Portrait of Pan Chao, by Jim Guliang. Early Qing Dynasty, woodcut published around 1690. This image is obviously the artist's invention. *What does it suggest about the ongoing image of Pan Chao? How does the image relate to Pan Chao's own ideas about women?* (Wan-go Weng Inc., NY.)

Being careless, and by nature stupid, I taught and trained (my children) without system. Consequently I fear that my son Ku may bring disgrace upon the Imperial Dynasty by whose Holy Grace he has unprecedentedly received the extraordinary privilege of wearing the Gold and the Purple, a privilege for the attainment of which (by my son, I) a humble subject never even hoped. Nevertheless, now that he is a man and able to plan his own life, I need not again have concern for him. But I do grieve that you, my daughters, just now at the age for marriage, have not at this time had gradual training and advice; that you still have not learned the proper customs for married women. I fear that by failure in good manners in other families you will humiliate both your ancestors and your clan. I am now seriously ill, life is uncertain. As I have thought of you all in so untrained a state, I have been uneasy many a time for you. At hours of leisure I have composed in seven chapters these instructions under the title, "Lessons for Women." In order that you may have something wherewith to benefit your persons, I wish every one of you, my daughters, each to write out a copy for yourself.

From this time on every one of you strive to practise these (lessons).

Chapter I: Humility

On the third day after the birth of a girl the ancients observed three customs: (first) to place the baby below the bed; (second) to give her a potsherd with which to play; and (third) to announce her birth to her ancestors by an offering. Now to lay the baby below the bed plainly indicated that she is lowly and weak, and should regard it as her primary duty to humble herself before others. To give her potsherds with which to play indubitably signified that she should practise labor and consider it her primary duty to be industrious. To announce her birth before her ancestors clearly meant that she ought to esteem as her primary duty the continuation of the observance of worship in the home.

These three ancient customs epitomize a woman's ordinary way of life and the teachings of the traditional ceremonial rites and regulations. Let a woman modestly yield to others; let her respect others; let her put others first, herself last. Should she do something good, let her not mention it; should she do something bad, let her not deny it. Let her bear disgrace; let her even endure when others speak or do evil to her. Always let her seem to tremble and to fear. (When a woman follows such maxims as these,) then she may be said to humble herself before others.

Let a woman retire late to bed, but rise early to duties; let her not dread tasks by day or by night. Let her not refuse to perform domestic duties whether easy or difficult. That which must be done, let her finish completely, tidily, and systematically. (When a woman follows such rules as these,) then she may be said to be industrious.

Let a woman be correct in manner and upright in character in order to serve her husband. Let her live in purity and quietness (of spirit), and attend to her own affairs. Let her love not gossip and silly laughter. Let her cleanse and purify and arrange in order the wine and the food for the offerings to the ancestors. (When a woman observes such principles as these,) then she may be said to continue ancestral worship.

No woman who observes these three (fundamentals of life) has ever had a bad reputation or has fallen into disgrace. If a woman fail to observe them, how can her name be honored; how can she but bring disgrace upon herself?

Chapter II: Husband and Wife

The Way of husband and wife is intimately connected with *Yin* and *Yang*, and relates the individual to gods and ancestors. Truly it is the great principle of Heaven and Earth, and the great basis of human relationships. Therefore the "Rites" honor union of man and woman; and in the "Book of Poetry" the "First Ode" manifests the principle of marriage. For these reasons the relationship cannot but be an important one.

If a husband be unworthy then he possesses nothing by which to control his wife. If a wife be unworthy, then she possesses nothing with which to serve her husband. If a husband does not control his wife, then the rules of conduct manifesting his authority are abandoned and broken. If a wife does not serve her husband, then the proper relationship (between men and women) and the natural order of things are neglected and destroyed. As a matter of fact the purpose of these two (the controlling of women by men, and the serving of men by women) is the same.

Now examine the gentlemen of the present age. They only know that wives must be controlled, and that the husband's rules of conduct manifesting his authority must be established. They therefore teach their boys to read books and (study) histories. But they do not in the least understand that husbands and masters must (also) be served, and that the proper relationship and the rites should be maintained.

Yet only to teach men and not to teach women,—is that not ignoring the essential relation between them? According to the "Rites," it is the rule to begin to teach children to read at the age of eight years, and by the age of fifteen years they ought then to be ready for cultural training. Only why should it not be (that girls' education as well as boys' be) according to this principle?

Chapter III: Respect and Caution

As *Yin* and *Yang* are not of the same nature, so man and woman have different characteristics. The distinctive quality of the *Yang* is rigidity; the function of the *Yin* is yielding. Man is honored for strength; a woman is beautiful on account of her gentleness. Hence there arose the common saying: "A man though born like a wolf may, it is feared, become a weak monstrosity; a woman though born like a mouse may, it is feared, become a tiger."

Now for self-culture nothing equals respect for others. To counteract firmness nothing equals compliance. Consequently it can be said that the Way of respect and acquiescence is woman's most important principle of conduct. So respect may be defined as nothing other than holding on to that which is permanent; and acquiescence nothing other than being liberal and generous. Those who are steadfast in devotion know that they should stay in their proper places; those who are liberal and generous esteem others, and honor and serve (them).

If husband and wife have the habit of staying together, never leaving one another, and following each other around within the limited space of their own rooms, then they will lust after and take liberties with one another. From such action improper language will arise between the two. This kind of discussion may lead to licentiousness. Out of licentiousness will be born a heart of disrespect to the husband. Such a result comes from not knowing that one should stay in one's proper place.

Furthermore, affairs may be either crooked or straight; words may be either right or wrong. Straightforwardness cannot but lead to quarreling; crookedness cannot but lead to accusation. If there are really accusations and quarrels, then undoubtedly there will be angry affairs. Such a result comes from not esteeming others, and not honoring and serving (them).

(If wives) suppress not contempt for husbands, then it follows (that such wives) rebuke and scold (their husbands). (If husbands) stop not short of anger, then they are certain to beat (their wives). The correct relationship between husband and wife is based upon harmony and intimacy, and (conjugal) love is grounded in proper union. Should actual blows be dealt, how could matrimonial relationship be preserved? Should sharp words be spoken, how could (conjugal) love exist? If love and proper relationship both be destroyed, then husband and wife are divided.

Chapter IV: Womanly Qualifications

A woman (ought to) have four qualifications: (1) womanly virtue; (2) womanly words; (3) womanly bearing; and (4) womanly work. Now what is called womanly virtue need not be brilliant ability, exceptionally different from others. Womanly words need be neither clever in debate nor keen in conversation. Womanly appearance requires neither a pretty nor a perfect face and form. Womanly work need not be work done more skilfully than that of others.

To guard carefully her chastity; to control circumspectly her behavior; in every motion to exhibit modesty; and to model each act on the best usage, this is womanly virtue.

To choose her words with care; to avoid vulgar language; to speak at appropriate times; and not to weary others (with much conversation), may be called the characteristics of womanly words.

To wash and scrub filth away; to keep clothes and ornaments fresh and clean; to wash the head and bathe the body regularly, and to keep the person free from disgraceful filth, may be called the characteristics of womanly bearing.

With whole-hearted devotion to sew and to weave; to love not gossip and silly laughter; in cleanliness and order (to prepare) the wine and food for serving guests, may be called the characteristics of womanly work.

These four qualifications characterize the greatest virtue of a woman. No woman can afford to be without them. In fact they are very easy to possess if a woman only treasure them in her heart. The ancients had a saying: "Is Love afar off? If I desire love, then love is at hand!" So can it be said of these qualifications.

Chapter V: Whole-Hearted Devotion

Now in the "Rites" is written the principle that a husband may marry again, but there is no Canon that authorizes a woman to be married the second time. Therefore it is said of husbands as of Heaven, that as certainly as people cannot run away from Heaven, so surely a wife cannot leave (a husband's home).

If people in action or character disobey the spirits of Heaven and of Earth, then Heaven punishes them. Likewise if a woman errs in the rites and in the proper mode of conduct, then her husband esteems her lightly. The ancient book, "A Pattern for Women," . . . says: "To obtain the love of one man is the crown of a woman's life; to lose the love of one man is to miss the aim in woman's life." For these reasons a woman cannot but seek to win her husband's heart. Nevertheless, the beseeching wife need not use flattery, coaxing words, and cheap methods to gain intimacy.

Decidedly nothing is better (to gain the heart of a husband) than whole-hearted devotion and correct manners. In accordance with the rites and the proper mode of conduct, (let a woman) live a pure life. Let her have ears that hear not licentiousness; and eyes that see not depravity. When she goes outside her own home, let her not be conspicuous in dress and manners. When at home let her not neglect her dress. Women should not assemble in groups, nor gather together (for gossip and silly laughter). They should not stand watching in the gateways. (If a woman follows) these rules, she may be said to have whole-hearted devotion and correct manners.

If, in all her actions, she is frivolous, she sees and hears (only) that which pleases herself. At home her hair is dishevelled, and her dress is slovenly. Outside the home she emphasizes her femininity to attract attention; she says what ought not to be said; and she looks at what ought not to be seen. (If a woman does such as) these, (she may be) said to be without whole-hearted devotion and correct manners.

STUDY QUESTIONS

1. According to Pan Chao, what were women's roles and purposes? How did Pan Chao's approach fit the definition of patriarchalism?
2. What was Confucian about Pan Chao's approach?
3. How good is this source as a means of determining women's situation in classical China? What social classes would this advice best describe, and why?
4. What was the relationship between these recommendations and Pan Chao's own life?
5. How could women use Pan Chao's ideas to some advantage, in winning certain protections and benefits within a patriarchal system?

9

"To Fight in a Righteous War": *Varna* and Moral Duty in India

Historians think that the caste system in India emerged gradually during the thousand years prior to the beginning of the Common Era. An Indo-European speaking people, the Aryans, who may have come from the grasslands north of the Caspian Sea, took the lead in creating a four-part division of social classes called *varnas* (a Sanskrit word meaning "color").

The new social system was strongly hierarchical. Priests (*brahmans*) ranked the highest and warriors (*kshatriyas*) came next. Merchants, artisans, and peasants (*vaishyas*) ranked third. The fourth *varna* was composed of the servants (*sudras*) of the three higher groups. A fifth category, made up of all those who were engaged in occupations defined as "unclean," stood outside the system of *varnas;* these people were known as "untouchables." (When the Portuguese arrived in India around 1500 C.E. they translated *varna* as "caste"; the "caste system" is thus a later European term for describing Indian social realities.)

The *brahmans* taught that each *varna* had its own sacred or moral duty (*dharma*) to perform. The example that we will consider in this chapter is that of the warriors; their sacred duty was to fight. A vivid illustration of the *dharma* of the warriors can be found in the most famous literary text from early India, the *Bhagavad Gita (Song of God)*. The *Bhagavad Gita* is a portion of a much longer Indian classic, the *Mahabharata,* the epic tale of a war between two branches of the same family in the distant past. In its present form the *Bhagavad Gita* dates from the second century B.C.E.

From *The Bhagavad Gita*, translated by Juan Mascaro (Baltimore, Md.: Penguin Books, 1962), pp. 45–51. Copyright © 1962 by Juan Mascaro. Reproduced by permission of Penguin Books Ltd.

The central theme of the *Bhagavad Gita* is the dialogue between the warrior Arjuna, who is on the eve of a great battle, and his chariot driver Krishna, who is actually the Hindu god Vishnu. The following passages capture the essence of the conversation between Arjuna and Krishna.

CHAPTER 1

. . .

Arjuna

21   Drive my chariot, Krishna immortal, and place it between the
      two armies.

22   That I may see those warriors who stand there eager for battle,
      with whom I must now fight at the beginning of this war.

23   That I may see those who have come here eager and ready to
      fight, in their desire to do the will of the evil son of Dhrita-rashtra.

Sanjaya

24   When Krishna heard the words of Arjuna he drove their
      glorious chariot and placed it between the two armies.

25   And facing Bhishma and Drona and other royal rulers he said:
      "See, Arjuna, the armies of the Kurus, gathered here on this
      field of battle."

26   Then Arjuna saw in both armies fathers, grandfathers, sons,

27   grandsons; fathers of wives, uncles, masters;

28   brothers, companions and friends.
      When Arjuna thus saw his kinsmen face to face in both lines of
      battle, he was overcome by grief and despair and thus he
      spoke with a sinking heart.

Arjuna

      When I see all my kinsmen, Krishna, who have come here on
      this field of battle,

29   Life goes from my limbs and they sink, and my mouth is sear
      and dry; a trembling overcomes my body, and my hair
      shudders in horror;

30   My great bow Gandiva falls from my hands, and the skin of my
      flesh is burning; I am no longer able to stand, because my mind
      is whirling and wandering.

31   And I see forebodings of evil, Krishna. I cannot foresee any
      glory if I kill my own kinsmen in the sacrifice of battle.

32 Because I have no wish for victory, Krishna, nor for a kingdom,
nor for its pleasures. How can we want a kingdom, Govinda,
or its pleasures or even life,

33 When those for whom we want a kingdom, and its pleasures,
and the joys of life, are here in this field of battle about to give
up their wealth and their life?

34 Facing us in the field of battle are teachers, fathers and sons;
grandsons, grandfathers, wives' brothers; mothers' brothers
and fathers of wives.

35 These I do not wish to slay, even if I myself am slain. Not even
for the kingdom of the three worlds: how much less for a
kingdom of the earth!

36 If we kill these evil men, evil shall fall upon us: what joy in
their death could we have, O Janardana, mover of souls?

37 I cannot therefore kill my own kinsmen, the sons of king
Dhrita-rashtra, the brother of my own father. What happiness
could we ever enjoy, if we killed our own kinsmen in battle?

38 Even if they, with minds overcome by greed, see no evil in the
destruction of a family, see no sin in the treachery to friends;

39 Shall we not, who see the evil of destruction, shall we not
refrain from this terrible deed?

40 The destruction of a family destroys its rituals of righteousness,
and when the righteous rituals are no more, unrighteousness
overcomes the whole family.

41 When unrighteous disorder prevails, the women sin and are
impure; and when women are not pure, Krishna, there is
disorder of castes, social confusion.

42 This disorder carries down to hell the family and the
destroyers of the family. The spirits of their dead suffer in
pain when deprived of the ritual offerings.

43 Those evil deeds of the destroyers of a family, which cause
this social disorder, destroy the righteousness of birth and the
ancestral rituals of righteousness.

44 And have we not heard that hell is waiting for those whose
familiar rituals of righteousness are no more?

45 O day of darkness! What evil spirit moved our minds when for
the sake of an earthly kingdom we came to this field of battle
ready to kill our own people?

46 Better for me indeed if the sons of Dhrita-rashtra, with arms in
hand, found me unarmed, unresisting, and killed me in the
struggle of war.

Sanjaya

47 Thus spoke Arjuna in the field of battle, and letting fall his bow
and arrows he sank down in his chariot, his soul overcome by
despair and grief.

CHAPTER 2

Sanjaya

1 Then arose the Spirit of Krishna and spoke to Arjuna, his
   friend, who with eyes filled with tears, thus had sunk into
   despair and grief.

Krishna

2 Whence this lifeless dejection, Arjuna, in this hour, the hour of
   trial? Strong men know not despair, Arjuna, for this wins
   neither heaven nor earth.

3 Fall not into degrading weakness, for this becomes not a man
   who is a man. Throw off this ignoble discouragement, and arise
   like a fire that burns all before it.

Arjuna

4 I owe veneration to Bhishma and Drona. Shall I kill with my
   arrows my grandfather's brother, great Bhishma? Shall my
   arrows in battle slay Drona, my teacher?

5 Shall I kill my own masters who, though greedy of my
   kingdom, are yet my sacred teachers? I would rather eat in
   this life the food of a beggar than eat royal food tasting of
   their blood.

6 And we know not whether their victory or ours be better for
   us. The sons of my uncle and king, Dhrita-rashtra, are here
   before us: after their death, should we wish to live?

7 In the dark night of my soul I feel desolation. In my self-pity
   I see not the way of righteousness. I am thy disciple, come to
   thee in supplication: be a light unto me on the path of my duty.

8 For neither the kingdom of the earth, nor the kingdom of the
   gods in heaven, could give me peace from the fire of sorrow
   which thus burns my life.

Sanjaya

9 When Arjuna the great warrior had thus unburdened his
   heart, "I will not fight, Krishna," he said, and then fell silent.

10 Krishna smiled and spoke to Arjuna—there between the two
   armies the voice of God spoke these words:

Krishna

11 Thy tears are for those beyond tears; and are thy words words
   of wisdom? The wise grieve not for those who live; and they
   grieve not for those who die—for life and death shall pass away.

12 Because we all have been for all time: I, and thou, and those
   kings of men. And we all shall be for all time, we all for ever
   and ever.

13   As the Spirit of our mortal body wanders on in childhood, and youth and old age, the Spirit wanders on to a new body: of this the sage has no doubts.

14   From the world of the senses, Arjuna, comes heat and comes cold, and pleasure and pain. They come and they go: they are transient. Arise above them, strong soul.

15   The man whom these cannot move, whose soul is one, beyond pleasure and pain, is worthy of life in Eternity.

16   The unreal never is: the Real never is not. This truth indeed has been seen by those who can see the true.

17   Interwoven in his creation, the Spirit is beyond destruction. No one can bring to an end the Spirit which is everlasting.

18   For beyond time he dwells in these bodies, though these bodies have an end in their time; but he remains immeasurable, immortal. Therefore, great warrior, carry on thy fight.

19   If any man thinks he slays, and if another thinks he is slain, neither knows the ways of truth. The Eternal in man cannot kill: the Eternal in man cannot die.

20   He is never born, and he never dies. He is in Eternity: he is for evermore. Never-born and eternal, beyond times gone or to come, he does not die when the body dies.

21   When a man knows him as never-born, everlasting, never-changing, beyond all destruction, how can that man kill a man, or cause another to kill?

22   As a man leaves an old garment and puts on one that is new, the Spirit leaves his mortal body and then puts on one that is new.

23   Weapons cannot hurt the Spirit and fire can never burn him. Untouched is he by drenching waters, untouched is he by parching winds.

24   Beyond the power of sword and fire, beyond the power of waters and winds, the Spirit is everlasting, omnipresent, never-changing, never-moving, ever One.

25   Invisible is he to mortal eyes, beyond thought and beyond change. Know that he is, and cease from sorrow.

26   But if he were born again and again, and again and again he were to die, even then, victorious man, cease thou from sorrow.

27   For all things born in truth must die, and out of death in truth comes life. Face to face with what must be, cease thou from sorrow.

28   Invisible before birth are all beings and after death invisible again. They are seen between two unseens. Why in this truth find sorrow?

29   One sees him in a vision of wonder, and another gives us words of his wonder. There is one who hears of his wonder; but he hears and knows him not.

30   The Spirit that is in all beings is immortal in them all: for the
        death of what cannot die, cease thou to sorrow.
31   Think thou also of thy duty and do not waver. There is no
        greater good for a warrior than to fight in a righteous war.
32   There is a war that opens the doors of heavens, Arjuna!
        Happy the warriors whose fate is to fight such war.
33   But to forgo this fight for righteousness is to forgo thy duty and
        honour: is to fall into transgression.
34   Men will tell of thy dishonour both now and in times to come.
        And to a man who is in honour, dishonour is more than death.
35   The great warriors will say that thou hast run from the battle
        through fear; and those who thought great things of thee will
        speak of thee in scorn.
36   And thine enemies will speak of thee in contemptuous words
        of ill-will and derision, pouring scorn upon thy courage. Can
        there be for a warrior a more shameful fate?
37   In death thy glory in heaven, in victory thy glory on earth.
        Arise therefore, Arjuna, with thy soul ready to fight. . . .

STUDY QUESTIONS

1. Why is Arjuna reluctant to fight?
2. What reasons does Krishna give for urging Arjuna into battle?
3. What clues regarding gender relations in India do you see in these passages?
    Do you see evidence of how masculinity and femininity were defined?
4. How did the *Bhagavad Gita* reinforce the system of *varnas*?
5. The *Bhagavad Gita* has fascinated the people of India for 2000 years. Why do
    you think this is the case? What other religions rely heavily on stories?
6. How would a Buddhist respond to Arjuna's ethical dilemma? (See Chapter 10.)
7. How does the advice from Krishna compare with the thinking of Confucius?
    (See Chapter 5.) What does this comparison suggest about how concepts of
    male "virtue" differed in classical India and China?

10

Buddhism and the Four Noble Truths

Buddhism, the oldest of the major world religions, arose in India during the sixth century B.C.E., at about the same time as the *varna* system also was taking shape there. Scholars think that the founder of the new faith, the future Buddha (i.e., Enlightened One), was probably born into the *kshatriya* (warrior) *varna* around 560 B.C.E. in the region north of the Ganges plain. His father may have been the local ruler. At about age 30 the young prince relinquished his power and privileges to become a wandering ascetic. After about six years of experimenting with various approaches to obtaining spiritual satisfaction, he achieved enlightenment while resting under a fig tree, which became known as the *bodhi* (wisdom) tree. The Buddha devoted the rest of his long life to teaching, dying in the 480s B.C.E.

The Buddha must have been a compelling teacher because he soon attracted devoted followers. After his death they kept his teaching alive by holding conferences, forming monastic communities, building temples, and establishing special sacred sites where relics of the Buddha—now deified—could be worshipped. In the third century B.C.E. the Indian emperor Ashoka (reigned 269–232) converted to Buddhism and encouraged the spread of the faith throughout his empire.

A few centuries later, around the beginning of the Common Era, Buddhist monks began to take their ideas and style of life from India to central Asia and China. Chinese monks then carried the faith to Korea and Japan. Meanwhile, Indian monks were traveling by sea to Southeast Asia. In general, Buddhist teachings were welcomed throughout East Asia.

Despite astonishing successes in winning converts in distant lands, Buddhist proselytizers experienced some setbacks during the first millennium. Expansion westward into Persia and beyond was blocked initially by the power of Zoroastrianism and then by the rise of Islam. In China, the Tang emperors turned against Buddhism around 850, permanently destroying its political influence, though not its continuing importance in Chinese cultural and social life. Finally, in India, where it had begun, by 1000 C.E. Buddhism had begun to fade out and to become increasingly absorbed into the other great religion to emerge in India—Hinduism.

Reprinted with permission of the publishers from *Buddhism in Translations: Passages from the Buddhist Sacred Books*, translated by Henry Clarke Warren (Cambridge, MA.: Harvard University Press), pp. 368–374. Copyright © 1953 by the President and Fellows of Harvard College.

The passages that follow are from the Four Noble Truths, the core of the Buddha's first sermon after his enlightenment. Although a rich tradition of theological exposition developed in Buddhism following the death of the founder, Buddhists nonetheless regard the Four Noble Truths as the touchstone of their faith.

1. The Truth Concerning Misery

And how, O priests, does a priest live, as respects the elements of being, observant of the elements of being in the four noble truths?

Whenever, O priest, a priest knows the truth concerning misery, knows the truth concerning the origin of misery, knows the truth concerning the cessation of misery, knows the truth concerning the path leading to the cessation of misery.

And what, O priests, is the noble truth of misery?

Birth is misery; old age is misery; disease is misery; death is misery; sorrow, lamentation, misery, grief, and despair are misery; to wish for what one cannot have is misery; in short, all the five attachment-groups are misery . . .

This, O priests, is called the noble truth of misery.

2. The Truth of the Origin of Misery

And what, O priests, is the noble truth of the origin of misery?

It is desire leading to rebirth, joining itself to pleasure and passion, and finding delight in every existence,—desire, namely, for sensual pleasure, desire for permanent existence, desire for transitory existence.

But where, O priests, does this desire spring up and grow? where does it settle and take root?

Where anything is delightful and agreeable to men, there desire springs up and grows, there it settles and takes root.

And what is delightful and agreeable to men, where desire springs up and grows, where it settles and takes root?

The eye is delightful and agreeable to men; there desire springs up and grows, there it settles and takes root.

The ear . . . the nose . . . the tongue . . . the body . . . the mind is delightful and agreeable to men; there desire springs up and grows, there it settles and takes root.

The Six Organs of Sense.

Forms . . . sounds . . . odors . . . tastes . . . things tangible . . . ideas are delightful and agreeable to men; there desire springs up and grows, there it settles and takes root.

The Six Objects of Sense.

Eye-consciousness . . . ear-consciousness . . . nose-consciousness . . . tongue-consciousness . . . body-consciousness . . . mind-consciousness is delightful and agreeable to men; there desire springs up and grows, there it settles and takes root.

The Six Consciousnesses.

Contact of the eye . . . ear . . . nose . . . tongue . . . body . . . mind is delightful and agreeable to men; there desire springs up and grows, there it settles and takes root.

The Six Contacts.

Sensation produced by contact of the eye . . . ear . . . nose . . . tongue . . . body . . . mind is delightful and agreeable to men; there desire springs up and grows, there it settles and takes root.

The Six Sensations.

Perception of forms . . . sounds . . . odors . . . tastes . . . things tangible . . . ideas is delightful and agreeable to men; there desire springs up and grows, there it settles and takes root.

The Six Perceptions.

Thinking on forms . . . sounds . . . odors . . . tastes . . . things tangible . . . ideas is delightful and agreeable to men; there desire springs up and grows, there it settles and takes root.

The Six Thinkings.

Desire for forms . . . sounds . . . odors . . . tastes . . . things tangible . . . ideas is delightful and agreeable to men; there desire springs up and grows, there it settles and takes root.

The Six Desires.

Reasoning on forms . . . sounds . . . odors . . . tastes . . . things tangible . . . ideas is delightful and agreeable to men; there desire springs up and grows, there it settles and takes root.

The Six Reasonings.

Reflection on forms . . . sounds . . . odors . . . tastes . . . things tangible . . . ideas is delightful and agreeable to men; there desire springs up and grows, there it settles and takes root.

The Six Reflections.

This, O priests, is called the noble truth of the origin of misery.

3. The Truth of the Cessation of Misery

And what, O priests, is the noble truth of the cessation of misery?

It is the complete fading out and cessation of this desire, a giving up, a losing hold, a relinquishment, and a nonadhesion.

But where, O priests, does this desire wane and disappear? where is it broken up and destroyed?

Where anything is delightful and agreeable to men; there desire wanes and disappears, there it is broken up and destroyed.

And what is delightful and agreeable to men, where desire wanes and disappears, where it is broken up and destroyed?

The eye is delightful and agreeable to men; there desire wanes and disappears, there it is broken up and destroyed.

[Similarly respecting the other organs of sense, the six objects of sense, the six consciousnesses, the six contacts, the six sensations, the six perceptions, the six thinkings, the six desires, the six reasonings, and the six reflections.]

This, O priests, is called the noble truth of the cessation of misery.

4. The Truth of the Path Leading to the Cessation of Misery

And what, O priests, is the noble truth of the path leading to the cessation of misery?

It is this noble eightfold path, to wit, right belief, right resolve, right speech, right behavior, right occupation, right effort, right contemplation, right concentration.

And what, O priests, is right belief?

The knowledge of misery, O priests, the knowledge of the origin of misery, the knowledge of the cessation of misery, and the knowledge of the path leading to the cessation of misery, this, O priests, is called "right belief."

And what, O priests, is right resolve?

The resolve to renounce sensual pleasures, the resolve to have malice towards none, and the resolve to harm no living creature, this, O priests, is called "right resolve."

And what, O priests, is right speech?

To abstain from falsehood, to abstain from backbiting, to abstain from harsh language, and to abstain from frivolous talk, this, O priests, is called "right speech."

And what, O priests, is right behavior?

To abstain from destroying life, to abstain from taking that which is not given one, and to abstain from immorality, this, O priests, is called "right behavior."

And what, O priests, is right occupation?

Whenever, O priests, a noble disciple, quitting a wrong occupation, gets his livelihood by a right occupation, this, O priests, is called "right occupation."

And what, O priests, is right effort?

Whenever, O priests, a priest purposes, makes an effort, heroically endeavors, applies his mind, and exerts himself that evil and demeritorious qualities not yet arisen may not arise; purposes, makes an effort, heroically endeavors, applies his mind, and exerts himself that evil and demeritorious qualities already arisen may be abandoned; purposes, makes an effort, heroically endeavors, applies his mind, and exerts himself that meritorious qualities not yet arisen may arise; purposes, makes an effort, heroically endeavors, applies his mind, and exerts himself for the preservation, retention, growth, increase, development, and perfection of meritorious qualities already arisen, this, O priest, is called "right effort."

And what, O priests, is right contemplation?

Whenever, O priests, a priest lives, as respects the body, observant of the body, strenuous, conscious, contemplative, and has rid himself of lust and grief; as respects sensations, observant of sensations, strenuous, conscious, contemplative, and has rid himself of lust and grief; as respects the mind, observant of the mind, strenuous, conscious, contemplative, and has rid himself of lust and grief; as respects the elements of being, observant of the elements of being, strenuous, conscious, contemplative, and has rid himself of lust and grief, this, O priests, is called "right contemplation."

And what, O priests, is right concentration?

Whenever, O priests, a priest, having isolated himself from sensual pleasures, having isolated himself from demeritorious traits, and still exercising reasoning, still exercising reflection, enters upon the first trance which is produced by isolation and characterized by joy and happiness; when, through the subsidence of reasoning and reflection, and still retaining joy and happiness, he enters upon the second trance, which is an interior tranquilization and intentness of the thoughts, and is produced by concentration; when, through the paling of joy, indifferent, contemplative, conscious, and in the experience of bodily happiness—that state which eminent men describe when they say, "Indifferent, contemplative, and living happily"—he enters upon the third trance; when, through the abandonment of happiness, through the abandonment of misery, through the disappearance of all antecedent gladness and grief, he enters upon the fourth trance, which has neither misery nor happiness, but is contemplation as refined by indifference, this, O priests, is called "right concentration."

This, O priests, is called the noble truth of the path leading to the cessation of misery.

STUDY QUESTIONS

1. According to the Four Noble Truths, what is the great problem that humans face?
2. Is there a solution to this problem in the Four Noble Truths? If so, what is it?
3. According to the Four Noble Truths, what does it mean to be a good person?
4. What is the attitude toward human emotions in the Four Noble Truths?
5. Is there a particular kind of social structure or set of gender relationships implied in the Four Noble Truths?
6. How might the ideas represented by Krishna in the *Bhagavad Gita* have contributed to the waning of Buddhism in India? (See Chapter 9.)
7. How do the teachings in the Four Noble Truths compare with those of Confucius? (See Chapter 5.) What similarities and what differences do you see?
8. Do the Four Noble Truths provide clues to the reasons why Buddhism spread so widely in East Asia and Southeast Asia?

11

State, Society, and Economy in India: The *Arthashastra*

The period from 500 to 200 B.C.E. was extraordinarily creative across Eurasia with regard to the development of political thinking. In China the Confucians and the Legalists formulated the ideas that have shaped political thinking in East Asia for the past 2000 years (see Chapters 5 and 6). In Greece—where the term *politics* was invented—Plato, Aristotle, and numerous other thinkers developed ideas of lasting importance for Europeans and, more recently, for people in other parts of the world (see Chapter 13.)

Innovative thinking about political issues was also part of the process that led to the establishment of India's first great empire around 300 B.C.E. By this time Chandragupta Maurya, originally the ruler of a small state on the Ganges plain, had conquered the rest of northern India and established the Mauryan Empire. Chandragupta's successors, especially Emperor Ashoka (reigned 269–232 B.C.E.), expanded the borders of the Mauryan state until it embraced nearly all of mainland South Asia. The empire founded by Chandragupta Maurya lasted until 185 B.C.E., when it broke up into regional polities.

During the reign of Emperor Chandragupta a major work of political thinking, the *Arthashastra (Treatise on Material Gain),* was written in India. Essentially a series of policy recommendations, the *Arthashastra* has been traditionally attributed to Kautilya, Chandragupta's key advisor. By studying this work we can learn much about political thinking and political circumstances in India during the late first millennium B.C.E. In addition, the *Arthashastra* contains a great deal of valuable information about economic and social realities in India. Representative passages from this work follow.

Chapter 10: On Spies

Advised and assisted by a tried council of officers, the ruler should proceed to institute spies.

Spies are in the guise of pseudo-student, priest, householder, trader, saint practising renunciation, classmate or colleague, desperado, poisoner and woman mendicant.

An artful person, capable of reading human nature, is a pseudo-student. Such a person should be encouraged with presents and purse and be told by the officer: "Sworn to the ruler and myself you shall inform us what wickedness you find in others."

One initiated in scripture and of pure character is a priest-spy. This spy should carry on farming, cattle culture and commerce with resources given to him. Out of the produce and profit accrued, he should encourage other priests to live with him and send them on espionage work. The other priests also should send their followers on similar errands.

A householder-spy is a farmer fallen in his profession but pure in character. This spy should do as the priest [above].

A trader-spy is a merchant in distress but generally trustworthy. This spy should carry on espionage, in addition to his profession.

A person with proper appearance and accomplishments as an ascetic is a saint-spy. He surrounds himself with followers and may settle down in the suburb of a big city and may pretend prayer and fasting in public. Trader-spies may associate with this class of spies. He may practise fortune-telling, palmistry, and pretend supernatural and magical powers by predictions. The followers will adduce proof for the predictions of their saint. He may even foretell official rewards and official changes, which the officers concerned may substantiate by reciprocating.

Rewarded by the rulers with money and titles, these five institutions of espionage should maintain the integrity of the country's officers.

Chapter 14: Administrative Councils

Deliberation in well-constituted councils precedes administrative measures. The proceedings of a council should be in camera and deliberations made top secret so that not even a bird can whisper. The ruler should be guarded against disclosure.

Whoever divulges secret deliberations should be destroyed. Such guilt can be detected by physical and attitudinal changes of ambassadors, ministers and heads.

Secrecy of proceedings in the council and guarding of officers participating in the council must be organised.

The causes of divulgence of counsels are recklessness, drink, talking in one's sleep and infatuation with women which [sic] assail councillors.

He of secretive nature or who is not regarded well will divulge council matters. Disclosure of council secrets is of advantage to persons other than the ruler and his high officers. Steps should be taken to safeguard deliberations. . . .

Chapter 20: Personal Security

The ruler should employ as his security staff only such persons as have noble and proven ancestry and are closely related to him and are well trained and loyal. No foreigners, or anonymous persons, or persons with clouded antecedents are to be employed as security staff for the ruler.

In a securely guarded chamber, the chief should supervise the ruler's food arrangements.

Special precautions are to be taken against contaminated and poisoned food. The following reveal poison: rice sending out deep blue vapour; unnaturally coloured and artificially dried-up and hard vegetables; unusually bright and dull vessels; foamy vessels; streaky soups, milk and liquor; white streaked honey; strange-tempered food;

carpets and curtains stained with dark spots and threadbare; polishless and lustreless metallic vessels and gems.

The poisoner reveals himself by parched and dry mouth, hesitating talk, perspiration, tremour, yawning, evasive demeanour and nervous behaviour.

Experts in poison detection should be in attendance on the ruler. The physicians attending the ruler should satisfy themselves personally as to the purity of the drugs which they administer to the ruler. The same precaution is indicated for liquor and beverages which the ruler uses. Scrupulous cleanliness should be insisted on in persons in charge of the ruler's dress and toilet requisites. This should be ensured by seals. . . .

In any entertainment meant for the amusement of the ruler, the actors should not use weapons, fire and poison. Musical instruments and accoutrements for horses, elephants and vehicles should be secured in the palace.

The ruler should mount beasts and vehicles only after the traditional rider or driver has done so. If he has to travel in a boat, the pilot should be trustworthy and the boat itself secured to another boat. There should be a proper convoy on land or water guarding the ruler. He should swim only in rivers which are free of larger fishes and crocodiles and hunt in forests free from snakes, man-eaters and brigands.

He should give private audience only attended by his security guards. He should receive foreign ambassadors in his full ministerial council. While reviewing his militia, the ruler should also attend in full battle uniform and be on horseback or on the back of an elephant. When he enters or exits from the capital city, the path of the ruler should be guarded by staffed officers and cleared of armed men, mendicants and the suspicious. He should attend public performances, festivals, processions or religious gatherings accompanied by trained bodyguards. The ruler should guard his own person with the same care with which he secures the safety of those around him through espionage arrangements.

Chapter 21: Building of Villages

The ruler may form villages either on new sites or on old sites, either by shifting population from heavily populated areas in his own state or by causing population to immigrate into his state.

Villages should consist of not less than a hundred and not more than five hundred families of cultivators of the service classes. The villages should extend from about one and a half miles to three miles each [in circumference] and should be capable of defending each other. Village boundaries may consist of rivers, hills, forests, hedges, caves, bridges and trees.

Each eight hundred villages should have a major fort. There should be a capital city for every four hundred villages, a market town for every two hundred villages, and an urban cluster for every ten villages.

The frontiers of the state should have fortifications protected by internal guards, manning the entrances to the state. The interior of the state should be guarded by huntsmen, armed guards, forest tribes, fierce tribes and frontier men.

Those who do social service by sacrifices, the clergy, and the intellectuals should be settled in the villages on tax-free farms.

Officers, scribes, cattlemen, guards, cattle doctors, physicians, horse-trainers and news purveyors should be given life interest in lands.

Lands fit for cultivation should be given to tenants only for life. Land prepared for cultivation by tenants should not be taken away from them.

Lands not cultivated by the landholders may be confiscated and given to cultivators. Or they may be cultivated through hired labourers or traders to avoid loss to the state. If cultivators pay their taxes promptly, they may be supplied with grains, cattle and money.

The ruler should give to cultivators only such farms and concessions as will replenish the treasury and avoid denuding it.

A denuded exchequer is a grave threat to the security of the state. Only on rare occasions like settlement of new areas or in grave emergencies should tax-remissions be granted. The ruler should be benevolent to those who have conquered the crisis by remission of taxes.

He should facilitate mining operations. He should encourage manufacturers. He should help exploitation of forest wealth. He should provide amenities for cattle breeding and commerce. He should construct highways both on land and on water. He should plan markets.

He should build dikes for water either perennial or from other sources. He should assist with resources and communications those who build reservoirs or construct works of communal comfort and public parks.

All should share in corporate work, sharing the expenditure but not claiming profit.

The ruler should have suzerainty over all fishing, transport and grain trade, reservoirs and bridges.

Those who do not recognise the rights of their servants, hirelings and relatives should be made to do so.

The ruler should maintain adolescents, the aged, the diseased and the orphans. He should also provide livelihood to deserted women with prenatal care and protection for the children born to them. . . .

The ruler should abstain from taking over any area which is open to attack by enemies and wild tribes and which is visited by frequent famines and pests. He should also abstain from extravagant sports.

He should protect cultivation from heavy taxes, slave labour and severe penalties, herds of cattle from cattle lifters, wild animals, venomous creatures and diseases.

He should clear highways of the visitation of petty officials, workmen, brigands and guards. He should not only conserve existing forests, buildings and mines, but also develop new ones.

Chapter 41: Decay, Stabilisation, and Progress of States

A state should always observe such a policy as will help it strengthen its defensive fortifications and life-lines of communications, build plantations, construct villages, and exploit the mineral and forest wealth of the country, while at the same time preventing fulfilment of similar programmes in the rival state.

Any two states hostile to each other, finding that neither has an advantage over the other in fulfilment of their respective programmes, should make peace with each other.

When any two states which are rivals expect to acquire equal possessions over the same span of time, they should keep peace with each other.

A state can indulge in armed invasion only:

Where, by invasion, it can reduce the power of an enemy without in any way reducing its own potential, by making suitable arrangements for protection of its own strategic works. . . .

Chapter 54: Restoration of Lost Balance of Power

When an invader is assailed by an alliance of his enemies, he should try to purchase the leader of the alliance with offers of gold and his own alliance and by diplomatic camouflage of the threat of treachery from the alliance of powers. He should instigate the leader of the allied enemies to break up his alliance.

The invader should also attempt to break the allied enemies' formation by setting up the leader of the alliance against the weaker of his enemies, or attempt to forge a combination of the weaker allies against their leader. He may also form a pact with the leader through intrigue, or offer of resources. When the confederation is shattered, he may form alliances with any of his former enemies.

If a state is weak in treasury or in striking power, attention should be directed to strengthen both through stabilisation of authority. Irrigational projects are a source of agricultural prosperity. Good highways should be constructed to facilitate movements of armed might and merchandise. Mines should be developed, as they supply ammunition. Forests should be conserved, as they supply material for defence, communication and vehicles. Pasture lands are the source of cattle wealth.

Thus, a state should build up its striking power through development of the exchequer, the army and wise counsel; and, till the proper time, should conduct itself as a weak power towards its neighbours, to evade conflict or envy from enemy or allied states. If the state is deficient in resources, it should acquire them from related or allied states. It should attract to itself capable men from corporations, from wild and ferocious tribes, and foreigners, and organise espionage that will damage hostile powers.

STUDY QUESTIONS

1. According to the *Arthashastra*, what policies should a ruler adopt in order to be successful?
2. What does the advice to employ spies and to devote considerable attention to personal security suggest about political conditions in India during the Mauryan dynasty?
3. What do you learn from these passages about the Indian economy?
4. According to the *Arthashastra*, what should be the foreign policy goals of a ruler? What steps should be taken to realize those goals?
5. How might the attempts by Indian political leaders to establish strong and enduring states have been assisted or impeded by the values represented by Krishna in the *Bhagavad Gita*? (See Chapter 9.)
6. How do the goals suggested in the *Arthashastra* compare with those in Buddhism? (See Chapter 10.)
7. How does the *Arthashastra* compare with Chinese Legalism? (See Chapter 6.) Did the Indian ideas and the Chinese ideas emerge in a similar context?
8. Why was there so much important political thinking during the period 500 to 300 B.C.E. in India, China, and Greece?

12

Gender Relations in India: Three Types of Evidence

The sharp lines between social groups that were characteristic of the *varna* system as it developed in India during the first millennium B.C.E. had their counterpart in the system of strongly patriarchal gender relations that arose at about the same time. Although it is true that the documentary evidence regarding relationships between men and women in early India is extremely fragmentary and often indirect, a variety of written sources nonetheless suggest that well before the beginning of the Common Era the principle of female subordination had become a central element in South Asian life.

In this chapter we look at three types of documentation that help us to grasp the character of gender relations in India around the beginning of the Common Era. First, we will examine a few songs from the *Therigatha,* a collection of more than 500 songs originally composed by Buddhist nuns (*theris*) who were contemporaries of the Buddha. Scholars think that the songs in the *Therigatha* were first put into writing in the first century B.C.E.

The second kind of evidence we consider comes from the *Laws of Manu,* an influential philosophical-legal treatise dating from the beginning of the Common Era. The anonymous authors of the *Laws of Manu* were *brahmans* whose purpose in writing the book was, in part, to outline prescribed modes of behavior. In the selections from the *Laws of Manu* which follow the focus is on gender relations.

Finally, we draw for a second time from the great Indian epic, the *Mahabharata,* which, as we have seen in Chapter 9, was transformed from oral tradition into writing during the late first millennium B.C.E. The selection which follows, "Savatri and the God of Death," has long been one of the most popular episodes in the *Mahabharata.*

Selection 1 reprinted by permission of the Feminist Press at the City University of New York, from Susie Tharu and K. Lalita, *Women Writing in India: Volume I: 600 B.C. to the Early Twentieth Century,* edited by Susie Tharu and K. Lalita. Copyright 1991 by Susie Tharu and K. Lalita, pp. 68–70. Selection 2 from Barbara N. Ramusack, "Women in South and Southeast Asia," in *Restoring Women to History,* edited by Organization of American Historians (Bloomington, Ind.: Organization of American Historians, 1988), p. 9. Selection 3 from Roy C. Amore and Larry D. Shinn, *Lustful Maidens and Ascetic Kings: Buddhist and Hindu Stories of Life* (New York: Oxford University Press, 1981), pp. 28–30, 32–33. Copyright © 1981 by Oxford University Press. Reprinted by permission.

Gender Imagery in India. An amorous couple, detail of the reliefs at the entrance to the Buddhist worship site at Karli, Maharashtra, India, second century C.E. *What does this work of art suggest about idealized differences between men and women?* (Borromeo/Art Resource, NY.)

1. SONGS COMPOSED BY BUDDHIST NUNS

Mutta
[So free am I, so gloriously free]

So free am I, so gloriously free,
Free from three petty things—
From mortar, from pestle and from my twisted lord,
Freed from rebirth and death I am,
And all that has held me down
Is hurled away.

Ubbiri
["O Ubbiri, who wails in the wood"]

"O Ubbiri, who wails in the wood
'O Jiva! Dear daughter!'
Return to your senses, in this charnel field
Innumerable daughters, once as full of life as Jiva,
Are burnt. Which of them do you mourn?"
The hidden arrow in my heart plucked out,
The dart lodged there, removed.
The anguish of my loss,
The grief that left me faint all gone,
The yearning stilled,
To the Buddha, the Dhamma [Moral Law], and the Sangha [Community of
    Buddhists]
I turn, my heart now healed.

Sumangalamata
[A woman well set free! How free I am]

A woman well set free! How free I am,
How wonderfully free, from kitchen drudgery.
Free from the harsh grip of hunger,
And from empty cooking pots,
Free too of that unscrupulous man,
The weaver of sunshades.
Calm now, and serene I am,
All lust and hatred purged.
To the shade of the spreading trees I go
And contemplate my happiness.

Mettika
[Though I am weak and tired now]

Though I am weak and tired now,
And my youthful step long gone,
Leaning on this staff,
I climb the mountain peak.
My cloak cast off, my bowl overturned,
I sit here on this rock.
And over my spirit blows
The breath
Of liberty
I've won, I've won the triple gems [the Buddha, the Dhamma and the Sangha]
The Buddha's way is mine.

2. THE LAWS OF MANU

In childhood a female must be subject to her father, in youth to her husband, and when
her lord is dead, to her sons; a woman must never be independent [Manu, V, 184].

Though destitute of virtue, or seeking pleasure (elsewhere), or devoid of good qualities, (yet) a husband must be constantly worshipped as a god by a faithful wife [Manu, V, 154].

A virtuous wife who after the death of her husband constantly remains chaste, reaches heaven, though she have no son, just like those chaste men [Manu, V, 160].

But a woman who from a desire to have offspring violates her duty towards her dead husband, brings on herself disgrace in this world, and loses her place with her husband in heaven [Manu V, 161].

A wife, a son and a slave, these three are declared to have no property: the wealth which they earn is (acquired) for him to whom they belong [Manu, VIII, 416].

(When creating them) Manu allotted to women (a love of their) bed, (of their) seat and (of) ornament, impure desires, wrath, dishonesty, malice, and bad conduct [Manu, IX, 17].

In the sacred texts which refer to marriage the appointment (of widows) is nowhere mentioned, nor is the remarriage of widows prescribed in the rules concerning marriage [Manu, IX, 65].

A man, aged thirty years, shall marry a maiden of twelve who pleases him, or a man of twenty-four a girl eight years of age; if the performance of his duties would otherwise be impeded, he must marry sooner [Manu, IX, 94]

3. SAVATRI AND THE GOD OF DEATH

Ashvapati, the virtuous king of Madras, grew old without offspring to continue his royal family. Desiring a son, Ashvapati took rigid vows and observed long fasts to accumulate merit. It is said that he offered 10,000 oblations to the goddess Savatri in hopes of having a son. After eighteen years of constant devotion, Ashvapati was granted his wish for an offspring even though the baby born was a girl.

The king rejoiced at his good fortune and named the child Savatri in honor of the goddess who gave him this joy to brighten his elder years.

Savatri was both a beautiful and an intelligent child. She was her father's delight and grew in wisdom and beauty as the years passed. As the age approached for Savatri to be given in marriage as custom demanded, no suitor came forward to ask her father for her hand—so awed were all the princes by the beauty and intellect of this unusual maiden. Her father became concerned lest he not fulfill his duty as father and incur disgrace for his failure to provide a suitable husband for his daughter. At last, he instructed Savatri herself to lead a procession throughout the surrounding kingdoms and handpick a man suitable for her.

Savatri returned from her search and told her father that she had found the perfect man. Though he was poor and an ascetic of the woods, he was handsome, well educated, and of kind temperament. His name was Satyavan and he was actually a prince whose blind father had been displaced by an evil king. Ashvapati asked the venerable sage Narada whether Satyavan would be a suitable spouse for Savatri. Narada responded that there was no one in the world more worthy than Satyavan. However, Narada continued, Satyavan had one unavoidable flaw. He was fated to live a short life and would die exactly one year from that very day. Ashvapati then tried to dissuade Savatri from marrying Satyavan by telling her of the impending death of her loved one. Savatri held firm to her choice, and the king and Narada both gave their blessings to this seemingly ill-fated bond.

After the marriage procession had retreated from the forest hermitage of Savatri's new father-in-law, Dyumatsena, the bride removed her wedding sari and donned the ocher robe and bark garments of her ascetic family. As the days and weeks passed, Savatri busied herself by waiting upon the every need of her new family. She served her husband, Satyavan, cheerfully and skillfully. Satyavan responded with an even-tempered love which enhanced the bond of devotion between Savatri and himself. Yet the dark cloud of Narada's prophecy cast a shadow over this otherwise blissful life.

When the fateful time approached, Savatri began a fast to strengthen her wifely resolve as she kept nightly vigils while her husband slept. The day marked for the death of Satyavan began as any other day at the hermitage. Satyavan shouldered his axe and was about to set off to cut wood for the day's fires when Savatri stopped him to ask if she could go along saying, "I cannot bear to be separated from you today." Satyavan responded, "You've never come into the forest before and the paths are rough and the way very difficult. Besides, you've been fasting and are surely weak." Savatri persisted, and Satyavan finally agreed to take her along. Savatri went to her parents-in-law to get their permission saying she wanted to see the spring blossoms which now covered the forest. They too expressed concern over her health but finally relented out of consideration for her long period of gracious service to them.

Together Satyavan and Savatri entered the tangled woods enjoying the beauty of the flowers and animals which betoken spring in the forest. Coming to a fallen tree, Satyavan began chopping firewood. As he worked, he began to perspire heavily and to grow weak. Finally, he had to stop and lie down telling Savatri to wake him after a short nap. With dread in her heart, Savatri took Satyavan's head in her lap and kept a vigil knowing Satyavan's condition to be more serious than rest could assuage. In a short time, Savatri saw approaching a huge figure clad in red and carrying a small noose. Placing Satyavan's head upon the ground, Savatri arose and asked the stranger of his mission. The lord of death replied, "I am Yama and your husband's days are finished. I speak to you, a mortal, only because of your extreme merit. I have come personally instead of sending my emissaries because of your husband's righteous life."

Without a further word, Yama then pulled Satyavan's soul out of his body with the small noose he was carrying. The lord of death then set off immediately for the realm of the dead in the south. Grief stricken and yet filled with wife devotion, Savatri followed Yama at a distance. Hours passed yet hunger and weariness could not slow Savatri's footsteps. She persisted through thorny paths and rocky slopes to follow Yama and his precious burden. As Yama walked south he thought he heard a woman's anklets tingling on the path behind him. He turned around to see Savatri in the distance following without pause. He called out to her to return to Satyavan's body and to perform her wifely duties of cremating the dead. Savatri approached Yama and responded, "It is said that those who walk seven steps together are friends. Certainly we have traveled farther than that together. Why should I return to a dead body when you possess the soul of my husband?"

Yama was impressed by the courage and wisdom of this beautiful young woman. He replied, "Please stop following me. Your wise words and persistent devotion for your husband deserve a boon. Ask of me anything except that your husband's life be restored, and I will grant it." Savatri asked that her blind father-in-law be granted new sight. Yama said that her wish would be granted, and then he turned to leave only to find that Savatri was about to continue following. Yama again praised her devotion and offered a second, and then a third boon. Savatri told Yama of the misfortune of her father-in-law's lost kingdom and asked that Yama assist in ousting the evil king from Dyumatsena's throne. Yama agreed. Then Savatri utilized her third boon to ask that her own father be given one hundred sons to protect his royal line, and that too was granted by Yama.

Yama then set off in a southerly direction only to discover after a short while that Savatri still relentlessly followed him. Yama was amazed at the thoroughly self-giving attitude displayed by Savatri and agreed to grant one last boon if Savatri would promise to return home. Yama again stipulated that the bereaved wife could not ask for her husband's soul. Savatri agreed to the two conditions and said, "I only ask for myself one thing, and that is that I may be granted one hundred sons to continue Satyavan's royal family." Yama agreed only to realize, upon prompting from Savatri, that the only way Satyavan's line could be continued would be for him to be restored to life. Although he had been tricked by the wise and thoughtful Savatri, Yama laughed heartily and said, "So be it! Auspicious and chaste lady, your husband's soul is freed by me." Loosening his noose Yama permitted the soul of Satyavan to return to its earthly abode and Savatri ran without stopping back to the place where Satyavan had fallen asleep. Just as Savatri arrived at the place where her husband lay, he awoke saying, "Oh, I have slept into the night, why did you not waken me?"

STUDY QUESTIONS

1. What are the main themes in the songs by the Buddhist nuns? How do the songs illustrate points in the Four Noble Truths? (See Chapter 10.)
2. What clues to the character of gender relations in India do you see in the songs?
3. How do the Laws of Manu define womanhood and manhood? How do these definitions compare?
4. What is the attitude toward woman's sexuality in the Laws of Manu? How do you explain this attitude on the part of the authors?
5. How do men and women relate to one another in the story of Savatri? How does Savatri relate to Yama, the "lord of death"?
6. Are Savatri's actions consistent with the Laws of Manu?
7. Based on your reading of the documents in this chapter, what generalizations, however tentative, seem reasonable regarding gender relations in India around the beginning of the Common Era?
8. Compare the Laws of Manu with Hammurabi's Code. (See Chapter 2.)
9. Compare gender relations in India and China.

13

The Greek Political Tradition

As with all the classical civilizations, the culture that developed along Europe's Mediterranean shores produced important political institutions and principles. The key political form, in Greece and later in republican Rome, was the city-state. Within its bounds, the portion of the population with political rights was supposed to participate actively in the affairs of state, to which it owed loyalty and service. Within this context, however, a variety of political structures arose. Some evolved toward democracy (though with many residents excluded from rights). In this Athens led the way, providing not only participant assemblies but also considerable support for individual freedom and legal rights. Other Greek city-states, however, stressed the power of government. Sparta, which would finally clash with Athens in the Peloponnesian War, set up a rigid militaristic regime designed to transform each male or female citizen into an absolute servant of the government. When Athens and Sparta warred at the end of the fifth century B.C.E., the conflict involved not only power, but also two clashing views of political life.

The Spartan system, described in the first selection, was set up by the lawmaker Lycurgus after 650 B.C.E., in large part to keep a vast slave (helot) population under control. The description comes from the writings of Plutarch (ca. 45–125 C.E.], in a biography of Lycurgus. The contrasting Athenian ideal was articulated by its great leader Pericles during the fifth century B.C.E., in the early stages of the Peloponnesian War, as part of a famous funeral oration that appears in the history by Thucydides.

The two selections thus allow a clear comparison between the ideas of the two city-states. It is important to realize that most articulate Greeks (including both

Selection 1 from Plutarch, *The Library of Original Sources.* Vol. II*: The Greek World,* edited by Oliver J. Thatcher (University Research Extension Co., Milwaukee, Wis.,: n.d.), pp. 118–119, 122, 128. Selection 2 from Thucydides, *History of the Peloponnesian War,* translated by Richard Crawley (London, 1896), Book 2, pp. 111–114.

Thucydides and Plutarch) preferred Spartan values; why might this be so? Are there any shared features beneath the obvious contrasts of Athens and Sparta? What resulted, in classical Greece itself and in the later Greek heritage, from such sharply differentiated systems within a common culture?

1. SPARTA

In order to [promote] the good education of their youth (which . . . he [Lyeurgus] thought the most important and noblest work of a lawgiver), he went so far back as to take into consideration their very conception and birth, by regulating their marriages. For Aristotle is wrong in saying, that, after he had tried all ways to reduce the women to more modesty and sobriety, he was at last forced to leave them as they were, because that, in the absence of their husbands, who spent the best part of their lives in the wars, their wives, whom they were obliged to leave absolute mistresses at home, took great liberties and assumed the superiority; and were treated with overmuch respect and called by the title of lady or queen. The truth is, he took in their case, also, all the care that was possible; he ordered the maidens to exercise themselves with wrestling, running, throwing and quoit, and casting the dart, to the end that the fruit they conceived might, in strong and healthy bodies, take firmer root and find better growth, and withal that they, with this greater vigor, might be the more able to undergo the pains of childbearing. And to the end he might take away their overgreat tenderness and fear of exposure to the air, and all acquired womanishness, he ordered that the young women should go naked in the processions, as well as the young men, and dance, too, in that condition, at certain solemn feasts, singing certain songs, whilst the young men stood around, seeing and hearing them. On these occasions, they now and then made, by jests, a befitting reflection upon those who had misbehaved themselves in the wars; and again sang encomiums upon those who had done any gallant action, and by these means inspired the younger sort with an emulation of their glory. Those that were thus commended went away proud, elated, and gratified with their honor among the maidens; and those who were rallied were as sensibly touched with it as if they had been formally reprimanded; and so much the more, because the kings and the elders, as well as the rest of the city, saw and heard all that passed. Nor was there anything shameful in this nakedness of the young women; modesty attended them, and all wantonness was excluded. It taught them simplicity and a care for good health, and gave them some taste of higher feelings, admitted as they thus were to the field of noble action and glory. Hence it was natural for them to think and speak as Gorgo, for example, the wife of Leonidas, is said to have done, when some foreign lady, as it would seem, told her that the women of Lacedœmon were the only women of the world who could rule men; "With good reason," she said, "for we are the only women who bring forth men."

　　These public processions of the maidens, and their appearing naked in their exercises and dancings, were incitements to marriage, operating upon the young with the rigor and certainty, as Plato says, of love, if not of mathematics. But besides all this, to promote it yet more effectually, those who continued bachelors were in a degree disfranchised by law; for they were excluded from the sight of those public processions in which the young men and maidens danced naked, and, in winter-time, the officers compelled them to march naked themselves round the market-place, singing as they went a certain song to their own disgrace, that they justly suf-fered this punishment for disobeying the laws. Moreover, they were denied that respect and observance which the younger men paid their elders; and no man, for example, found fault with what was said to Dercyllidas, though so eminent a com-mander; upon whose approach one day, a young man, instead of rising, retained his seat, remarking, "No child of yours will make room for me." . . .

Nor was it lawful, indeed, for the father himself to breed up the children after his own fancy; but as soon as they were seven years old, they were to be enrolled in certain companies and classes, where they all lived under the same order and disci-pline, doing their exercises and taking their play together. Of these, he who showed the most conduct and courage was made captain; they had their eyes always upon him, obeyed his orders, and underwent patiently whatsoever punishment he inflicted; so that the whole course of their education was one continued exercise of a ready and perfect obedience. The old men, too, were spectators of their perfor-mances, and often raised quarrels and disputes among them, to have a good op-portunity of finding out their different characters, and of seeing which would be valiant, which a coward, when they should come to more dangerous encounters. Reading and writing they gave them, just enough to serve their turn; their chief care was to make them good subjects, and to teach them to endure pain and con-quer in battle. To this end, as they grew in years, their discipline was proportion-ately increased; their heads were close-clipped, they were accustomed to go bare-foot, and for the most part to play naked.

After they were twelve years old, they were no longer allowed to wear any un-dergarment; they had one coat to serve them a year; their bodies were hard and dry, with but little acquaintance of baths and unguents; these human indulgences they were allowed only on some few particular days in the year. They lodged to-gether in little bands upon beds made of the rushes which grew by the banks of the river Eurotas, which they were to break off with their hands without a knife; if it were winter, they mingled some thistle-down with their rushes, which it was thought had the property of giving warmth. By the time they were come to this age, there was not any of the more hopeful boys who had not a lover to bear him company. The old men, too, had an eye upon them, coming often to the grounds to hear and see them contend either in wit or strength with one another, and this as seriously and with as much concern as if they were their fathers, their tutors, or their magis-trates; so that there scarcely was any time or place without some one present to put them in mind of their duty, and punish them if they had neglected it. . . .

Their discipline continued still after they were full-grown men. No one was al-lowed to live after his own fancy; but the city was a sort of camp, in which every man had his share of provisions and business set out, and looked upon himself not so much born to serve his own ends as the interest of his country. Therefore, if they were commanded nothing else, they went to see the boys perform their exercises, to teach them something useful, or to learn it themselves of those who knew better. And, indeed, one of the greatest and highest blessings Lycurgus procured his peo-ple was the abundance of leisure, which proceeded from his forbidding to them the exercise of any mean and mechanical trade. Of the money-making that depends on troublesome going about and seeing people and doing business, they had no need at all in a state where wealth obtained no honor or respect. The Helots tilled their ground for them, and paid them yearly in kind the appointed quantity, without any trouble of theirs. To this purpose there goes a story of a Lacedœmonian [Spartan] who, happening to be at Athens when the courts were sitting, was told of a citizen that had been fined for living an idle life, and was being escorted home in much distress of mind by his condoling friends; the Lacedœmonian was much surprised at it, and desired his friend to show him the man who was condemned for living like a freeman. So much beneath them did they esteem the frivolous devotion of time and attention to the mechanical arts and to money-making.

2. PERICLEAN ATHENS

Our constitution does not copy the laws of neighbouring states; we are rather a pattern to others than imitators ourselves. Its administration favours the many instead of the few; this is why it is called a democracy. If we look to the laws, they afford equal justice to all in their private differences; if to social standing, advancement in public life falls to reputation for capacity, class considerations not being allowed to interfere with merit; nor again does poverty bar the way, if a man is able to serve the state, he is not hindered by the obscurity of his condition. The freedom which we enjoy in our government extends also to our ordinary life. There, far from exercising a jealous surveillance over each other, we do not feel called upon to be angry with our neighbour for doing what he likes, or even to indulge in those injurious looks which cannot fail to be offensive, although they inflict no positive penalty. But all this ease in our private relations does not make us lawless as citizens. Against this fear is our chief safeguard, teaching us to obey the magistrates and the laws, particularly such as regard the protection of the injured, whether they are actually on the statute book, or belong to that code which, although unwritten, yet cannot be broken without acknowledged disgrace.

Further, we provide plenty of means for the mind to refresh itself from business. We celebrate games and sacrifices all the year round, and the elegance of our private establishments forms a daily source of pleasure and helps to banish the spleen; while the magnitude of our city draws the produce of the world into our harbour, so that to the Athenian the fruits of other countries are as familiar a luxury as those of his own.

If we turn to our military policy, there also we differ from our antagonists. We throw open our city to the world, and never by alien acts exclude foreigners from any opportunity of learning or observing, although the eyes of an enemy may occasionally profit by our liberality; trusting less in system and policy than to the native spirit of our citizens; while in education, where our rivals from their very cradles by a painful discipline seek after manliness, at Athens we live exactly as we please, and yet are just as ready to encounter every legitimate danger. In proof of this it may be noticed that the Lacedœmonians do not invade our country alone, but bring with them all their confederates; while we Athenians advance unsupported into the territory of a neighbour, and fighting upon a foreign soil usually vanquish with ease men who are defending their homes. Our united force was never yet encountered by an enemy, because we have at once to attend to our marine and to despatch our citizens by land upon a hundred different services; so that, wherever they engage with some such fraction of our strength, a success against a detachment is magnified into a victory over the nation, and a defeat into a reverse suffered at the hands of our entire people. And yet if with habits not of labour but of ease, and courage not of art but of nature, we are still willing to encounter danger, we have the double advantage of escaping the experience of hardships in anticipation and of facing them in the hour of need as fearlessly as those who are never free from them.

Nor are these the only points in which our city is worthy of admiration. We cultivate refinement without extravagance and knowledge without effeminacy; wealth we employ more for use than for show, and place the real disgrace of poverty not in owning to the fact but in declining the struggle against it. Our public men have, besides politics, their private affairs to attend to, and our ordinary citizens, though occupied with the pursuits of industry, are still fair judges of public matters; for, unlike any other nation, regarding him who takes no part in these duties not as unambitious but as useless, we Athenians are able to judge at all events if we cannot originate, and instead of looking on discussion as a stumbling-block in the way of action, we think it an indispensable preliminary to any wise action at all. Again, in our enterprises we present the singular spectacle of daring and deliberation, each carried to its highest point, and both united in the same persons; although usually decision is the fruit of ignorance, hesitation of reflexion. But the palm of courage will surely be adjudged most justly to those who best know the difference between hardship and pleasure and yet are never tempted to shrink from danger. In generosity we are equally singular, acquiring our friends by conferring not by receiving favours. Yet, of course, the doer of the favour is the firmer friend of the two, in order by continued kindness to keep the recipient in his debt; while the debtor feels less keenly from the very consciousness that the return he makes will be a payment, not a free gift. And it is only the Athenians who, fearless of consequences, confer their benefits not from calculations of expediency, but in the confidence of liberality.

In short, I say that as a city we are the school of Hellas; while I doubt if the world can produce a man, who where he has only himself to depend upon, is equal to so many emergencies, and graced by so happy a versatility as the Athenian. And that this is no mere boast thrown out for the occasion, but plain matter of fact, the power of the state acquired by these habits proves. For Athens alone of her contemporaries is found when tested to be greater than her reputation, and alone gives no occasion to her assailants to blush at the antagonist by whom they have been worsted, or to her subjects to question her title by merit to rule. Rather, the admiration of the present and succeeding ages will be ours, since we have not left our power without witness, but have shown it by mighty proofs; and far from needing a Homer for our panegyrist, or others of his craft whose verses might charm for the moment only for the impression they gave to melt at the touch of fact, we have forced every sea and land to be the highway of our daring, and everywhere, whether for evil or for good, have left imperishable monuments behind us. Such is the Athens for which these men, in the assertion of their resolve not to lose her, nobly fought and died; and well may every one of their survivors be ready to suffer in her cause.

STUDY QUESTIONS

1. What was the nature of family regulation in Sparta? What were the reasons for it?
2. How does Pericles define the nature and purpose of the Athenian state?
3. What were the differences between Athenian and Spartan systems of military recruitment and motivation for service?
4. Were Sparta and Athens forerunners of contemporary government systems, or would this be a misleading assessment?
5. Were there any similarities between Spartan and Athenian values and goals?
6. How do Athenian political principles compare with Confucian ideals and goals? Why was Confucianism more successful? (See Chapter 5.)

14

Mediterranean Social and Family Structure

In these selections, the philosopher Aristotle (384–322 B.C.E.) describes some widely accepted Greek principles of social organization that also came to be current in Rome. He is obviously intent on justifying a social hierarchy; how does he divide functions? Why does he prefer that manual labor (at least in agriculture) be done by slaves? The idea of hierarchy also extends to the family, with clear divisions between men and women; were these unusual in classical civilizations? Does Aristotle's definition of the purposes of family organization differ from those in China and India?

Aristotle was an ardent defender of most Athenian political principles, including a degree of democracy as the Athenians defined it. How do his arguments for social and family hierarchy relate to Greek politics?

Social divisions existed in all the classical civilizations, of course. Were the kinds of divisions Aristotle described comparable to social structures elsewhere in the classical world—for example, in India's caste system?

I. POLITICS

We stated above that the land ought to be possessed by those who have arms and enjoy full participation in the constitution, and why the cultivators should be different from the owners, also the nature and extent of the territory required. We must speak first about the division of the land for the purposes of cultivation and about those who will cultivate it, who and of what type they will be. We do not agree with those who have said that all land should be communally owned, but we do believe that there should be a friendly arrangement for sharing the usufruct [profits] and that none of the citizens should be without means of support. Next as to communal feeding, it is generally agreed that this is a very useful institution in a well-ordered society; why we too are of this opinion we will say later. In any case, where commu-

Selection 1 from Aristotle, *The Politics,* translated by T. A. Sinclair (Harmmondsworth, England: Penguin Classics edition, 1962). Copyright © 1962 by the Estate of T. A. Sinclair. Reprinted by permission of Penguin Books Ltd. Selection 2 from Aristotle, *Economics,* Book I, in Vol. 10 of *The Oxford Translation of Aristotle,* edited by W. D. Ross (Oxford: Oxford University Press, 1921).

nal meals exist, all citizens should partake of them, though it is not easy for those who are badly off to pay the contribution fixed and keep a household going at the same time. Another thing that should be a charge on the whole community is the public worship of the gods. Thus it becomes necessary to divide the land into two parts, one publicly owned, the other privately. Each of these has to be further divided into two. One part of the public land will support the service of the gods, the other the communal feeding. Of the privately owned land one part will be near the frontier, the other near the city, so that every citizen will have two portions, one in each locality. This is not only in accordance with justice and equality but makes also for greater unity in the face of wars with bordering states. Without this dual arrangement some make too little of hostilities on the border, others too much, some underestimate the dangers of frontier quarrels, others take them too seriously, even sacrificing honour in order to avoid them. Hence in some countries it is the custom that when war against a neighbour is under consideration, those who live near to the border should be excluded from the discussion as being too closely involved to be able to give honest advice. It is therefore important that the territory should for the reasons given be divided in the manner stated. As for those who are to till the land, they should, if possible, be slaves (and we are building as we would wish). They should not be all of one stock nor men of spirit; this will ensure that they will be good workers and not prone to revolt. An alternative to slaves is foreigners settled on the countryside, men of the same type as the slaves just mentioned. They fall into two groups according to whether they work privately on the land of individual owners of property, or publicly on the common land. I hope later on to say how slaves ought to be used in agriculture and why it is a good thing that all slaves should have before them the prospect of receiving their freedom as a reward.

2. ECONOMICS

As regards the human part of the household, the first care is concerning a wife; for a common life is above all things natural to the female and to the male. For we have elsewhere laid down the principle that nature aims at producing many such forms of association, just as also it produces the various kinds of animals. But it is impossible for the female to accomplish this without the male or the male without the female, so that their common life has necessarily arisen. Now in the other animals this intercourse is not based on reason, but depends on the amount of natural instinct which they possess and is entirely for the purpose of procreation. But in the civilized and more intelligent animals the bond of unity is more perfect (for in them we see more mutual help and goodwill and co-operation), above all in the case of man, because the female and the male co-operate to ensure not merely existence but a good life. And the production of children is not only a way of serving nature but also of securing a real advantage; for the trouble which parents bestow upon their helpless children when they are themselves vigorous is repaid to them in old age when they are helpless by their children, who are then in their full vigour. At the same time also nature thus periodically provides for the perpetuation of mankind as a species, since she cannot do so individually. Thus the nature both of the man and of the woman has been preordained by the will of heaven to live a common life. For they are distinguished in that the powers which they possess are not applicable to purposes in all cases identical, but in some respects their functions are opposed to one another though they all tend to the same end. For nature has made the one sex stronger, the other weaker, that the latter through fear may be the more cautious, while the former by its courage is better able to ward off attacks; and that the one may acquire possessions outside the house, the other preserve those within. In the performance of work, she made one sex able to lead a sedentary life and not strong enough to endure exposure, the other less adapted for quiet pursuits but well constituted for outdoor activities; and in relation to offspring she has made both share in the procreation of children, but each render its peculiar service towards them, the woman by nurturing, the man by educating them.

First, then, there are certain laws to be observed towards a wife, including the avoidance of doing her any wrong; for thus a man is less likely himself to be wronged. This is inculcated by the general law, as the Pythagoreans say, that one least of all should injure a wife as being "a suppliant and seated at the hearth." Now wrong inflicted by a husband is the formation of connexions outside his own house. As regards sexual intercourse, a man ought not to accustom himself not to need it at all nor to be unable to rest when it is lacking, but so as to be content with or without it. The saying of Hesiod is a good one:

A man should marry a maiden, that habits discreet he may teach her.

For dissimilarity of habits tends more than anything to destroy affection. As regards adornment, husband and wife ought not to approach one another with false affectation in their person any more than in their manners; for if the society of husband and wife requires such embellishment, it is no better than play-acting on the tragic stage.

Of possessions, that which is the best and the worthiest subject of economics comes first and is most essential—I mean, man. It is necessary therefore first to provide oneself with good slaves. Now slaves are of two kinds, the overseer and the worker. And since we see that methods of education produce a certain character in the young, it is necessary when one has procured slaves to bring up carefully those to whom the higher duties are to be entrusted. The intercourse of a master with his slaves should be such as not either to allow them to be insolent or to irritate them. To the higher class of slaves he ought to give some share of honour, and to the workers abundance of nourishment. And since the drinking of wine makes even freemen insolent, and many nations even of freemen abstain therefrom (the Carthaginians, for instance, when they are on military service), it is clear that wine ought never to be given to slaves, or at any rate very seldom. Three things make up the life of a slave, work, punishment, and food. To give them food but no punishment and no work makes them insolent; and that they should have work and punishment but no food is tyrannical and destroys their efficiency. It remains therefore to give them work and sufficient food; for it is impossible to rule over slaves without offering rewards, and a slave's reward is his food. And just as all other men become worse when they get no advantage by being better and there are no rewards for virtue and punishments for vice, so also is it with slaves. Therefore we must take careful notice and bestow or withhold everything, whether food or clothing or leisure or punishments, according to merit, in word and deed following the practice adopted by physicians in the matter of medicine, remembering at the same time that food is not medicine because it must be given continually.

The slave who is best suited for his work is the kind that is neither too cowardly nor too courageous. Slaves who have either of these characteristics are injurious to their owners; those who are too cowardly lack endurance, while the highspirited are not easy to control. All ought to have a definite end in view; for it is just and beneficial to offer slaves their freedom as a prize, for they are willing to work when a prize is set before them and a limit of time is defined.

STUDY QUESTIONS

1. Why does Aristotle find slavery necessary?
2. How does the discussion of slavery or the use of foreigners mesh with Athenian political values? Would Aristotle and Pericles have argued about these issues?
3. Are Aristotle's gender values patriarchal? How do they compare with the gender system of Sparta, described earlier by Lycurgus? (See Chapter 13.)
4. How do Greek gender values compare with those of classical India and China? Were they more or less severe?
5. How do Aristotle's views on social inequality compare with Confucian and Hindu views? What are the key similarities? How do all these social theories compare with characteristic modern discussions on the reasons and justifications for social inequality?

15

Principles of Roman Political Virtue: Plutarch

The Roman Republic and early Empire produced many vigorous statesmen, including leaders of the famous Senate, and many enunciations of basic political principles. Although some leaders seized power by military force or by manipulating support, others were selected because they seemed to exemplify sound political virtues. Unlike Athenians, who in their democratic period chose many officials by lot, most Roman republican leaders were elected by the Senate or the popular assembly, and this prompted frequent discussions of what qualities a good statesman should possess. Correspondingly, when political life in the Republic became more contentious, ultimately yielding to the formation of the Empire, and again later when the Empire itself began to function badly, many observers blamed a deterioration of leadership quality rather than any larger problems.

The following passages were written by a Greek politician and writer, Plutarch, who was born between 40 and 45 C.E., in the early stages of the Empire when republican values continued to be widely touted even though institutions were changing. Entitled *Precepts of Statecraft,* they were designed to distill examples of success and failure for the training of a Greek aristocrat, Menemachus. Plutarch belonged to a wealthy family in the Greek city of Chaerona. He was fascinated with Roman political affairs, because the Romans had ruled his region for some time. He compiled a host of biographies of Roman emperors and other political figures, advised the emperor Trajan, and ultimately became both a citizen of Rome and an ambassador. Plutarch's method, using historical example to illustrate and deriving basic lessons in political behavior, included abundant references to past figures such as Pericles (whom Plutarch admired) or the popular but ultimately assassinated Roman reformers, the Gracchus brothers (whom Plutarch judged unwise for disrupting the late Republic).

Plutarch's summary of Mediterranean political values at the height of the Roman period obviously deserves comparison with earlier statements from leaders of Greek city-states and with political philosophers in other classical civilizations, such as Confucius.

Reprinted by permission of the publishers and the Loeb Classical Library from *Moralia, Plutarch: Volume x, xv,* translated by Harold North Fowler (Cambridge, MA., Harvard University Press, 1936), pp. 159–163, 169–171, 215–217, 229–231, 243, 289–293.

First, then, at the base of political activity there must be, as a firm and strong foundation, a choice of policy arising from judgement and reason, not from mere impulse due to empty opinion or contentiousness or lack of other activities. For just as those who have no useful occupation at home spend most of their time in the market-place, even if there is nothing they need there, just so some men, because they have no business of their own that is worth serious attention, throw themselves into public affairs, treating political activity as a pastime, and many who have become engaged in public affairs by chance and have had enough of them are no longer able to retire from them without difficulty; they are in the same predicament as persons who have gone aboard a vessel to be rocked a bit and then have been driven out into the open sea; they turn their gaze outside, seasick and much disturbed, but obliged to stay where they are and endure their present plight.

> Over the bright calm sea
> The fair-faced loves went past them to the mad
> Outrage of the ship's oars that plough the deep.

These men cast the greatest discredit upon public life by regretting their course and being unhappy when, after hoping for glory, they have fallen into disgrace or, after expecting to be feared by others on account of their power, they are drawn into affairs which involve dangers and popular disorders. But the man who has entered upon public life from conviction and reasoning, as the activity most befitting him and most honourable, is not frightened by any of these things, nor is his conviction changed. For neither is it right to enter upon public life as a gainful trade, as Stratocles and Dromoclcides and their set used to invite each other to come to the golden harvest (for so they called the orators' platform in jest); nor ought we to enter upon it as if we were suddenly seized by an onset of strong emotion, as Gaius Gracchus did, who, when his brother's misfortunes were still fresh, withdrew so far as possible from public affairs and then, inflamed by anger because certain persons insulted and reviled him, rushed into public life. . . .

So, then, the statesman who already has attained to power and has won the people's confidence should try to train the character of the citizens, leading them gently towards that which is better and treating them with mildness; for it is a difficult task to change the multitude. But do you yourself, since you are henceforth to live as on an open stage, educate your character and put it in order; and if it is not easy wholly to banish evil from the soul, at any rate remove and repress those faults which are most flourishing and conspicuous. For you know the story that Themistocles, when he was thinking of entering upon public life, withdrew from drinking-parties and carousals; he was wakeful at night, was sober and deeply thoughtful. . . .

And Pericles also changed his personal habits of life, so that he walked slowly, spoke gently, always showed a composed countenance, kept his hand under his cloak, and trod only one path—that which led to the assembly and the senate. For a populace is not a simple and easy thing for any chance person to subject to that control which is salutary; but one must be satisfied if the multitude accept authority without shying, like a suspicious and capricious beast, at face or voice. Since, then, the statesman must not treat even these matters carelessly, ought he to neglect the things which affect his life and character, that they may be clear of blame and ill report of every kind? For not only are men in public life held responsible for their public words and actions, but people busy themselves with all their concerns: dinner, love affair, marriage, amusement, and every serious interest. . . .

For, just as a mole or a wart on the face is more unpleasant than brand-marks, mutilations, or scars on other parts of the body, so small faults appear great when observed in the lives of leaders and statesmen on account of the opinion which the majority has of governing and public office, regarding it as a great thing which ought to be clean of all eccentricities and errors. . . . For if it is a noble thing and the mark of an exalted spirit to exclaim

> I love my children, but I love my country more,

would it not have been easier for each of them to say, "I hate so-and-so and wish to do him harm, but I love my country more"? For to be unwilling to make peace with a personal enemy for the sake of those things for which we ought even to give up a friend is shockingly uncivilized and as low as the beasts. . . .

For the statesman should not regard any fellow-citizen as an enemy, unless some man . . . should appear who is a pest and a running sore to the State. Those who are in other ways out of harmony he should, like a skilful musician, bring into unison by gently tightening or relaxing the strings of his control, not attacking angrily and insultingly those who err, but making an appeal designed rather to make a moral impression. . . .

For so far as goodwill and solicitude for the common weal are concerned, a statesman should not hold aloof from any part of public affairs, but should pay attention to them all and inform himself about all details; nor should he, as the ship's gear called sacred is stowed apart, hold himself aloof, waiting for the extreme necessities and fortunes of the State; but just as pilots do some things with their own hands but perform other duties by means of different instruments operated by different agents, thus giving a turn or a twist to the instruments while they sit apart, and they make use of sailors, look-out men, and boatswains, some of whom they often call to the stern and entrust with the tiller, just so it is fitting that the statesman should yield office to others and should invite them to the orators' platform in a gracious and kindly manner, and he should not try to administer all the affairs of the State by his own speeches, decrees, and actions, but should have good, trustworthy men and employ each of them for each particular service according to his fitness. . . .

Or should we correct Euripides when he chants the sentiment that if a man must spend sleepless nights and haunt another man's court and subject himself to an intimacy with a great man, it is best to do so for the sake of his native land, but otherwise it is best to welcome and hold fast friendships based on equality and justice?

However, the statesman, while making his native State readily obedient to its sovereigns, must not further humble it . . . [T]hose who invite the sovereign's decision on every decree, meeting of a council, granting of a privilege or administrative measure, force their sovereign to be their master more than he desires. And the cause of this is chiefly the greed and contentiousness of the foremost citizens; for either, in cases in which they are injuring their inferiors, they force them into exile from the State, or, in matters concerning which they differ among themselves. . . .

Now those who are skilled in tending and keeping bees think that the hive which hums loudest and is most full of noise is thriving and in good condition; but he to whom God has given the care of the rational and political swarm will judge of its happiness chiefly by the quietness and tranquillity of the people; he will accept and imitate to the best of his ability the other precepts of Solon, but will wonder in great perplexity why that great man prescribed that in case of factional disorder whoever joined neither faction should be deprived of civic rights. For in a body afflicted with disease, the beginning of a change to health does not come from the diseased parts, but it comes when the condition in the healthy parts gains strength and drives out that which is contrary to nature; and in a people afflicted with faction, if it is not dangerous and destructive but is destined to cease sometime, there must be a strong, permanent, and permeating admixture of sanity and soundness; for to this element there flows from the men of understanding that which is akin to it, and then it permeates the part which is diseased; but States which have fallen into complete disorder are utterly ruined unless they meet with some external necessity and chastisement and are thus forcibly compelled by their misfortunes to be reasonable. . . .

But the best thing is to see to it in advance that factional discord shall never arise among them and to regard this as the greatest and noblest function of what may be called the art of statesmanship. For observe that of the greatest blessings which States can enjoy,—peace, liberty, plenty, abundance of men, and concord,—so far as peace is concerned the peoples have no need of statesmanship at present; for all war, both Greek and foreign, has been banished from among us and has disappeared; and of liberty the peoples have as great a share as our rulers grant them, and perhaps more would not be better for them; but bounteous productiveness of the soil, kindly tempering of the seasons, that wives may bear "children like to their sires," and that the offspring may live in safety—these things the wise man will ask the gods in his prayers to grant his fellow-citizens.

There remains, then, for the statesman, of those activities which fall within his province, only this—and it is the equal of any of the other blessings:—always to instil concord and friendship in those who dwell together with him and to remove strifes, discords, and all enmity. . . .

STUDY QUESTIONS

1. What are the main qualities a good leader should aspire to, according to Plutarch?
2. What are the main functions of a good leader and a good state? Why would Plutarch have been so attracted to Roman—which was, to him, foreign—rule?
3. Why was Plutarch relatively uninterested in the specific structure of a state? Was this a potential weakness in his political approach?
4. How do his principles for leadership compare with those earlier implied by Pericles? What would Plutarch have thought of attempts to form a democracy?
5. What are the similarities and differences between Plutarch's concept of leadership and that of Confucius? Which approach was most useful for forming an effective bureaucracy?
6. How do Plutarch's political principles and his goals for the state compare with more modern formulations?

16

Global Contacts: Whistling Arrows and Chinese Emperors

One of the most important developments in world history during the first millennium B.C.E. was the rise of the pastoral nomads in central Asia. From 300 B.C.E. onward successive groups of horseriders dominated the wide swath of grasslands stretching from Mongolia in the east to the Ukraine in the west along the fiftieth degree of latitude. For nearly two millennia the success or failure of rulers in China, India, Persia, and Russia often depended on their ability to mobilize effective defenses against—or trade with—the nomadic horseriders.

The first of the great nomadic confederations or "states" in central Asia was created around 200 B.C.E. by the people known to the Chinese as the Hsiung-nu. The Hsiung-nu, whose home was the plains of present-day Inner Mongolia, were herders and hunters who occasionally engaged in trade with Chinese merchants. However, in times of hardship on the prairie the Hsiung-nu raided the silos of Chinese peasants to obtain supplies of newly harvested grain.

For the Hsiung-nu the unification of China in 221 B.C.E. by Emperor Ch'in Shih-huang-ti was an ominous development. Soon after establishing his rule, the First Emperor had walls built along the northern frontier of China. (Much later these separate walls were joined together to form the Great Wall.) The Chinese walls were built to fence out the nomads and, equally important to the First Emperor, to fence in potential Chinese allies of the nomads.

As the Chinese walls went up, the Hsiung-nu began to unite their traditionally conflict-prone neighbors on the grasslands into a formidable military force. For the

Selections 1, 2, and 3 from *Records of the Grand Historian of China*, Burton Watson, tr. © 1961 (New York: Columbia University Press), pp. 155–156, 160–161, 163–165, 167–170. Reprinted with permission of the publisher. Selection 4 from Yu, Ying-shih, *Trade and Expansion in Han China: A Study in the Structure of Sino-Barbarian Economic Relations* (Berkeley: University of California Press, 1967), p. 47.

next 250 years, until the Hsiung-nu confederation unraveled in the first century of the Common Era, the emperors of the Han dynasty were compelled to devote considerable attention to relations with the Hsiung-nu. Indeed, relations with the nomadic successors of the Hsiung-nu remained a major priority for Chinese emperors until after 1700 C.E.

Because the Hsiung-nu did not have a system of writing, and therefore left no records for historians to examine, our richest sources of documentary evidence about them come from the writings of ancient Chinese historians. The following account of the rise of the Hsiung-nu comes from the work of the greatest of the early Chinese historians, Ssu-ma Ch'ien (ca. 145–90 B.C.E.). A table on Chinese "gifts" of silk to the Hsiung-nu, which comes from a book by a present-day historian, follows the excerpts from Ssu-ma Ch'ien. How do these documents help us to understand the Hsiung-nu and their contacts with the Chinese?

I. THE HSIUNG-NU

The ancestor of the Hsiung-nu was a descendant of the rulers of the Hsia dynasty [ca. 2000–1750 B.C.E.] by the name of Ch'un-wei. As early as the time of Emperors Yao and Shun and before, we hear of these people, known as Mountain Barbarians, . . . living in the region of the northern barbarians and wandering from place to place pasturing their animals. The animals they raise consist mainly of horses, cows, and sheep, but include such rare beasts as camels, asses, mules, and wild horses. . . . They move about in search of water and pasture and have no walled cities or fixed dwellings, nor do they engage in any kind of agriculture. Their lands, however, are divided into regions under the control of various leaders. They have no writing, and even promises and agreements are only verbal. The little boys start out by learning to ride sheep and shoot birds and rats with a bow and arrow, and when they get a little older they shoot foxes and hares, which are used for food. Thus all the young men are able to use a bow and act as armed cavalry in time of war. It is their custom to herd their flocks in times of peace and make their living by hunting, but in periods of crisis they take up arms and go off on plundering and marauding expeditions. This seems to be their inborn nature. For long-range weapons they use bows and arrows, and swords and spears at close range. If the battle is going well for them they will advance, but if not, they will retreat, for they do not consider it a disgrace to run away. Their only concern is self-advantage, and they know nothing of propriety or righteousness.

From the chiefs of the tribe on down, everyone eats the meat of the domestic animals and wears clothes of hide or wraps made of felt or fur. The young men eat the richest and best food, while the old get what is left over, since the tribe honors those who are young and strong and despises the weak and aged. On the death of his father, a son will marry his stepmother, and when brothers die, the remaining brothers will take the widows for their own wives. . . .

Under the *Shan-yü* [i.e., the Hsiung-nu emperor] are the Wise Kings of the Left and Right, the left and right Lu-li kings, left and right generals, left and right commandants, left and right household administrators, and left and right Ku-tu marquises. The Hsiung-nu word for "wise" is "*t'u-ch'i*," so that the heir of the *Shan-yü* is customarily called the "*T'u-ch'i* King of the Left." Among the other leaders, from the wise kings on down to the household administrators, the more important ones command ten thousand horsemen and the lesser ones several thousand, numbering twenty-four leaders in all, though all are known by the title of "Ten Thousand Horsemen." The high ministerial offices are hereditary, being filled from generation to generation by the members of the Hu-yen and Lan families, and in more recent times by the Hsü-pu family. These three families constitute the aristocracy of the nation. The kings and other leaders of the left live in the eastern sector, the region from Shang-ku east to the lands of the Hui-mo and Ch'ao-hsien peoples. The kings and leaders of the right live in the west, the area from Shang Province west to the territories of the Yüeh-chih and Ch'iang tribes. The *Shan-yü* has his court in the region north of Tai and Yün-chung. Each group has its own area, within which it moves about from place to place looking for water and pasture. The Left and Right Wise Kings and Lu-li kings are the most powerful, while the Ku-tu marquises assist the *Shan-yü* in the administration of the nation. Each of the twenty-four leaders in turn appoints his own "chiefs of a thousand," "chiefs of a hundred," and "chiefs of ten," as well as his subordinate kings, prime ministers, chief commandants, household administrators, *chü-ch'ü* officials, and so forth.

In the first month of the year the various leaders come together in a small meeting of the *Shan-yü*'s court to perform sacrifices, and in the fifth month a great meeting is held at Lung-ch'eng at which sacrifices are conducted to the Hsiung-nu ancestors, Heaven and Earth, and the gods and spirits. In the autumn, when the horses are fat, another great meeting is held at the Tai Forest when a reckoning is made of the number of persons and animals.

According to Hsiung-nu law, anyone who in ordinary times draws his sword a foot from the scabbard is condemned to death. Anyone convicted of theft has his property confiscated. Minor offenses are punished by flogging and major ones by death. No one is kept in jail awaiting sentence longer than ten days, and the number of imprisoned men for the whole nation does not exceed a handful.

At dawn the *Shan-yü* leaves his camp and makes obeisance to the sun as it rises, and in the evening he makes a similar obeisance to the moon. In seating arrangements the left side or the seat facing north is considered the place of honor. The days *wu* and *chi* of the ten-day week are regarded as most auspicious.

In burials the Hsiung-nu use an inner and an outer coffin, with accessories of gold, silver, clothing, and fur, but they do not construct grave mounds or plant trees on the grave, nor do they use mourning garments. When a ruler dies, the ministers and concubines who were favored by him and who are obliged to follow him in death often number in the hundreds or even thousands.

Whenever the Hsiung-nu begin some undertaking, they observe the stars and the moon. They attack when the moon is full and withdraw their troops when it wanes. After a battle those who have cut off the heads of the enemy or taken prisoners are presented with a cup of wine and allowed to keep the spoils they have captured. Any prisoners that are taken are made slaves. Therefore, when they fight, each man strives for his own gain. They are very skillful at using decoy troops to lure their opponents to destruction. When they catch sight of the enemy, they swoop down like a flock of birds, eager for booty, but when they find themselves hard pressed and beaten, they scatter and vanish like the mist. Anyone who succeeds in recovering the body of a comrade who has fallen in battle receives all of the dead man's property. . . .

2. THE RISE OF MO-TUN

At this time [around 210 B.C.E.] the Eastern Barbarians were very powerful and the Yüeh-chih were likewise flourishing. The *Shan-yü* or chieftain of the Hsiung-nu was named T'ou-man. T'ou-man, unable to hold out against the Ch'in [i.e., Chinese] forces, had withdrawn to the far north, where he lived with his subjects for over ten years. After Meng T'ien died and the feudal lords revolted against the Ch'in, plunging China into a period of strife and turmoil, the convicts which the Ch'in had sent to the northern border to garrison the area all returned to their homes. The Hsiung-nu, the pressure against them relaxed, once again began to infiltrate south of the bend of the Yellow River until they had established themselves along the old border of China.

T'ou-man's oldest son, the heir apparent to his position, was named Mo-tun, but the *Shan-yü* also had a younger son by another consort whom he had taken later and was very fond of. He decided that he wanted to get rid of Mo-tun and set up his younger son as heir instead, and he therefore sent Mo-tun as a hostage to the Yüeh-chih nation. Then, after Mo-tun had arrived among the Yüeh-chih, T'ou-man made a sudden attack on them. The Yüeh-chih were about to kill Mo-tun in retaliation, but he managed to steal one of their best horses and escape, eventually making his way back home. His father, struck by his bravery, put him in command of a force of ten thousand cavalry.

Mo-tun had some arrows made that whistled in flight and used them to drill his troops in shooting from horseback. "Shoot wherever you see my whistling arrow strike!" he ordered, "and anyone who fails to shoot will be cut down!" Then he went out hunting for birds and animals, and if any of his men failed to shoot at what he himself had shot at, he cut them down on the spot. After this, he shot a whistling arrow at one of his best horses. Some of his men hung back and did not dare shoot at the horse, whereupon Mo-tun at once executed them. A little later he took an arrow and shot at his favorite wife. Again some of his men shrank back in terror and failed to discharge their arrows, and again he executed them on the spot. Finally he went out hunting with his men and shot a whistling arrow at one of his father's finest horses. All his followers promptly discharged their arrows in the same direction, and Mo-tun knew that at last they could be trusted. Accompanying his father, the *Shan-yü* T'ou-man, on a hunting expedition, he shot a whistling arrow at his father and every one of his followers aimed their arrows in the same direction and shot the *Shan-yü* dead. Then Mo-tun executed his stepmother, his younger brother, and all the high officials of the nation who refused to take orders from him, and set himself up as the new *Shan-yü* [reigned 209–174 B.C.E.]. . . .

3. AN EXCHANGE OF LETTERS

When Emperor Wen [of the Han dynasty] came to the throne he renewed the peace treaty with the Hsiung-nu. In the fifth month of the third year of his reign [177 B.C.E.], however, the Hsiung-nu Wise King of the Right invaded the region south of the Yellow River, plundering the loyal barbarians of Shang Province who had been appointed by the Han to guard the frontier, and murdering and carrying off a number of the inhabitants. Emperor Wen ordered the chancellor Kuan Ying to lead a force of eighty-five thousand carriages and cavalry to Kao-nu, where they attacked the Wise King of the Right. The latter fled beyond the frontier.

The emperor in person visited T'ai-yüan, at which time the king of Chi-pei revolted. When the emperor returned to the capital he disbanded the army which Kuan Ying had used in the attack on the barbarians.

The following year the *Shan-yü* [i.e., Mo-tun] sent a letter to the Han court which read:

> The great *Shan-yü* whom Heaven has set up respectfully inquires of the emperor's heath. Formerly the emperor broached the question of a peace alliance, and I was most happy to comply with the intentions expressed in his letter. Certain of the Han border officials, however, imposed upon and insulted the Wise King of the Right, and as a result he heeded the counsel of Hou-i, Lu-hou, Nan-chih, and others of his generals and, without asking my permission, engaged in a skirmish with the Han officials, thus violating the pact between the rulers of our two nations and rupturing the bonds of brotherhood that joined us. The emperor has twice sent letters complaining of this situation and I have in turn dispatched an envoy with my answer, but my envoy has not been allowed to return, nor has any envoy come from the Han. As a result, the Han has broken off peaceful relations and our two neighboring countries are no longer bound in alliance.
>
> Because of the violation of the pact committed by the petty officials, and the subsequent events, I have punished the Wise King of the Right by sending him west to search out the Yüeh-chih people and attack them. Through the aid of Heaven, the excellence of his fighting men, and the strength of his horses, he has succeeded in wiping out the Yüeh-chih, slaughtering or forcing to submission every member of the tribe. In addition he has conquered the Lou-lan, Wu-sun, and Hu-chieh tribes, as well as the twenty-six states nearby, so that all of them have become a part of the Hsiung-nu nation. All the people who live by drawing the bow are now united into one family and the entire region of the north is at peace.
>
> Thus I wish now to lay down my weapons, rest my soldiers, and turn my horses to pasture; to forget the recent affair and restore our old pact, that the peoples of the border may have peace such as they enjoyed in former times, that the young may grow to manhood, the old live out their lives in security, and generation after generation enjoy peace and comfort.
>
> However, I do not as yet know the intentions of the emperor. Therefore I have dispatched my palace attendant Hsi-hu-ch'ien to bear this letter. At the same time I beg to present one camel, two riding horses, and eight carriage horses. If the emperor does not wish the Hsiung-nu to approach his frontier, then he should order the officials and people along the border to withdraw a good distance back from the frontier. When my envoy has arrived and delivered this, I trust that he will be sent back to me.

The envoy bearing the letter arrived in the region of Hsin-wang during the sixth month. When it was delivered to the emperor, he began deliberations with his ministers as to whether it was better to attack or make peace. The high officials all stated, "Since the *Shan-yü* has just conquered the Yüeh-chih and is riding on a wave of victory, he cannot be attacked. Moreover, even if we were to seize the Hsiung-nu lands, they are all swamps and saline wastes, not fit for habitation. It would be far better to make peace."

The emperor agreed with their opinion and in the sixth year of the former part of his reign [174 B.C.E.] he sent an envoy to the Hsiung-nu with a letter which read as follows:

The emperor respectfully inquires about the health of the great *Shan-yü*. Your palace attendant Hsi-hu-ch'ien has brought us a letter which states: "The Wise King of the Right, without asking my permission, heeded the counsel of Hou-i, Lu-hou, Nan-chih, and others of his generals, violating the pact between the rulers of our two nations and rupturing the bonds of brotherhood that joined us, and as a result the Han has broken off peaceful relations with me, and our two neighboring countries are no longer bound in alliance. Because of the violation of the pact committed by the petty officials, I have punished the Wise King of the Right by sending him west to attack the Yüeh-chih. Having completed the conquest of the region, I wish to lay down my weapons, rest my soldiers, and turn my horses to pasture; to forget the recent affair and restore our old pact so that the peoples of the border may have peace, the young may grow to manhood, the old live out their lives in security, and generation after generation enjoy peace and comfort."

We heartily approve these words. This indeed is the way the sage rulers of antiquity would have spoken.

The Han has made a pact of brotherhood with the Hsiung-nu, and for this reason we have sent generous gifts to you. Any violations of the pact or ruptures of the bonds of brotherhood have been the work of the Hsiung-nu. However, as there has been an amnesty since the affair of the Wise King of the Right occurred, you need not punish him too severely. If your intentions are really those expressed in your letter, and if you will make them clearly known to your various officials so that they will henceforth act in good faith and commit no more violations of the pact, then we are prepared to honor the terms of your letter.

Your envoy tells us that you have led your troops in person to attack the other barbarian nations and have won merit, suffering great hardship on the field of battle. We therefore send you from our own wardrobe an embroidered robe lined with patterned damask, an embroidered and lined underrobe, and a brocaded coat, one each; one comb; one sash with gold ornaments; one gold-ornamented leather belt; ten rolls of embroidery; thirty roles of brocade; and forty rolls each of heavy red silk and light green silk, which shall be delivered to you by our palace counselor I and master of guests Chien.

4. HAN CHINESE GIFTS OF SILK TO THE HSIUNG-NU

Year (B.C.E.)	Silk Floss (catties)	Silk Fabrics (pieces)
51	6,000	8,000
49	8,000	9,000
33	16,000	18,000
25	20,000	20,000
1	30,000	30,000

Note: 1 catty equals approximately $\frac{1}{2}$ lb.

STUDY QUESTIONS

1. What are Ssu-ma Ch'ien's most important points about the Hsiung-nu? What does he observe about the Hsiung-nu economy, their political system, their social classes, and their religion?

2. According to Ssu-ma Ch'ien, what seems to explain the rise of Mo-tun as the Hsiung-nu *Shan-yü*? How does the account of Mo-tun's rise to power add to our understanding of the culture and political institutions of the Hsiung-nu?

3. What are the main points in the letters exchanged between Mo-tun and Emperor Wen? Do Mo-tun and Emperor Wen agree on the reasons for the conflict between the Hsiung-nu and the Chinese?

4. What do the two letters reveal about the level of political thinking among the Hsiung-nu and the Chinese?

5. Do you see elements of Confucian thinking in the letter from Emperor Wen? In the letter from Mo-tun? How do you explain this?

6. What "gifts" do Emperor Wen and Mo-tun exchange? Does the exchange seem equal to you? What other terms besides "gift-giving" might be used to describe this exchange?

7. What does the trend in Chinese silk sent to the Hsiung-nu, as indicated by the table, suggest about Chinese perceptions of the nomads? What does the same trend suggest about the importance of the silk industry in China?

8. Why do you think Ssu-ma Ch'ien devoted so much attention to the Hsiung-nu? How do you think he obtained his information about the nomads? Why might we expect that a Chinese historian's account of the Hsiung-nu might be biased? Do you detect any bias in Ssu-ma Ch'ien? Is it possible to write "objective" history?

17

Global Contacts: Precious Commodities and Cultural Interchange

Rome, Arabia, India, and China

During the Han dynasty (206 B.C.E.–220 C.E.) Chinese emperors began to send large amounts of silk—for both diplomatic and commercial reasons—to the nomads of central Asia. Within a short time some of this silk found its way, by means of a type of relay trade, to the overland trade routes running west to Rome. Historians refer to these routes collectively as the Silk Road. By 100 C.E. the land routes linking China to Rome also had a maritime counterpart. Seaborne commerce flourished between Rome and India via the Red Sea and the Arabian Sea. Farther east, shipping routes connected Indian ports with harbors in Southeast Asia and on the coast of China.

A great Afro-Eurasian commercial network had now come into being. Silk from China (the only country which produced it until after 500 C.E.), pepper and jewels from India, and incense from Arabia were sent to the Mediterranean region on well-traveled routes which terminated in Roman ports such as Alexandria, Tyre, and Ephesus. In exchange for these precious commodities, the Romans, albeit somewhat reluctantly, sent large amounts of silver, bronze, and gold eastward to destinations in Asia.

Since the long-distance trade of the classical period was mainly in luxuries rather than in articles of daily use, its overall economic impact was probably limited. (However, see the contrary view that follows by the Roman writer Pliny the Elder.) Most present-day historians think, contrary to the views of Pliny, that the Rome-India-China trade was significant primarily because of its role in promoting the spread of religions, styles of art, technologies, and epidemic diseases.

Selection 1 from Suetonius, *The Twelve Caesars: Gaius Suetonius Tranquillus,* translated by Robert Graves (Baltimore: Penguin Books, 1957), p. 175. Permission granted by W. P. Watt Ltd on behalf of The Trustees of the Robert Graves Copyright Trust. Selections 2 and 3 reprinted by permission of the publishers and the Loeb Classical Library from *Strabo, Geography, Volume I,* pp. 453, 455; *Volume VII,* pp. 125, 127, 129, translated by Horace L. Jones, (Cambridge, MA.: Harvard University Press, 1917; 1930). Selections 4 and 5 reprinted by permission of the publishers and the Loeb Classical Library from *Pliny, Natural History, Volume IV,* translated by H. Rackham, (Cambridge, MA.: Harvard University Press, 1942), pp. 19, 21, 41, 43, 45, 47, 61, 63. Selection 6 from *The Travels of Fa-hsien (399–414 A.D.),* or *Record of the Buddhistic Kingdoms,* translated by H. A. Giles (Cambridge: Cambridge University Press, 1923), pp. 76–79, 81.

Sculptural styles that developed in many parts of Asia during the first millennium C.E. are an especially striking case of this process of cultural lending and borrowing. Many of the earliest Indian (Gandhara school) representations of the Buddha, dating from early in the Common Era, are sculptures that show the Buddha wearing a Greco-Roman style toga. Moreover, present-day museums in Pakistan, India, central Asia, northern China, and Japan display numerous examples of other types of sculpture dating from the first millennium which clearly show the influence of Greco-Roman models. It is this kind of evidence that has led scholars to conclude that the significance of the Silk Road was not economic but rather primarily cultural (and perhaps biological, if we take into account the probable spread of diseases along the trade routes).

In various ways the passages that follow illustrate the existence of East-West contacts during the early centuries of the Common Era. Two characteristics of the documents should be kept in mind as you read them. The excerpts are necessarily fragmentary because, so far as historians know, there is no single narrative of a journey from Rome to China or vice versa from the classical period. In addition, the readings are heavily weighted toward the Roman end of the trade network because documentation from Asian sources is either nonexistent or extremely fragmentary.

1. A ROMAN EMPEROR'S FASHION STATEMENT

[*Suetonius, the author of the following passage on the notorious emperor Caligula (reigned 37 to 41 C.E.), was a Roman historian of the second century.*]

Caligula paid no attention to traditional or current fashions in his dress; ignoring male conventions and even the human decencies. Often he made public appearances in a cloak covered with embroidery and encrusted with precious stones, a long-sleeved tunic and bracelets; or in silk (which men were forbidden by law to wear) or even in a woman's robe; and came shod sometimes with slippers, sometimes with buskins, sometimes with military boots, sometimes with women's shoes. Occasionally he affected a golden beard and carried Jupiter's thunderbolt, Neptune's trident, or Mercury's serpent-twined staff. He even dressed up as Venus and, long before his expedition, wore the uniform of a triumphant general, often embellished with the breastplate which he had stolen from Alexander the Great's tomb at Alexandria. . . .

2. A REPORT ON AMBASSADORS FROM INDIA TO ROME

[*The following passage is from Strabo (born 64 B.C.E.), the Greek geographer. Nicolaus of Damascus (born 64 B.C.E.) was a historian and philosopher.*]

[Nicolaus of Damascus] says that at Antioch, near Daphne, he chanced to meet the Indian ambassadors who had been despatched to Caesar Augustus; that the letter [they carried] plainly indicated more than three ambassadors, but that only three had survived (whom he says he saw), but the rest, mostly by reason of the long journeys, had died; and that the letter was written in Greek on a skin; and that it plainly showed that Porus was the writer, and that, although he was ruler of six hundred kings, still he was anxious to be a friend to Caesar, and was ready, not only to allow him a passage through his country, wherever he wished to go, but also to co-operate

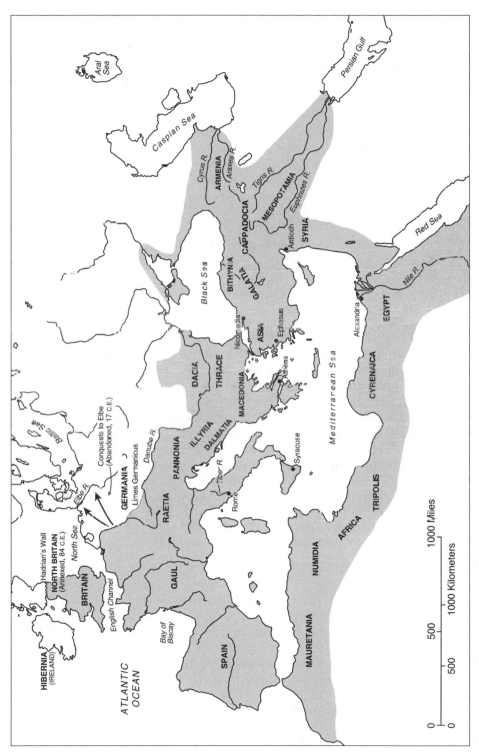

The Roman Empire at Its Greatest Extent, 98–117 C.E.

with him in anything that was honourable. Nicolaus says that this was the content of the letter to Caesar, and that the gifts carried to Caesar were presented by eight naked servants, who were clad only in loin-cloths besprinkled with sweet-smelling odours; and that the gifts consisted of the Hermes, a man who was born without arms, whom I myself have seen, and large vipers, and a serpent ten cubits in length, and a river tortoise three cubits in length, and a partridge larger than a vulture; and they were accompanied also, according to him, by the man who burned himself up at Athens; and that whereas some commit suicide when they suffer adversity, seeking release from the ills at hand, others do so when their lot is happy, as was the case with that man; for, he adds, although that man had fared as he wished up to that time, he thought it necessary then to depart this life, lest something untoward might happen to him if he tarried here; and that therefore he leaped upon the pyre with a laugh, his naked body anointed, wearing only a loin-cloth; and that the following words were inscribed on his tomb: "Here lies Zarmanochegas, an Indian from Bargosa, who immortalised himself in accordance with the ancestral customs of Indians."

3. STRABO'S REPORT ON ROMAN SHIPS SAILING TO INDIA

Again, since the Romans have recently invaded Arabia Felix with an army, of which Aelius Gallus, my friend and companion, was the commander, and since the merchants of Alexandria are already sailing with fleets by way of the Nile and of the Arabian Gulf as far as India, these regions also have become far better known to us of to-day than to our predecessors. At any rate, when Gallus was prefect of Egypt, I accompanied him and ascended the Nile as far as Syene and the frontiers of Ethiopia, and I learned that as many as one hundred and twenty vessels were sailing from Myos Hormos [an Egyptian port on the Red Sea] to India, whereas formerly, under the Ptolemies, only a very few ventured to undertake the voyage and to carry on traffic in Indian merchandise.

4. A ROMAN NATURALIST ON THE CULTIVATION OF INCENSE IN ARABIA.

[*The following two selections are from Pliny the Elder's* Natural History, *a work that runs to 37 books and was written in the first century C.E.*]

It used to be the custom, when there were fewer opportunities of selling frankincense, to gather it only once a year, but at the present day trade introduces a second harvesting. The earlier and natural gathering takes place at about the rising of the Dogstar, when the summer heat is most intense. They make an incision where the bark appears to be fullest of juice and distended to its thinnest; and the bark is loosened with a blow, but not removed. From the incision a greasy foam spurts out, which coagulates and thickens, being received on a mat of palm-leaves where the nature of the ground requires this, but in other places on a space round the tree that has been rammed hard. The frankincense collected in the latter way is in a purer state, but the former method produces a heavier weight; while the residue adhering to the tree is scraped off with an iron tool, and consequently contains fragments of bark. The forest is divided up into definite portions, and owing to the mutual honesty of the owners is free from trespassing, and though nobody keeps guard over the trees after an incision has been made, nobody steals from his neighbour. At Alexandria, on the other hand, where the frankincense is worked up for sale, good heavens! no vigilance is sufficient to guard the factories. A seal is put upon the workmen's aprons, they have to wear a mask or a net with a close mesh on their heads, and before they are allowed to leave the premises they have to take off all their clothes: so much less honesty is displayed with regard to the produce with them than as to the forests with the growers. The frankincense from the summer crop is collected in autumn; this is the purest kind, bright white in colour. The second crop is harvested in the spring, cuts having been made in the bark during the winter in preparation for it; the juice that comes out on this occasion is reddish, and not to be compared with the former taking, the name for which is carfiathum, the other being called dathiathum. Also the juice produced by a sapling is believed to be whiter, but that from an older tree has more scent . . .

Frankincense after being collected is conveyed to Sabota on camels, one of the gates of the city being opened for its admission; the kings have made it a capital offence for camels so laden to turn aside from the high road. At Sabota a tithe estimated by measure and not by weight is taken by the priests for the god they call Sabis, and the incense is not allowed to be put on the market until this has been done; this tithe is drawn on to defray what is a public expenditure, for actually on a fixed number of days the god graciously entertains guests at a banquet. It can only be exported through the country of the Gebbanitae [in southwest Arabia], and accordingly a tax is paid on it to the king of that people as well. Their capital is Thomna, which is 1487½ miles distant from the town of Gaza in Judaea on the Mediterranean coast; the journey is divided into 65 stages with halts for camels. Fixed portions of the frankincense are also given to the priests and the king's secretaries, but beside these the guards and their attendants and the gate-keepers and servants also have their pickings: indeed all along the route they keep on paying, at one place for water, at another for fodder, or the charges for lodging at the halts, and the various octrois [i.e., toll stations]; so that expenses mount up to 688 denarii [i.e., silver coins] per camel before the Mediterranean coast is reached; and then again payment is made to the customs officers of our empire. Consequently the price of the best frankincense is 6, of the second best 5, and the third best 3 denarii a pound. It is tested by its whiteness and stickiness, its fragility and its readiness to catch fire from a hot coal; and also it should not give to pressure of the teeth, and should rather crumble into grains. Among us it is adulterated with drops of white resin, which closely resemble it, but the fraud can be detected by the means specified. . . .

These people have not got cinnamon or casia, and nevertheless Arabia is styled 'Happy' [the Roman name for southwestern Arabia was "Arabia Felix," i.e., "Happy Arabia"]—a country with a false and ungrateful appellation, as she puts her happiness to the credit of the powers above, although she owes more of it to the power below. Her good fortune has been caused by the luxury of mankind even in the hour of death, when they burn over the departed the products which they had originally understood to have been created for the gods. Good authorities declare that Arabia does not produce so large a quantity of perfume in a year's output as was burned by the Emperor Nero in a day at the obsequies of his consort Poppaea. Then reckon up the vast number of funerals celebrated yearly throughout the entire world, and the perfumes such as are given to the gods a grain at a time, that are piled up in heaps to the honour of dead bodies! Yet the gods used not to regard with less favour the worshippers who petitioned them with salted spelt, but rather, as the facts show, they were more benevolent in those days. But the title 'happy' belongs still more to the Arabian Sea, for from it come the pearls which that country sends us. And by the lowest reckoning India, China and the Arabian peninsula take from our empire 100 million sesterces [i.e., bronze coins] every year—that is the sum which our luxuries and our women cost us; for what fraction of these imports, I ask you, now goes to the gods, or to the powers of the lower world? . . .

5. PLINY THE ELDER ON PEPPER FROM INDIA

The olive-tree of India is barren, except for the fruit of the wild olive. But trees resembling our junipers that bear pepper occur everywhere, although some writers have reported that they only grow on the southern face of the Caucasus. The seeds differ from those of the juniper by being in small pods, like those which we see in the case of the kidney-bean; these pods when plucked before they open and dried in the sun produce what is called 'long pepper,' but if left to open gradually, when ripe they disclose white pepper, which if afterwards dried in the sun changes colour and wrinkles up. Even these products, however, have their own special infirmity, and inclement weather shrivels them up and turns the seeds into barren husks, called *bregma,* which is an Indian word meaning 'dead.' Of all kinds of pepper this is the most pungent and the lightest, and it is pale in colour. Black pepper is more agreeable, but white pepper is of a milder flavour than either the black or the 'long' pepper . . .

Long pepper is sold at 15 denarii [i.e., silver coins] a pound, white pepper at 7, and black at 4. It is remarkable that the use of pepper has come so much into favour, as in the case of some commodities their sweet taste has been an attraction, and in others their appearance, but pepper has nothing to recommend it in either fruit or berry. To think that its only pleasing quality is pungency and that we go all the way to India to get this! . . .

6. SAILING FROM SRI LANKA TO CHINA:
THE HOMEWARD JOURNEY OF A BUDDHIST MONK.

[*Fa-hsien, the author of the following passages, was a Chinese Buddhist monk who set out for India via central Asia in 399. Fifteen years later he returned to China by sea. Fa-hsien's travel book is the earliest-known narrative of Chinese travel to and from India.*]

Fa-hsien remained in this country [i.e., Sri Lanka] for two years; and after repeated search he obtained a copy of the Disciplines according to the school of "The Faith Prevailing"; also copies of the long Agamas on cosmogony, and of the miscellaneous Agamas on ecstatic contemplation, and subsequently of a collection of extracts from the Canon, all of which China was without. When he had obtained these in Sanskrit, he took passage on board a large merchant-vessel, on which there were over two hundred souls, and astern of which there was a smaller vessel in tow, in case of accident at sea and destruction of the big vessel. Catching a fair wind,

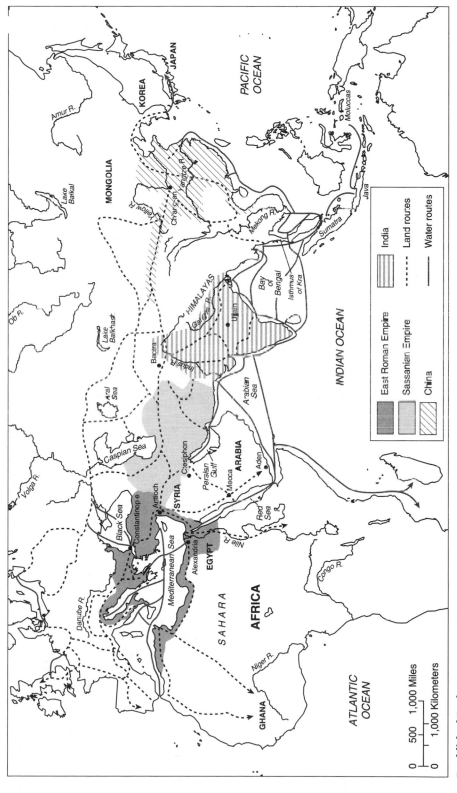

Established Trade Routes, ca. 600 C.E.

they sailed eastward for two days; then they encountered a heavy gale, and the vessel sprang a leak. The merchants wished to get aboard the smaller vessel; but the men on the latter, fearing that they would be swamped by numbers quickly cut the tow-rope in two. The merchants were terrified, for death was close at hand; and fearing that the vessel would fill, they promptly took what bulky goods there were and threw them into the sea. Fa-hsien also took his pitcher and ewer, with whatever else he could spare, and threw them into the sea; but he was afraid that the merchants would throw over his books and his images, and accordingly fixed his whole thoughts upon Kuan Yin [i.e., Guanyin, the compassionate Bodhisattva], the Hearer of Prayers, and put his life into the hand of the Catholic [i.e., Buddhist] Church in China, saying, "I have journeyed far on behalf of the Faith. Oh that by your awful power you would grant me a safe return from my wanderings."

The gale blew on for thirteen days and nights, when they arrived alongside of an island, and then, at ebb-tide, they saw the place where the vessel leaked and forthwith stopped it up, after which they again proceeded on their way.

This sea is infested with pirates, to meet whom is death. The expanse of ocean is boundless, east and west are not distinguishable; only by observation of the sun, moon, and constellations, is progress to be made. In cloudy and rainy weather, our vessel drifted at the mercy of the wind, without keeping any definite course. In the darkness of night nothing was to be seen but the great waves beating upon one another and flashing forth light like fire, huge turtles, sea-lizards, and such-like monsters of the deep. Then the merchants lost heart, not knowing whither they were going, and the sea being deep, without bottom, they had no place where they could cast their stone-anchor and stop. When the sky had cleared, they were able to tell east from west and again to proceed on their proper course; but had they struck a hidden rock, there would have been no way of escape.

And so they went on for more than ninety days until they reached a country named Java, where heresies and Brahmanism were flourishing, while the Faith of Buddha was in a very unsatisfactory condition.

After having remained in this country for five months or so, Fa-hsien again shipped on board another large merchant-vessel which also carried over two hundred persons. They took with them provisions for fifty days and set sail on the 16th of the 4th moon, and Fa-hsien went into retreat on board the vessel.

A north-east course was set in order to reach Canton; and over a month had elapsed when one night in the second watch (9–11 P.M.) they encountered a violent gale with tempestuous rain, at which the travelling merchants and traders who were going to their homes were much frightened. However, Fa-hsien once more invoked the Hearer of Prayers and the Catholic [Buddhist] Church in China, and was accorded the protection of their awful power until day broke. As soon as it was light, the Brahmans took counsel together and said, "Having this Shaman on board has been our undoing, causing us to get into this trouble. We ought to land the religious mendicant on some island; it is not right to endanger all our lives for one man." A "religious protector" of Fa-hsien's replied, saying, "If you put this religious mendicant ashore, you shall also land me with him; if not, you had better kill me, for supposing that you land him, when I reach China I will report you to the king who is a reverent believer in the Buddhist Faith and honours religious mendicants." At this the merchants wavered and did not dare to land him just then.

Meanwhile, the sky was constantly darkened and the captain lost his reckoning. So they went on for seventy days until the provisions and water were nearly exhausted, and they had to use seawater for cooking, dividing the fresh water so that each man got about two pints. When all was nearly consumed, the merchants consulted together and said, "The ordinary time for the voyage to Canton is exactly fifty days. We have now exceeded that limit by many days; must we not have gone out of our course?"

Thereupon they proceeded in a northwesterly direction, seeking for land; and after twelve days and nights arrived south of the Lao mountain (on the Shantung promontory) at the boundary of the Prefecture of Ch'ang-kuang (the modern Kiao-chou), where they obtained fresh water and vegetables.

And now, after having passed through much danger, difficulty, sorrow, and fear, suddenly reaching this shore and seeing the old familiar vegetables, they knew it was their fatherland. . . .

Fa-hsien spent six years in travelling from Ch'ang-an [i.e., the ancient Chinese capital] to Central India; he stayed there six years, and it took him three more to reach Ch'ing-chou. The countries he passed through amounted to rather fewer than thirty. From the Sandy Desert westwards all the way to India, the dignified deportment of the priesthood and the good influence of the Faith were beyond all expression in detail. As, however, the ecclesiastics at home had had no means of hearing about these things, Fa-hsien had given no thought to his own unimportant life, but came home across the sea, encountering still more difficulties and dangers. Happily, he was accorded protection by the divine majesty of the Precious [Buddhist] Trinity, and was thus preserved in the hour of danger. Therefore he wrote down on bamboo tablets and silk an account of what he had been through, desiring that the gentle reader should share this information.

STUDY QUESTIONS

1. How do we know that the Romans wore silk? How did the Romans obtain this fabric?
2. What evidence is there in the passages by Strabo and Pliny the Elder that Indians were traveling to Rome and Romans were traveling to India? What were the reasons for these journeys?
3. What evidence is there in the passages from Pliny to suggest that the Romans placed a high value on incense? How does Pliny's description of the trade in incense help to explain its high cost? How was incense used by the Romans?
4. Compare Pliny's report on incense with his report on pepper. Does pepper grow on trees? How do you explain this confusion in Pliny? What were Pliny's likely sources of information about the cultivation of incense and pepper?
5. When Fa-hsien decided to return to China, how did he travel? What does his mode of travel (and the difficulties that he encountered during his journey) suggest about trade between India and China?
6. To what extent does Fa-hsien seem to subscribe to the ideals of the Four Noble Truths? (See Chapter 10.)
7. What evidence do you see in these documents of connections between commerce and religion?

8. Note the evidence of disapproval in Suetonius and Pliny with regard to the use of silk, incense, and pepper by the Romans. Why do you think some Romans objected to the use of these commodities? How does the disapproval of Asian luxuries provide clues to the nature of Roman gender relations? How does the suggestion of disapproval relate to characteristic Roman political principles, as discussed in Chapter 15?

9. How did the long-distance trade illustrated in these documents relate to changes in Rome as empire replaced republic and then matured?

Section Three

The Postclassical Period, 500 to 1500 C.E.: Expansions and Contacts

After the collapse of key classical dynasties or empires, new influences arose in many older centers—particularly with the rise of Islam and the spread of Buddhism. Civilization also expanded from older centers—thus the rise of a Japanese form of East Asian culture and the development of civilization in northwestern Europe and in Russia, with links, however, to earlier Mediterranean forms. Civilizations also expanded in portions of the Americas and sub-Saharan Africa.

During most of the postclassical period, Islamic civilization, centered in the Middle East and North Africa, became the leading force. Other themes included the sheer spread of major religions—particularly Islam, Christianity and Buddhism—and the resultant impact on the arts and politics. International trade expanded rapidly, as did imitation of older centers by regions solidifying the forms of civilization for the first time, such as northern Europe and Japan. The expansion of trade led to new kinds of questions about merchants and merchants' motives, although different societies offered different resolutions. Toward the end of the period, Mongol conquests and a brief flurry of Chinese trading expeditions intensified international contacts, including technology exchange from Asia and the spread of epidemic disease.

The chapters in this section focus on developments within major civilizations, as the roster expanded. Two chapters then deal with growing trade and the Mongol conquests as sources of change; then two final chapters take up the expanding range of international contacts.

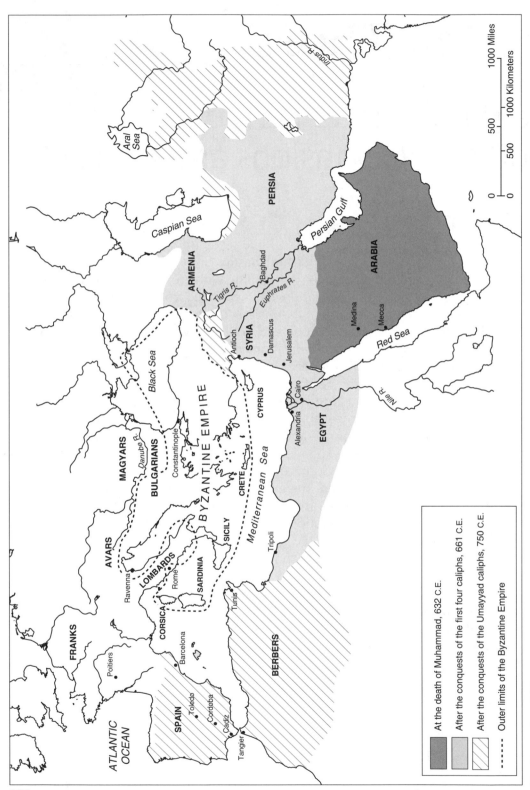

The Expansion of Islam

Legend:
- At the death of Muhammad, 632 C.E.
- After the conquests of the first four caliphs, 661 C.E.
- After the conquests of the Umayyad caliphs, 750 C.E.
- Outer limits of the Byzantine Empire

Map labels:
ATLANTIC OCEAN, SPAIN, Toledo, Córdoba, Cádiz, Tangier, Barcelona, CORSICA, SARDINIA, Poitiers, FRANKS, BERBERS, Tunis, Mediterranean Sea, SICILY, Rome, Ravenna, LOMBARDS, AVARS, BULGARIANS, MAGYARS, Danube R., Constantinople, BYZANTINE EMPIRE, CRETE, CYPRUS, Black Sea, Caspian Sea, Aral Sea, ARMENIA, Tigris R., Euphrates R., Baghdad, PERSIA, Indus R., Persian Gulf, ARABIA, Medina, Mecca, Red Sea, Nile R., EGYPT, Alexandria, Cairo, Jerusalem, Damascus, Antioch, SYRIA, Tripoli

Scale: 1000 Miles / 1000 Kilometers / 500

18

The Koran and the Family

The canonical source of Islam (*al-Islâm*, meaning "surrender") is the Koran [*Qur'ān*], which contains revelations from Allah, "the God of Abraham, Ishmael, Isaac, and Jacob, and the Tribes [of Israel] . . . and Jesus," to the Prophet Muhammad [ca. 570–632 C.E.]. Transmitted through the intermediary of the angel Gabriel during the 20 years of Muhammad's apostolate, these full and complete revelations embodied Allah's "eternal knowledge and judgment of all things" and a perfection of all previous religions. As the ultimate authority in Islam and the "supreme self-manifestation of God to His creatures," the Koran was early reduced to writing. Yet an official, authoritative edition did not appear until after the Prophet's death in 632 C.E. Divided into 114 chapters (*suras*) and containing 77,639 words, the text of the Koran is arranged in order of decreasing length with complete disregard for chronology. Internally each *sura* consists of verses [*'ayāt'*, meaning "signs" or "tokens"] with post-Muhammad headings derived from key terms in the text. Written in classical Arabic, the Koran adheres to a metrical style and was designed to be heard. In the selections below from Sura IV ("Women") the focus is on women, children, orphans, and inheritances, with injunctions to males in the Islamic patriarchal society regarding them.

The following passages obviously invite judgments about what kind of family life and gender relations were urged in Islamic society; we can compare these with other versions of a patriarchal system in classical India and China (see Chapters 8 and 12). These passages also show how Islamic religion developed specific regulations, not just general ethics, for personal and family behavior, harking back to older Middle Eastern traditions in this area (see Chapters 2 and 4). Finally, the passages also show something of the Islamic view of God, in whose name men and women were to regulate their relationships.

From Arthur J. Arberry, *The Koran Interpreted*, 2 vols. (London: George Allen and Unwin, Ltd., 1955), Vol. I, pp. 100–106, 119–120. Copyright © George Allen and Unwin, 1955. Reprinted by permission of HarperCollins Publishers, Inc.

In the Name of God, the Merciful, the Compassionate

. . .

Give the orphans their property, and do not
exchange the corrupt for the good; and devour
not their property with your property; surely that is a great crime.
If you fear that you will not act justly
toward the orphans, marry such women
as seem good to you, two, three, four;
but if you fear you will not be equitable,
then only one, or what your right hands own;
so it is likelier you will not be partial.
And give the women their dowries as a gift
spontaneous; but if they are pleased
to offer you any of it, consume it with wholesome appetite.
But do not give to fools their property
that God has assigned to you to manage;
provide for them and clothe them out of it,
and speak to them honourable words.
Test well the orphans, until they reach
the age of marrying; then, if you perceive
in them right judgment, deliver to them
their property; consume it not wastefully and hastily
ere they are grown. If any man is rich,
let him be abstinent; if poor, let him consume in reason.
And when you deliver to them their property,
take witnesses over them; God suffices for a reckoner.

To the men a share of what parents and kinsmen
leave, and to the women a share of what
parents and kinsmen leave, whether it be
little or much, a share apportioned;
and when the division is attended by
kinsmen and orphans and the poor,
make provision for them out of it,
and speak to them honourable words.
And let those fear who, if they left
behind them weak seed, would be afraid
on their account, and let them fear
God, and speak words hitting the mark.
Those who devour the property of orphans
unjustly, devour Fire in their bellies,
and shall assuredly roast in a Blaze.
God charges you, concerning your children:
to the male the like of the portion
of two females, and if they be women
above two, then for them two-thirds
of what he leaves, but if she be one

then to her a half; and to his parents
to each one of the two the sixth
of what he leaves, if he has children;
but if he has no children, and his
heirs are his parents, a third to his
mother, or, if he has brothers, to his
mother a sixth, after any bequest
he may bequeath, or any debt.
Your fathers and your sons—you know not
which out of them is nearer in profit
to you. So God apportions; surely God is
    All-knowing, All-wise.

And for you a half of what your wives
leave, if they have no children; but
if they have children, then for you of what
they leave a fourth, after any bequest
they may bequeath, or any debt.
And for them a fourth of what you leave,
if you have no children; but if you
have children, then for them of what
you leave an eighth, after any bequest
you may bequeath, or any debt.
If a man or a woman have no heir
direct, but have a brother or a sister,
to each of the two a sixth; but if they
are more numerous than that, they share
equally a third, after any bequest
he may bequeath, or any debt not
prejudicial; a charge from God. God is
    All-knowing, All-clement.

Those are God's bounds. Whoso obeys God
and His Messenger, He will admit him
to gardens underneath which rivers flow,
therein dwelling forever; that is the mighty triumph.
But whoso disobeys God, and His Messenger,
and transgresses His bounds, him He will
admit to a Fire, therein dwelling
forever, and for him there awaits a humbling chastisement.

Such of your women as commit indecency,
call four of you to witness against them;
and if they witness, then detain them
in their houses until death takes them
or God appoints for them a way.
And when two of you commit indecency,
punish them both; but if they repent
and make amends, then suffer them to be;

God turns, and is All-compassionate.
God shall turn only towards those who do
evil in ignorance, then shortly repent;
God will return towards those; God is
    All-knowing, All-wise.
But God shall not turn towards those
who do evil deeds until, when one of them
is visited by death, he says, "Indeed
now I repent," neither to those who die
disbelieving; for them We have prepared a painful chastisement.

O believers, it is not lawful for you
to inherit women against their will;
neither debar them, that you may go off
with part of what you have given them,
except when they commit a flagrant indecency.
Consort with them honourably; or if
you are averse to them, it is possible
you may be averse to a thing, and God set in it much good.
And if you desire to exchange a wife
in place of another, and you have given
to one a hundredweight, take of it nothing.
What, will you take it by way of calumny and manifest sin?
How shall you take it, when each of you has been
privily with the other, and they have taken from you a solemn compact?
And do not marry women that your fathers
married, unless it be a thing of the past;
surely that is indecent and hateful, an evil way.

Forbidden to you are your mothers and daughters,
your sisters, your aunts paternal and maternal,
your brother's daughters, your sister's daughters,
your mothers who have given suck to you,
your suckling sisters, your wives' mothers,
your stepdaughters who are in your care
being born of your wives you have been in to—
but if you have not yet been in to them
it is no fault in you—and the spouses
of your sons who are of your loins,
and that you should take to you two sisters
together, unless it be a thing of the past;
God is All-forgiving, All compassionate;
and wedded women, save what your right hands own.
So God prescribes for you. Lawful for you,
beyond all that, is that you may seek,
using your wealth, in wedlock and not
in licence. Such wives as you enjoy thereby,
give them their wages apportionate; it is no

fault in you in your agreeing together,
after the due apportionate. God is
    All-knowing, All-wise.

Any one of you who has not the affluence
to be able to marry believing freewomen
in wedlock, let him take believing handmaids
that your right hands own; God knows very well
your faith; the one of you is as the other.
So marry them, with their people's leave,
and give them their wages honourably
as women in wedlock, not as in licence or taking lovers.
But when they are in wedlock, if they
commit indecency, they shall be liable
to half the chastisement of freewomen.
That provision is for those of you who fear
fornication; yet it is better for you
to be patient. God is All-forgiving
    All-compassionate.
God desires to make clear to you, and to
guide you in the institutions of those
before you, and to turn towards you; God is
    All-knowing, All-wise;
and God desires to turn towards you, but
those who follow their lusts desire you
to swerve away mightily. God desires
to lighten things for you, for man was created a weakling. . . .

Do not covet that whereby God in bounty
has preferred one of you above another.
To the men a share from what they have earned,
and to the women a share from what they
have earned. And ask God of his bounty;
    God knows everything.

To everyone We have appointed heirs
of that which parents and kinsmen leave,
and those with whom you have sworn compact.
So give to them their share; God is witness over everything.

Men are the managers of the affairs of women
for that God has preferred in bounty
one of them over another, and for that
they have expended of their property.
Righteous women are therefore obedient,
guarding the secret for God's guarding.
And those you fear may be rebellious
admonish; banish them to their couches,
and beat them. If they then obey you,

look not for any way against them; God is
    All-high, All-great.
And if you fear a breach between the two,
bring forth an arbiter from his people
and from her people an arbiter, if they
desire to set things right; God will
compose their differences; surely God is
    All-knowing, All-aware. . . .

If a woman fear rebelliousness or aversion
in her husband, there is no fault in them
if the couple set things right between them;
right settlement is better; and souls are very
prone to avarice. If you do good
and are godfearing, surely God is aware of
    the things you do.
You will not be able to be equitable
between your wives, be you ever so eager;
yet do not be altogether partial
so that you leave her as it were suspended.
If you set things right, and are godfearing,
God is All-forgiving, All-compassionate.
But if they separate, God will enrich
each of them of His plenty; God is
    All-embracing, All-wise.

STUDY QUESTIONS

1. Did Islam enforce a patriarchal gender system?
2. What were the key protections for women, and how did they compare with protective features in the earlier classical and river-valley civilizations?
3. Were women spiritually equal to men in Islam? How was this reconciled with patriarchal traditions?
4. What kinds of concerns did Islam emphasize concerning sexuality?

19

The Islamic Religion

Supplementing the Koran as a source for Islamic religious, social, and legal precepts is the Hadith (which means a story, tale, or report). These are collections of
traditions attributed to Muhammad, his companions, and early caliphs. Consisting of rules and practical social norms (*sunnah*) formulated by the prophet and
enforced by early leaders in the Islamic community, the Hadith contains prescribed rules and behaviors not offered in the Koran that guide Muslims. Pro
claimed in sermons or informally before witnesses, the apostolic traditions remained unwritten until the beginning of the seventh century. In response to
Caliph Oman II's orders for a formal collection of extant traditions, an Iranian sa-
vant, Abū 'Abdallah Muhammad (b. Ismāil al-Bukhārī, 810–870), traveled
throughout the Islamic World, where he uncovered more than 600,000. Joined
by other collectors, al-Bukhari devised a critical scientific method to separate
authentic traditions from the spurious. From this, he produced an authoritative
Hadith consisting of 7397 authentic traditions. His collection, along with those
by 'Abul Husain Muslim (819–874) and four less reliable collectors, acquired
canonical status among the orthodox Sunnis and is known as the *Sahīh* ("The
Genuine").

In the Hadith selections that follow, you can get a sense of what the main religious duties of a Muslim are and how the individual relates to Allah. What is distinctive about Muslim religious life? Why do so many people find Islam such a satisfac-
tory religion, often converting to it from other faiths?

Said the Apostle of Allah—upon whom be Allah's blessing and peace—: "The
[true] Muslim is he from whose tongue and whose hand [other] Muslims are
safe, and the [true] Muhājir is he who has fled from those things Allah has forbidden."

Islam is built upon five things: on testifying that there is no deity save Allah
and that Muhammad is his Apostle, on performing prayer, on paying the legal alms
(*zakāt*), on the pilgrimage [to Mecca], and on the fast of Ramadān.

From *A Reader on Islam,* edited by Arthur Jeffery (New York: Books for Libraries, A Division of
Arno Press, 1980), pp. 81–86. Copyright © Arno Press, 1980. Reprinted by permission.

The Apostle of Allah—upon whom be Allah's blessing and peace—was asked which [good] work was the most excellent, and he answered: "Belief in Allah and in His Apostle." He was asked: "And then which?" He replied: "Jihād in the way of Allah." He was again asked: "and then what?" and he replied: "An acceptable pilgrimage."

No one ever bears witness that there is no deity save Allah and that Muhammad is the Apostle of Allah, [testifying to it] sincerely from his heart, but Allah will preserve him from Hell-fire.

There is no Muslim who plants a tree or cultivates a plot from which birds of man or domestic beasts [may gather food to] eat, but has therein an act of charitable alms [recorded to his merit].

If a man seizes the property of others with intent to restore it, Allah will settle with him, but if he seizes it with intent to waste it Allah will make waste of him.

If a slave serves honestly his [earthly] master and worships earnestly his [heavenly] Lord, he will have a double recompense.

He who shows concern for the widows and the unfortunate [ranks as high] as one who goes on Jihād in the way of Allah, or one who fasts by day and who rises at night [for prayer].

A [true] believer views his sins as though he were sitting beneath a mountain which he fears may fall on him, but an evil-doer views his sins as a fly that moves across his nose.

In this world be as a stranger, or as one who is just passing along the road.

In two things an old man's heart never ceases to be that of a youth, in love of this world and in hoping long.

Were a man to possess two valleys full of gold he would be wanting a third, for nothing will ever really fill man's belly but the dust.

To look at a woman is forbidden, even if it is a look without desire, so how much the more is touching her.

Said he—upon whom be Allah's blessing and peace—: "Avoid seven pernicious things." [His Companions] said: "And what are they, O Apostle of Allah?" He answered: "Associating anything with Allah, sorcery, depriving anyone of life where Allah has forbidden that save for just cause, taking usury, devouring the property of orphans, turning the back on the day of battle, and slandering chaste believing women even though they may be acting carelessly."

No one who enters Paradise will ever want to return to this world, even could he possess the earth and all that is on it, save the martyrs who desire to return to this world and be killed ten times so great is the regard in which they find themselves held.

To be stationed on the frontier for one day during Holy War is better than [to possess] this world and all that is on it. A place in Paradise the size of one of your whip-lashes is better than this world and all that is on it. A night or a day that a man spends on Holy War is better than this world and all that is on it.

The similitude of a stingy man and a generous giver of alms is that of two men wearing cloaks of mail in which the hand-pieces are fastened to the collar-piece. Whenever the generous giver starts to give an alms it stretches for him so that it is as though it were not, but when the stingy man starts to give an alms every link clings to the one next it so contracting that his hands are kept tight by his collar-bone and however much he strives it will not stretch.

It is right to "hearken and obey" so long as one is not bidden disobey [Allah], but should the command be to disobedience let there be no "hearken and obey."

Travelling is part of one's punishment, for one is deprived of one's sleeping, one's eating, one's drinking thereby, so whenever any one of you has finished what he had to do let him hurry home.

Allah desires to meet those who desire to meet with Him, but is disinclined to meet those who are disinclined to meet with Him.

The man who has the lightest punishment on the Day will be the one who has live coals placed under the soles of his feet [so hot that] his brains will boil from the heat thereof.

If a man sees something in [the conduct of] his ruler which he dislikes let him put up with it patiently, for there is no one who separates himself even a span from the community and dies [in that separation], but dies a pagan death.

When Friday comes angels take their seat over every mosque gate and write down in order those who come in, but when the prayer leader sits they fold their sheets and come to hearken to the words.

Said the Prophet—upon whom be Allah's blessing and peace—: "I had a look into Paradise and I saw that the poor made up most of its inhabitants, and I had a look into Hell and saw that most of its inhabitants were women."

When [the month of] Ramadān begins the gates of heaven are set open, the gates of Hell are locked shut, and the satans are chained.

Treat women-folk kindly for woman was created of a rib. The crookedest part of a rib is its upper part. If you go to straighten it out you will break it, and if you leave it alone it will continue crooked. So treat women in kindly fashion.

Whosoever testifies that there is no deity save Allah, that Muhammad is His servant and His Apostle, that Jesus is His servant and His Apostle and His word which He cast to Mary and a Spirit from Him, that Paradise is a reality and Hell-fire a reality, him will Allah bring into Paradise in accordance with his works.

Only two men are really to be envied, namely, a man to whom Allah has given Scripture and who sits up at nights with it, and a man to whom Allah has given wealth which he distributes in charitable alms day and night.

Said the Apostle of Allah—upon whom be Allah's blessing and peace: "O band of youths, let him among you who is able to make a home get married, and let him who is not able betake himself to fasting for he will find in that a quencher [of his passions]."

The worst of foods is that of a feast to which the rich have been invited and the poor overlooked, yet anyone who overlooks an invitation is in rebellion against Allah and His Apostle.

Said the Apostle of Allah—upon whom be Allah's blessing and peace—: "Do not wear silks and satins, and do not drink from gold and silver vessels nor eat from dishes made thereof, for these things are theirs in this world but ours in the world to come."

Said the Apostle of Allah—upon whom be Allah's blessing and peace—: "Gabriel said to me: 'Whosoever of your community dies without ever having associated any other with Allah will enter Paradise' (or perhaps he said: 'will not enter Hell-fire'). Someone said: 'Even if he is an adulterer or a thief?' He replied: 'Even if.'"

The similitude of a good companion and a bad one is [that of] a man who carries musk and one who blows a blacksmith's bellows, for one who is carrying musk may give you a share, or you may purchase some of it, or in any case enjoy the delightful smell, but one who blows the blacksmith's bellows will either set your clothes on fire or accost you with an evil smell.

Said the Prophet—upon whom be Allah's blessing and peace—: "The first group to enter Paradise will have faces like the moon on the night of its fullness, will neither spit nor blow their noses or defecate therein, their utensils there will be of gold, their combs of gold and silver, their censers of aloes wood, their sweat will be musk, and each of them will have two spouses so beautiful that the marrow of their leg-bones will be visible through the flesh. There will be no differences or disputings among them for they will all be of one heart, glorifying Allah morning and evening."

"Ā'isha said: "I was stuffing a pillow for the Prophet—upon whom be Allah's blessing and peace—on which were images like those on a saddle-cushion, when he came and stood on the doorway. His countenance started to alter, so I said: 'What is it, O Apostle of Allah?' He said: 'What are you doing with this pillow?' 'It is a pillow,' I answered, 'that I have made for you on which you may recline.' Said he: 'Do you not know that angels will not enter a house in which there is a picture? On the Day makers of [such] pictures will be punished, for [Allah] will say to them: 'Give life to that which you have created.'"

Among the signs of the coming of the Hour are these: ignorance will be apparent and learning inconspicuous, fornication will be rampant and the drinking of wine, men will be few but women many so that fifty women will have but one husband between them.

Said the Prophet—upon whom be Allah's blessing and peace—: "He who drinks wine in this world and repents not of it will be forbidden it in the world to come."

There is no misfortune befalls a Muslim but Allah will atone for some sin of his thereby, even if it be only [so small a misfortune as] his being pricked by a thorn.

Said the Prophet—upon whom be Allah's blessing and peace—: "Visions are from Allah but dreams are from Satan, so if any one of you sees anything disagreeable [during sleep] let him spit three times when he wakens up and take refuge [with Allah] from its evil, and then it will do him no harm."

Said the Apostle of Allah—upon whom be Allah's blessing and peace—: "Among the greatest of mortal sins is that a man curse his parents." They said: "O Apostle of Allah, how could a man curse his parents?" He replied: "The man who reviles another man's parents is reviling his own father and mother." . . .

The Apostle of Allah—on whom be Allah's blessing and peace—once kissed al-Hasan the son of 'Alī while al-Aqra' b. Hābis of Tamīm was sitting there. Al-Aqra' said: "I have ten sons but never have kissed any one of them." The Apostle of Allah—upon whom be Allah's blessing and peace—looked at him, and then said: "He who does not show tenderness will not have tenderness shown him."

Said the Prophet—upon whom be Allah's blessing and peace—: "Whoever casts himself down from a mountain so as to kill himself will be in Hell continually casting himself down thus for ever and ever. Whoever sips poison so as to kill himself will in Hell have poison in his hand which he will go on sipping there for ever and ever. Whoever kills himself with a knife will in Hell have a knife in his hand which he will go on continually plunging into his bowels for ever and ever."

Said he—upon whom be Allah's blessing and peace—: "Let none of you wish for death because of any hardship that has befallen him. If he needs must say something, let him say: 'Allahumma! let me live so long as life is best for me, and let me pass away when passing away is the best thing for me.'"

Said the Prophet—upon whom be Allah's blessing and peace—: "Allah made mercy in a hundred parts. Ninety-nine of these parts He kept with Himself and one single part He sent down on earth. It is by reason of this one part that creatures show mercy to one another, so that a mare carefully lifts her hoof fearing lest with it she harm her foal."

Said the Apostle of Allah—on whom be Allah's blessing and peace—: "Let him who believes in Allah and the Last Day refrain from doing harm to his neighbour. Let him who believes in Allah and the Last Day see to it that he properly honours his guest. Let him who believes in Allah and the Last Day either speak what is good or hold his tongue."

Said the Prophet—upon whom be Allah's blessing and peace—: "No one will ever experience the sweetness of faith till he loves a man solely for the sake of Allah, till he feels that he would rather be cast into Hell-fire then return to unbelief once Allah has delivered him from it, till Allah and His Apostle are dearer to him than anything besides."

Muhammad b. Muqātil Abū'l-Hasan has related to me [saying]: 'Abdallah informed us on the authority of Humaid b. 'Abd ar-Rahmān, on the authority of Abū Huraira—with whom may Allah be pleased—that a man came to the Apostle of Allah—upon whom be Allah's blessing and peace—saying: "O Apostle of Allah, there is no hope for me." He replied: "Too bad for you." Said [the man]: "I had intercourse with my wife during Ramadān." [The Prophet] answered: "Then set free a slave." Said he: "I have none." [The Prophet] answered: "Then fast for two months on end." Said he: "But I could not." [The Prophet] answered: "Then feed sixty poor people." Said he: "I have not the wherewithall." Just then there was brought to [the Prophet] a basket of dates, so he said to the man: "Take this and distribute it as charitable alms [in expiation for your sin]." Said he: "O Apostle of Allah, [am I to distribute it] to other than my own family? when by Him in whose hand is my soul there is no one between the gateposts of the city more needy than I am." Thereat the Prophet laughed till his canine teeth showed, and he said: "Go along and take it."

STUDY QUESTIONS

1. What are some of the main religious obligations of Muslims, according to these passages? What were the goals of a proper religious life?

2. How do the gender values in these passages compare with the previous selections from the Koran? What might account for any differences?

3. What was the Islamic approach to social and economic inequality? To slavery? How did this approach compare with the social theories of the classical Mediterranean period? (See Chapter 14.)

4. What were some of the major offenses against Islamic rules?

5. Do these passages suggest some of the reasons for Islam's striking success as a world religion?

20

Religious and Political Organization in the Islamic Middle East

The office of imam, or leader, dates from Muhammad's death in 632, when a successor, or caliph, was elected. The word *imam* is also applied to local leaders of worship within a mosque. The following passage, from Al-Mawārdī's (d. 1058) *Ordinance of Government,* describes the central leadership of Islam during the centuries of Arab dominance in the office most commonly known as the caliphate. The statement of the duties and eligibility of the caliph comes from the majority, or Sunni Muslims. Minority Shiite Muslims split away in their belief that the caliphate was a divinely designated office inherited by descendants of Muhammad.

The orthodox Sunni view held that the imam or caliph was an elected and secular office that did, however, involve strict religious as well as political duties. The authority of the office was absolute so long as its holder adhered to the Koran and Hadith. Early elective procedures gave way to inheritance of the office in the Umayyad and Abbasid dynasties (661–750 and 750–1378), but the concept of the caliph's duties remained consistent. This office, then, was the chief political legacy of Islam during the centuries of Arab rule in the Middle East. In what sense was the caliphate a religious office? In what sense did it embrace nonreligious functions? What kind of government structure did the powers of the caliphate imply?

The office of Imam was set up in order to replace the office of Prophet in the defense of the faith and the government of the world. By general consensus [*ijmā‘*], from which only al-Aṣamm dissents, the investiture of whichsoever member of the community exercises the functions of Imam is obligatory. But there is disagreement as to whether this obligation derives from reason or from Holy Law. One group says it derives from reason, since it is in the nature of reasonable men to submit to a leader who will prevent them from injuring one another and who will settle quarrels and disputes, for without rulers men would live in anarchy and heedlessness like benighted savages. . . .

From *Islam from the Prophet Muhammed to the Capture of Constantinople,* edited and translated by Bernard Lewis (New York: Harper & Row, 1974), Vol. I, pp. 150–151, 171–179. Reprinted by permission of HarperCollins Publishers, Inc.

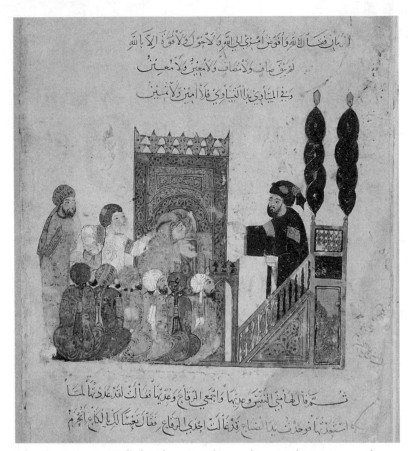

Islamic Imam or Caliph. Abou Zayd preaching in the Mosque of Samarkand (Central Asia). Persian artists took more liberties in representing the human form than did Arab artists, but the Arabic script and decorative detail are typical of mosque design. (From "Al Maquamat" ("The Meetings"), illustrated by Hariri, second quarter of 13th century, Persian literary texts. [Ms Ar 5847 f.18v]; Bibliothèque Nationale, Paris/The Bridgeman Art Library, London, New York.)

Another group says that the obligation derives from the Holy Law and not from reason, since the Imam deals with matters of Holy Law to which, in reason, he would be allowed not to devote himself, since reason does not make them obligatory. All that reason requires is that a reasonable man should refrain from mutual injury and conflict with his neighbor and act equitably in mutual fairness and good relations, conducting himself in accordance with his own reason, and not with someone else's. But it is the Holy Law which intervenes to entrust these affairs to its religious representative. . . .

The obligation of the Imamate, which is thus confirmed, is a collective duty, like the Holy War and the pursuit of knowledge, so that when it is performed by those whose charge it is, the general obligation of the rest of the community lapses. If no one discharges it, then two groups of people must be distinguished from the rest; first, the electors, who choose an Imam for the community; and second, those eligible for the Imamate, one of whom must be made Imam. The rest of the community, who belong neither to the one nor to the other group, commit no sin or offense if there is a delay in filling the Imamate. When these two groups are constituted and take over the collective obligation, each group must conform to the prescribed conditions. The conditions required in the electors are three:

1. Rectitude ['*adāla*] in all respects.
2. The knowledge to recognize the required qualifications for the Imamate.
3. The discernment and wisdom to choose the candidate best suited to the Imamate, the most capable and the best informed of the conduct of public affairs.

He who is in the city of the Imam has no privilege or precedence, because of this, over those in other places. That those who are present in the city of the Imam undertake the appointment of the new Imam is custom, not law; this happens because they are the first to hear of his death and because those who are best qualified to succeed him are usually to be found in his city.

The conditions of eligibility for the Imamate are seven:

1. Rectitude in all respects.
2. The knowledge to exercise personal judgment [*ijtihād*] in cases and decisions.
3. Soundness of hearing, sight, and tongue so that he may deal accurately with those matters which can only be attained by them.
4. Soundness of limb so that he has no defect which would prevent him from moving freely and rising quickly.
5. The discernment needed to govern the subjects and conduct public affairs.
6. The courage and vigor to defend the lands of Islam and to wage holy war against the enemy.
7. Descent, that is to say, he must be of the tribe of Quraysh, as is prescribed by a text and accepted by consensus. . . .

The Imamate is conferred in two ways: one is by the choice of the electors [literally, those competent to bind and to loosen], and the other is by the nomination of the previous Imam. . . .

When the electors meet, they scrutinize the qualified candidates and proceed to appoint that one among them who is the most worthy, who best meets the required conditions, and to whom the people are most willing to give obedience. They recognize him without delay. If the exercise of their judgment leads them to choose a particular person from the community, they offer him the Imamate. If he accepts, they swear allegiance to him, and the Imamate is vested in him by this procedure. Allegiance to him and obedience to him then become binding on the entire community. If he holds back and refuses and Imamate, it cannot be imposed upon him, since it is a contract by consent and choice and may not involve compulsion or constraint. In such case the Imamate is offered to another qualified candidate.

If two candidates are equally well qualified, the elder takes precedence in choice; however, seniority, where the parties are of age, is not a necessary condition, and if the younger is appointed, it is still valid. If one is wiser and the other braver, the choice should be determined by the needs of the time. If the need for courage is more urgent because of the disorder of the frontiers and the appearance of rebels, then the braver has a better claim. If the need for wisdom is more urgent because of the quiescence of the populace and the appearance of heretics, then it is the wiser who has a better claim. . . .

The duties of the Imam in the conduct of public affairs are ten:

1. To maintain the religion according to established principles and the consensus of the first generation of Muslims. If an innovator appears or if some dubious person deviates from it, the Imam must clarify the proofs of religion to him, expound that which is correct, and apply to him the proper rules and penalties so that religion may be protected from injury and the community safeguarded from error.

2. To execute judgments given between litigants and to settle disputes between contestants so that justice may prevail and so that none commit or suffer injustice.

3. To defend the lands of Islam and to protect them from intrusion so that people may earn their livelihood and travel at will without danger to life or property.

4. To enforce the legal penalties for the protection of God's commandments from violation and for the preservation of the rights of his servants from injury or destruction.

5. To maintain the frontier fortresses with adequate supplies and effective force for their defense so that the enemy may not take them by surprise, commit profanation there, or shed the blood, either of a Muslim or an ally [*mu'āhad*].

6. To wage holy war [*jihād*] against those who, after having been invited to accept Islam, persist in rejecting it, until they either become Muslims or enter the Pact [*dhimma*] so that God's truth may prevail over every religion [cf. Qur'ān, ix, 33].

7. To collect the booty and the alms [*sadaqa*] in conformity with the prescriptions of the Holy Law, as defined by explicit texts and by independent judgment [*ijtihād*], and this without terror or oppression.

8. To determine the salaries and other sums due from the treasury, without extravagance and without parsimony, and to make payment at the proper time, neither in advance nor in arrears.

9. To employ capable and trustworthy men and appoint sincere men for the tasks which he delegates to them and for the money which he entrusts to them so that the tasks may be competently discharged and the money honestly safeguarded.

10. To concern himself directly with the supervision of affairs and the scrutiny of conditions so that he may personally govern the community, safeguard the faith, and not resort to delegation in order to free himself either for pleasure or for worship, for even the trustworthy may betray and the sincere may deceive. God said, "O David, we have made you our vicegerent [*khalīfa*] on earth; therefore, judge justly among men and do not follow your caprice, which will lead you astray from God's path." [Qur'ān, xxxviii, 25]. In this, God was not content with delegation, but

required a personal performance and did not excuse the following of passions, which, He says, lead astray from His path, and this, though He considered David worthy to judge in legion and to hold His viceregency [*khilāfa*]. This is one of the duties of government of any shepherd. The Prophet of God, may God bless and save him, said, "You are all shepherds, and you are all answerable for your flocks."

. . .

The rules of the Imamate and its general jurisdiction over the interests of religion and the governance of the community, as we have described them, being established, and the investiture of an Imam being duly confirmed, the authority which comes from him to his deputies is of four kinds:

1. Those who have unlimited authority of unlimited scope. These are the viziers, for they are entrusted with all public affairs without specific attribution.
2. Those who have unlimited authority of limited scope. Such are the provincial and district governors, whose authority is unlimited within the specific areas assigned to them.
3. Those who have limited authority of unlimited scope. Such are the chief qādī, the commander of the armies, the commandant of the frontier fortresses, the intendant of the land tax, and the collector of the alms, each of whom has unlimited authority in the specific functions assigned to him.
4. Those with limited authority of limited scope, such as the *qādī* of a town or district, the local intendant of the land tax, collector of tithes, the frontier commandment, or the army commander, every one of whom has limited authority of limited scope.

STUDY QUESTIONS

1. How would a Muslim distinguish between good and bad government?
2. What kind of enforcement for good government does this document suggest?
3. What should a Muslim do when a ruler did not live up to his obligations?
4. What was the power, in principle, of a Muslim ruler? What kind of bureaucratic system did Al-Māwardī suggest?
5. How did Islamic political principles compare with those of Christianity?
6. Why do scholars disagree about the political implications and flexibility of Islam? Are there potential tensions about appropriate political behavior, in cases of a less than ideal government, embedded in this document?

China and Japan

21

"Unfit to Draw the Bow": Peasants and Poets in Tang China

During the Tang dynasty (618–907 C.E.) China experienced one of its golden ages. Chang'an, the Tang capital, had a population of about a million people within its huge walls, making it one of the world's great cities. For about 150 years, during the first half of the Tang dynasty, the borders of the Chinese empire stretched far into central Asia. The manufacture of silk and porcelain, partly for export across the revived overland routes leading westward, flourished. Buddhist temples and monasteries, often elaborately decorated with sculpture and paintings, were built throughout the country. In addition, during the Tang dynasty there was a great flowering of literary culture in China, most notably in poetry.

Some examples of the many thousands of poems written during the Tang dynasty follow. The authors of the poems were Tang officials, some of whom (particularly Tu Fu) are regarded by scholars as among the greatest Chinese writers of verse. The poems have been chosen for their value in helping scholars to understand the lives of ordinary people. Tang Chang'an—with its huge population, massive walls, thriving markets, and beautiful buildings—understandably attracts the attention of the historian. But most Chinese people during the Tang dynasty, about 85 percent of the population, were peasants living in small villages in the countryside. The Tang poets bring us close to their lives.

From "Recruiting Officer of Shih-hao," "Watching the Wheat-reapers," and "Bitter Cold, Living in the Village" translated by Irving Yucheng Lo; "The Old Man of Hsing-feng with the Broken Arm" and "An Old Charcoal Seller" translated by Eugene Eoyang; "Farmers," "On Covering the Bones of Chang Chin, the Hired Man" translated by Jan W. Walls; and "Lament of a Woman Acorn-gatherer" translated by William H. Niehauser. All poems from *Sunflower Splendor,* edited by Wu-chi Liu and Irving Yucheng Lo. Copyright © 1975 by Wu-chi Liu and Irving Lo. Reprinted by permission of the authors.

1. FROM TU FU (712–770)

Recruiting Officer of Shih-hao

At dusk I sought lodging at Shih-hao village,
When a recruiting officer came to seize men at night.
An old man scaled the wall and fled,
His old wife came out to answer the door.

How furious was the officer's shout!
How pitiable was the woman's cry!
I listened as she stepped forward to speak:
"All my three sons have left for garrison duty at Yeh;
From one of them a letter just arrived,
Saying my two sons had newly died in battle.
Survivors can manage to live on.
But the dead are gone forever.
Now there's no other man in the house,
Only a grandchild at his mother's breast.
The child's mother has not gone away;
She has only a tattered skirt for wear.
An old woman, I am feeble and weak,
But I will gladly leave with you tonight
To answer the urgent call at Ho-yang—
I can still cook morning gruel for your men."

The night drew on, but talking stopped;
It seemed I heard only half-concealed sobs.
As I got back on the road at daybreak,
Only the old man was there to see me off.

2. FROM PO CHÜ-YI (772–846)

Watching the Wheat-Reapers

Farm families have few leisure months,
In the fifth month chores double up.
When south wind rises at night,
Fields and dikes are covered with golden wheat.

Women old and young carry baskets of food,
Children and toddlers bring out porridge in pots,
Following each other with food for the farmhands,
Those stout fellows on the southern knoll.

Their feet steamed by the sultry vapor from the soil,
Their backs scorched by the sun's burning light;
Drained of all strength to feel any heat,
Their only regret, summer days are too short.

Then there are those poor womenfolk,
Their children clinging to their side.

With their right hand they pick up leftover grains;
On their left arm dangles a broken basket.

To hear their words of complaint—
All who listen will grieve for them:
Their family land stripped clean to pay tax,
They now glean the field to fill their stomach.

What deeds of merit have I done?
I've neither farmed nor raised silkworms;
My official's salary, three hundred piculs of rice,
And at year's end there is surplus grain to eat.

Thinking of this, I feel guilty and ashamed;
All day long I cannot keep it out of my mind.

Bitter Cold, Living in the Village

In the twelfth month of this Eighth Year,
On the fifth day, a heavy snow fell.
Bamboos and cypress all perished from the freeze.
How much worse for people without warm clothes!

As I looked around the village,
Of ten families, eight or nine were in need.
The north wind was sharper than the sword,
And homespun cloth could hardly cover one's body.
Only brambles were burnt for firewood,
And sadly people sat at night to wait for dawn.

From this I know that when winter is harsh,
The farmers suffer most.
Looking at myself, during these days—
How I'd shut tight the gate of my thatched hall,
Cover myself with fur, wool, and silk,
Sitting or lying down, I had ample warmth.
I was lucky to be spared cold or hunger,
Neither did I have to labor in the field.

Thinking of that, how can I not feel ashamed?
I ask myself what kind of man am I.

The Old Man of Hsin-feng with the Broken Arm

An old man from Hsin-feng, eighty-eight years old,
Hair on his temples and his eyebrows white as snow.
Leaning on his great-great-grandson, he walks to the front of the inn,
His left arm on the boy's shoulder, his right arm broken.
I ask the old man how long has his arm been broken,
And how it came about, how it happened.
The old man said he grew up in the Hsin-feng district.

He was born during blessed times, without war or strife,
And he used to listen to the singing and dancing in the Pear Garden,
Knew nothing of banner and spear, or bow and arrow.
Then, during the T'ien-pao period, a big army was recruited:
From each family, one was taken out of every three,
And of those chosen, where were they sent?
Five months, ten thousand miles away, to Yunnan,
Where, it is said, the Lu River runs,
Where, when flowers fall from pepper trees, noxious fumes rise;
Where, when a great army fords the river, with its seething eddies,
Two or three out of ten never reach the other side.

The village, north and south, was full of the sound of wailing,
Sons leaving father and mother, husbands leaving wives.
They all said, of those who went out to fight the barbarians,
Not one out of a thousand lived to come back.
At the time, this old man was twenty-four,
And the army had his name on their roster.

"Then, late one night, not daring to let anyone know,
By stealth, I broke my arm, smashed it with a big stone.
Now I was unfit to draw the bow or carry the flag,
And I would be spared the fighting in Yunnan.
Bone shattered, muscles ached, it wasn't unpainful,
But I could count on being rejected and sent home.

"This arm has been broken now for over sixty years:
I"ve lost one limb, but the body's intact.
Even now, in cold nights, when the wind and rain blow,
Right up to daybreak, I hurt so much I cannot sleep,
But I have never had any regrets.
At least, now I alone have survived.
Or else, years ago at the River Lu,
I would have died, my spirit fled, and my bones left to rot:
I would have wandered, a ghost in Yunnan looking for home,
Mourning over the graves of ten thousands."
So the old man spoke: I ask you to listen.
Have you not heard the Prime Minister of the K'ai-yüan period,
　　Sung K'ai-fu?
How he wouldn't reward frontier campaigns, not wanting to glorify war?
And, have you not heard of Yang Kuo-chung, the Prime Minister of the
　　T'ien-pao period,
Wishing to seek favor, achieved military deeds at the frontier,
But, before he could pacify the frontier, the people became disgruntled:
Ask the old man of Hsin-feng with the broken arm!

An Old Charcoal Seller

An old charcoal seller
Cuts firewood, burns coal by the southern mountain.

His face, all covered with dust and ash, the color of smoke,
The hair at his temples is gray, his ten fingers black.
The money he makes selling coal, what is it for?
To put clothes on his back and food in his mouth.
The rags on his poor body are thin and threadbare;
Distressed at the low price of coal, he hopes for colder weather.
Night comes, an inch of snow has fallen on the city,
In the morning, he rides his cart along the icy ruts,
His ox weary, he hungry, and the sun already high.
In the mud by the south gate, outside the market, he stops to rest.
All of a sudden, two dashing riders appear;
An imperial envoy, garbed in yellow (his attendant in white),
Holding an official dispatch, he reads a proclamation.
Then turns the cart around, curses the ox, and leads it north.
One cartload of coal—a thousand or more catties!
No use appealing to the official spiriting the cart away:
Half a length of red lace, a slip of damask
Dropped on the ox—is payment in full!

3. FROM LIU TSUNG-YÜAN (773–819)

Farmers

Beyond the bamboo fence, cooking fire and smoke,
an evening when neighboring farmers chat.
From courtyard's edge autumn insects chirrup,
scattered hempstalks, now desolate and alone.
Silk from the worms all surrendered as tax,
loom and shuttle lean idly on the wall.
An officer passes through one night,
and is served a feast of fowl and millet.
Everyone says the official is harsh,
his language full of reprimands.
East villagers are behind in their rent
and wagon wheels sink in mire and bog.
Officials' residences are short on mercy;
where whips and rods are given fiendish rein.
We must attend cautiously to our work,
for flesh and skin are to be pitied.
We welcome now the new year's arrival,
fearing only to tread on the former tracks.

On Covering the Bones of Chang Chin, the Hired Man

The cycle of life is a worrisome thing,
a single breath that gathers and scatters again.
We come by chance into a hubbub of joy and rage
and suddenly we're taking leave again.

To be an underling is no disgrace,
neither is nobility divine;
all at once when breathing stops,
fair and ugly disappear in decay.
You slaved in my stables all your life,
cutting fodder, you never complained you were tired.
When you died we gave you a cheap coffin
and buried you at the foot of the eastern hill.
But then, alas, there came a raging flood
that left you helter-skelter by the roadside.
Dry and brittle, your hundred bones baked in the sun,
scattered about, never to join again.
Luckily an attendant told me of this,
and the vision saddened me to tears,
for even cats and tigers rate a sacrificial offering,
and dogs and horses have their ragged shrouds.
Long I stand here mourning for your soul
yet how could you know of this act?
Basket and spade bear you to the grave
which waterways will keep from further harm.
My mind is now at ease
whether you know it or not.
One should wait for spring to cover up bones,
and propitious is the time now.
Benevolence for all things is not mine to confer;
just call it a personal favor for you.

4. FROM P'I JIH-HSIU (CA. 833–883)

Lament of a Woman Acorn-Gatherer

Deep into autumn the acorns ripen,
Scattering as they fall into the scrub on the hill.
Hunched over, a hoary-haired crone
Gathers them, treading the morning frost.
After a long time she's got only a handful,
An entire day just fills her basket.
First she suns them, then steams them,
To use in making late winter provisions.

At the foot of the mountain she has ripening rice,
From its purple spikes a fragrance pervades.
Carefully she reaps, then hulls the grain,
Kernel after kernel like a jade earring.
She takes the grain to offer as government tax,
In her own home there are no granary bins.
How could she know that well over a picul of rice
Is only five pecks in official measurement?

Those crafty clerks don't fear the law,
Their greedy masters won't shun a bribe.
In the growing season she goes into debt,
In the off season sends grain to government bin.
From winter even into spring,
With acorns she tricks her hungry innards.

· · ·

Aah, meeting this old woman acorn-gatherer,
Tears come uncalled to moisten my robe.

STUDY QUESTIONS

1. What do these poems suggest about the lives of the peasants during the Tang dynasty? Pay particular attention to the issues of material standards, working conditions, family life, and gender relations.
2. What do the poems tell us about Chinese agriculture (crops, technology, farming practices, etc.)?
3. What clues are there in these poems about the foreign policy of the Tang emperors?
4. What do you learn about Tang officials from these poems? Pay particular attention to the issues of tax collection, military recruitment, and the authorship of the poems.
5. How do you explain the overall point of view expressed in the poems?
6. Why were the Chinese peasants so poor?
7. Do you see any evidence in the poems that the peasants engaged in protest against their plight?
8. Compare the lives of the Chinese peasants with the lives of the Hsiung-nu nomads (see Chapter 16). What differences do you see?

22

"The Noble and Magnificent City of Hangzhou": Marco Polo in China

During the three centuries from 950 to 1250 C.E. the Chinese economy grew rapidly. There was a great increase in the mining of coal and in the manufacture of objects made of iron. The manufacture of silk and porcelain also expanded. In southern China the amount of rice harvested shot upward. In addition, major new overseas ports emerged on China's southeast coast. Chinese ships, making use of the mariner's compass (a Chinese invention), began to ply the waters of the South China Sea and the eastern half of the Indian Ocean as never before.

Marco Polo, a Venetian merchant, traveled to China near the end of this great economic boom. Polo, who had journeyed eastward via the overland routes across central Asia, arrived in China during the 1270s just as the Mongols were completing their long campaign of conquest in China. He remained in China for 20 years and traveled widely in the country; during part of his time in China Polo may have been employed by the Mongols as an official. In the 1290s Polo decided to return home and chose the maritime route, setting sail from the (then) great Chinese port of Quanzhou.

Scholars have long regarded Marco Polo's book, if used carefully, as an important historical document. Polo's account of his travels, which he dictated to a professional writer shortly after returning home, is a mixture of careful observation, a traveler's tendency to exaggerate (especially in regard to numbers), and fantastic "wonder" stories. In the following passages Polo reports on the city of Hangzhou.

Upon leaving Va-giu you pass, in the course of three days' journey, many towns, castles and villages, all of them well-inhabited and opulent. The people have an abundance of provisions. At the end of three days you reach the noble and magnificent city of Hangzhou, a name that signifies "The Celestial City." This name it merits from its pre-eminence, among all others in the world, in point of grandeur and beauty, as well as from its many charms, which might lead an inhabitant to imagine himself in paradise.

This city was frequently visited by Marco Polo, who carefully and diligently observed and inquired into every aspect of it, all of which he recorded in his notes, from which the following particulars are drawn. According to common estimate, this city is a hundred miles around. Its streets and canals are extensive, and there are squares or market places, which are frequented by a prodigious number of people and are exceedingly spacious. It is situated between a fresh, very clear lake and a river of great magnitude, the waters of which run via many canals, both large and small, through every quarter of the city, carrying all sewage into the lake and ultimately to the ocean. This furnishes communication by water, in addition to that by land, to all parts of the town, the canals being of sufficient width for boats and the streets for carriages.

It is commonly said that the number of bridges amounts to twelve thousand. Those which cross the principal canals and are connected with the main streets have arches so high and are built with so much skill that the masts of vessels can pass under them. At the same time, carts and horses can pass over them, so gradual is the upward slope of the arch. If they were not so numerous, there would be no way of crossing from one part to another.

Beyond the city, and enclosing it on that side, there is a moat about forty miles in length, very wide, and issuing from the river mentioned before. This was excavated by the ancient kings of the province so that when the river overflowed its banks, the floodwater might be drawn off into this channel. This also serves for defense. The earth dug from it was thrown to the inner side, and forms a mound around the place.

There are within the city ten principal squares or market places, besides innumerable shops along the streets. Each side of these squares is half a mile in length, and in front of them is the main street, forty paces in width and running in a straight line from one end of the city to the other. It is crossed by many low and convenient bridges. These market squares are four miles from each other. Parallel to the main street, but on the opposite side of the square, runs a very large canal. On the nearer bank of this stand large stone warehouses provided for merchants who arrive from India and other parts with their goods and effects. They are thus situated conveniently close to the market squares. In each of these, three days in every week, from forty to fifty thousand persons come to the markets and supply them with every article that could be desired.

There is a great deal of game of all kinds, such as roebuck, stags, fallow deer, hares, and rabbits, together with partridges, pheasants, quail, hens, capon, and ducks and geese beyond number, for so easily are they bred on the lake that, for the value of a Venetian silver groat, you may purchase a pair of geese and two pair of ducks. There, too, are the houses where they slaughter cattle, such as oxen, calves, kids, and lambs, to furnish the tables of the rich and of leading citizens. . . .

At all seasons there is in the markets a great variety of herbs and fruits, especially pears of an extraordinary size, weighing ten pounds each, that are white inside and very fragrant. There are also peaches in season, both the yellow and white kinds, and of a delicious flavor. . . . From the sea, fifteen miles distant, a vast quantity of fish is each day brought up the river to the city. There is also an abundance of fish in the lake, which gives employment at all times to a group of fisherman. . . .

Each of the ten market squares is surrounded with high dwelling houses, in the lower part of which are shops where every kind of manufacture is carried on and every article of trade is offered, including spices, drugs, trinkets, and pearls. In certain shops nothing is sold but the wine of the country, which they make continually and serve out fresh to their customers at a moderate price. Many streets connect with the market squares, and in some of them are many cold baths, attended by servants of both sexes. The men and women who frequent them have been accustomed from childhood to wash in cold water, which they consider highly conducive to health. At these baths, however, they have rooms provided with warm water for the use of strangers who cannot bear the shock of the cold. All are in the habit of washing themselves daily, and especially before their meals. . . .

On each side of the principal street mentioned earlier, which runs from one end of the city to the other, there are great houses and mansions with their gardens, and near these, the dwellings of the artisans who work in the shops of the various trades. At all hours you see such multitudes of people passing to and fro on their personal affairs that providing enough food for them might be thought impossible. But one notes that on every market day the squares are crowded with tradespeople and with articles brought by cart and boat—all of which they sell out. From the sale of a single article such as pepper, some notion may be formed of the vast quantity of meat, wine, groceries, and the like, required by the inhabitants of Hangzhou. From an officer in the Great Khan's customs, Marco Polo learned that the amount of pepper bought daily was forty-three loads, each load being 243 pounds.

The inhabitants of the city are idolaters [i.e. Buddhists, Daoists, and Confucians]. They use paper money as currency. The men as well as the women are fair-skinned and handsome. Most of them always dress themselves in silk, as a result of the vast quantity of that material produced in Hangzhou, exclusive of what the merchants import from other provinces.

Among the handicrafts in the city, twelve [which are not identified] are considered superior to the rest as being more generally useful. For each of these there are a thousand workshops, and each shop employs ten, fifteen, or twenty workmen, and in a few instances as many as forty, under their respective masters. . . .

There are on the lake a great number of pleasure vessels or barges that can hold ten, fifteen, or twenty persons. They are from fifteen to twenty paces in length, broad-beamed, and not liable to rock. Men who want to enjoy this pastime in the company either of women friends or other men can hire one of these barges, which are always kept in excellent order, and have suitable seats and tables and every other furnishing needed for a party. The cabins have a flat roof or upper deck, where the boatmen stand; and by means of long poles, which they thrust to the bottom of the lake (which is not more than one or two fathoms in depth), shove the barges along. These cabins are painted inside with various colors and figures; all parts of the vessel are likewise adorned with painting. There are windows on either side, which may be opened to allow the company, as they sit at table, to look out in every direction and feast their eyes on the variety and beauty of the passing scene. The pleasure of this exceeds any that can be derived from amusements on land; for as the lake extends the whole length of the city, you have a distant view, as you stand in the boat, of all its grandeur and beauty, its palaces, temples, large convents, and gardens with great trees growing down to the water's edge, while at the same time you can enjoy the sight of other similar boats continually passing you, filled in like manner with parties in pursuit of amusement. . . .

It must be observed . . . that the streets of Hangzhou are all paved with stone and brick, and so too are all the principal roads running from there through the province of Manzi [south China]. By means of these, travelers can go to every part without muddying their feet. But as his Majesty's couriers go on horseback in great haste and cannot ride on pavement, a strip of road is left unpaved for their benefit.

The main street of the city is paved with stone and brick to the width of ten paces on each side, the center strip being filled with gravel and having curved drains for carrying off rain water into nearby canals so that it remains always dry. On this gravel, carriages continually pass to-and-fro. . . .

In every street of this city there are stone buildings or towers. In case a fire breaks out in any quarter, which is by no means unusual since the houses are mostly made of wood, the inhabitants may move their possessions to the safety of these towers.

By a regulation of his Majesty, there is a guard of ten watchmen, stationed under cover on all the principal bridges, five on duty by day and five by night. Each of these guards is provided with a drumlike wooden instrument as well as one of metal, together with a water clock which tells the hours of the day and night. When the first hour of the night has passed, one of the watchmen strikes once on the wooden instrument, and also upon the gong. At the end of the second hour he strikes twice, and so on as the hours advance. The guard is not allowed to sleep and must be always on the alert. In the morning as soon as the sun rises, they strike a single stroke again, as in the evening before, and so on from hour to hour. . . .

In cases of rioting or insurrection among the citizens, this police guard is also utilized; but independently of them, his Majesty always keeps on hand a large body of troops, both infantry and cavalry, under the command of his ablest officers.

For the purposes of the nightly watch, towers of earth have been thrown up at a distance of more than a mile from each other. On top of these is a wooden drum, which, when struck with a mallet by the guard stationed there, can be heard at a great distance. If precautions of this nature were not taken there would be a danger that half the city would be consumed. The usefulness of these guards in case of a popular uprising is obvious. . . .

Every father, or head of a household, is required to list on the door of his house the names of each member of his family, as well as the number of his horses. When any person dies, or leaves the dwelling, the name is struck out; similarly, when anyone is born, the name is added to the list. Thus the authorities know at all times the exact number of inhabitants. The same practice is followed throughout the province of Cathay [north China] as well as Manzi. In like manner, all the keepers of inns and public hotels inscribe the names of those who stay with them, noting the day and the hour of their arrival and departure. A copy of this record is transmitted daily to the magistrates stationed in the market squares.

STUDY QUESTIONS

1. What does Marco Polo report about the size and layout of Hangzhou?
2. How important was commerce in Hangzhou? What evidence do you see of the role of Hangzhou in long-distance trade?
3. What evidence in Marco Polo's report do you see regarding the standard of living of the residents of Hangzhou?

4. What evidence is there that fire was a serious problem in Hangzhou? What provisions were made for detecting and suppressing fires?

5. What evidence is there to suggest that the Hangzhou authorities were worried about the possibility of riot or insurrection? What steps were taken to prevent such occurrences?

6. Was clock time important in Hangzhou?

7. How did the lives of Hangzhou residents compare with the lives of the peasants in the Tang poems? (See Chapter 21.) Are the differences attributable to changes over time or to the quality of urban life as opposed to rural life?

8. How does Marco Polo's report on Hangzhou provide us with evidence regarding the condition of the Chinese economy during the thirteenth century?

9. How does the Chinese economy compare with the European economy, ca. 950 to 1250?

10. How does Polo's report illustrate the importance of cross-cultural contacts during the Mongol era?

23

Valor and Fair Treatment:
The Rise of the Samurai

Beginning in 794 C.E. Japanese emperors ruled their country from Kyoto, a city that was built to look very much like Chang'an, the home of the Tang emperors in China. For about two centuries the Chinese style of governance worked effectively in Japan. Gradually, however, the Japanese emperors and their advisors began to lose power to landowners and warriors in the provinces that established lord-vassal relationships similar to those in feudal western Europe. The result of these long-term political and social changes was the emergence of a new social class in Japan, the *samurai* (literally, "those who serve").

By the twelfth century the effective authority of the court in Kyoto had almost disappeared. Two great coalitions of samurai warriors battled for control of the country. A turning point was reached when Minamoto Yoritomo (1147–1199) led one of the warrior coalitions to victory over its rivals. However, instead of deposing the emperor, as would likely have happened in China, Yoritomo allowed the emperor to remain in Kyoto and to continue to reign as the symbolic head of state. Meanwhile, Yoritomo established a second capital at Kamakura, near present-day Tokyo, becoming Japan's first shogun or supreme military ruler. As in China, Japanese emperors continued to succeed one another in their capital, but unlike China, Japan was now effectively ruled by its warrior class. The samurai had established a distinctive pattern of governance in Japan which lasted for the next seven centuries. Even today the memory of samurai rule remains part of the political culture in Japan.

The first of the following selections is taken from the *Tale of the Heike,* the most famous literary account of the rise of the samurai. Inspired by the wars that gave rise to the Kamakura shoguns, the *Tale of the Heike* took shape shortly after the events that it describes. In the selection here, Yoshinaka, a leader of the Minamoto forces, is killed by other Minamotos who are jealous of his success. The second reading comes from the set of instructions that Hojo Shigetoki, a leading samurai,

Selection 1 from *The Tale of the Heike,* translated by Hiroshi Kitagawa and Bruce T. Tsuchida (Tokyo: University of Tokyo Press, 1975), pp. 519–523. Copyright © 1975, The University of Tokyo Press. Reprinted by permission. Selection 2 excerpted from *A History of Japan to 1334,* by George Sansom, with the permission of the publishers. Stanford Univerity Press. © 1958 by the Board of Trustees of the Leland Stanford Junior University..

gave to his 18-year-old son in 1247, following the latter's appointment to a key post in the shogunal administration.

1. FROM THE *TALE OF THE HEIKE*

Yoshinaka had brought with him from Shinano Province two beautiful women, Tomoe and Yamabuki. Of the two, Yamabuki had become ill and had remained in the capital.

Tomoe was indescribably beautiful; the fairness of her face and the richness of her hair were startling to behold. Even so, she was a fearless rider and a woman skilled with the bow. Once her sword was drawn, even the gods and devils feared to fight against her. Indeed, she was a match for a thousand. Thus it was that whenever a war broke out, she armed herself with a strong bow and a great sword, and took a position among the leaders. In many battles she had won matchless fame. This time too she had survived, though all her companions had been killed or wounded. Tomoe was among the seven last riders.

At first the men of Yoritomo's force had thought that Yoshinaka would take the Tamba Road through Nagasaka or would cross over the Ryūge Pass toward the north. Instead, taking neither of these, Yoshinaka urged his horse toward Seta in search of Kanehira. Kanehira had held his position at Seta until Noriyori's repeated assaults had reduced his eight hundred men to fifty. He then ordered his men to roll up their banners and rode back toward the capital to ascertain his master's fate. He was galloping along the lakeshore of Uchide when he caught sight of Yoshinaka ahead of him at a distance of one chō. Recognizing each other, master and retainer spurred their horses to join each other. Seizing Kanehira's hands, Yoshinaka said: "I would have fought to the death on the banks of the Kamo at Rokujō. Simply because of you, however, I have galloped here through the enemy swarms."

"It was very kind of you, my lord," replied Kanehira. "I too would have fought to the death at Seta. But in fear of your uncertain fate, I have come this way."

"We are still tied by karma," said Yoshinaka. "There must be more of my men around here, for I have seen them scattered among the hills. Unroll the banner and raise it high!"

As soon as Kanehira unfurled the banner, many men who had been in flight from the capital and Seta saw it and rallied. They soon numbered more than three hundred.

"Since we still have so many men, let us try one last fight!" shouted Yoshinaka jubilantly. "Look! That band of soldiers over there! Whose army is that?"

"I hear," replied one of Yoshinaka's men, "that is Tadayori's army, my lord."

"How many men are there in his army?"

"About six thousand, my lord."

"Just right!" cried out Yoshinaka. "Since we are determined to fight to the death, let us ride neck and neck with our valiant foes and die gallantly in their midst. Forward!"

Shouting, Yoshinaka dashed ahead. That day he wore armor laced with twilled silk cords over a red battle robe. His helmet was decorated with long golden horns. At his side hung a great sword studded with gold. He carried his quiver a little higher than usual on his back. Some eagle-feathered arrows still remained. Gripping his rattan-bound bow, he rode his famous horse, Oniashige [Gray Demon].

Rising his in his stirrups, he roared at the enemy: "You have often heard of me. Now take a good look at the captain of the Imperial Stables of the Left and governor of Iyo Province—Rising-Sun General Minamoto no Yoshinaka, that is who I am! I know that among you is Kai no Ichijōjirō Tadayori. We are fit opponents for each other. Cut off my head and show it to Yoritomo!"

At this challenge, Tadayori shouted to his men: "Now, hear this! He is the commander of our enemy. Let him not escape! All men—to the attack!"

Tadayori tried to seize Yoshinaka by surrounding him with his many men. Yoshinaka fought desperately, urging his horse into the six thousand, galloping back and forth, left and right, like a spider's legs. When he had dashed through the enemy, he found that his three hundred men had been cut down to fifty. Then he encountered another army of two thousand led by Sanehira. He continued on, attacking several other small bands of one or two hundred here and there, until at last his men were reduced to four. Tomoe was among the survivors.

Yoshinaka called her to his side and said: "You are a woman—leave now for wherever you like, quickly! As for me, I shall fight to the death. If I am wounded, I will kill myself. How ashamed I would be if people said that Yoshinaka was accompanied by a woman in his last fight."

Tomoe would not stir. After repeated pleas, however, she was finally convinced to leave.

"I wish I could find a strong opponent!" she said to herself. "Then I would show my master once more how well I can fight." She drew her horse aside to wait for the right opportunity.

Shortly thereafter, Moroshige of Musashi, a warrior renowned for his great strength, appeared at the head of thirty horsemen. Galloping alongside Moroshige, Tomoe grappled with him, pulled him against the pommel of her saddle, and giving him no chance to resist, cut off his head. The fight concluded, she threw off her armor and fled to the eastern provinces.

Among the remaining retainers of Yoshinaka, Tezuka no Tarō was killed, and his uncle, Tezuka no Bettō, took flight, leaving only Kanehira. When Yoshinaka found himself alone with Kanehira, he sighed: "My armor has never weighed upon me before, but today it is heavy."

"You do not look tired at all, my lord," replied Kanehira, "and your horse is still fresh. What makes it feel so heavy? If it is because you are discouraged at having none of your retainers but me, please remember that I, Kanehira, am a match for a thousand. Since I still have seven or eight arrows left in my quiver, let me hold back the foe while you withdraw to the Awazu pine wood. Now I pray you to put a peaceful end to yourself."

No sooner had he spoken to his master than another band of soldiers confronted them. "Please go to the pine wood, my lord," said Kanehira again. "Let me fight here to keep them away from you."

"I would have died in the capital!" replied Yoshinaka. "I have come this far with no other hope but to share your fate. How can I die apart from you? Let us fight until we die together!"

With these words, Yoshinaka tried to ride neck and neck with Kanehira. Now Kanehira alighted from his horse, seized the bridle of his master's mount, and pleaded in tears: "Whatever fame a warrior may win, a worthless death is a lasting shame for him. You are worn out, my lord. Your horse is also exhausted. If you are surrounded by the enemy and slain at the hand of a low, worthless retainer of some unknown warrior, it will be a great shame for you and me in the days to come. How disgraceful it would be if such a nameless fellow could declare, 'I cut off the head of Yoshinaka, renowned throughout the land of Japan!'"

Yoshinaka finally gave in to Kanehira's entreaty and rode off toward the pine wood of Awazu. Kanehira, riding alone, charged into the band of some fifty horsemen. Rising high in his stirrups, he cried out in a thunderous voice: "You have often heard of me. Now take a good look. I am Imai no Shirō Kanehira, aged thirty-three, a foster brother of Lord Yoshinaka. As I am a valiant warrior among the men of Lord Yoshinaka, your master, Yoritomo, at Kamakura must know my name well. Take my head and show it to him!"

Kanehira had hardly uttered these words when he let fly his remaining eight arrows one after another without pause. Eight men were shot from their horses, either dead or wounded. He then drew his sword and brandished it as he galloped to and fro. None of his opponents could challenge him face to face, though they cried out: "Shoot him down! Shoot him down!"

Sanehira's soldiers let fly a shower of arrows at Kanehira, but his armor was so strong that none of them pierced it. Unless they aimed at the joints of his armor, he could never be wounded.

Yoshinaka was now all alone in the pine wood of Awazu. It was the twenty-first day of the first month. Dusk had begun to fall. Thin ice covered the rice fields and the marsh, so that it was hard to distinguish one from the other. Thus it was that Yoshinaka had not gone far before his horse plunged deep into the muddy slime. Whipping and spurring no longer did any good. The horse could not stir. Despite his predicament, he still thought of Kanehira. As Yoshinaka was turning around to see how he fared, Tamehisa, catching up with him, shot an arrow under his helmet. It was a mortal wound. Yoshinaka pitched forward onto the neck of his horse. Then two of Tamehisa's retainers fell upon Yoshinaka and struck off his head. Raising it high on the point of his sword, Tamehisa shouted: "Kiso no Yoshinaka, renowned throughout the land of Japan as a valiant warrior, has been killed by Miura no Ishida Jirō Tamehisa!"

Kanehira was fighting desperately as these words rang in his ears. At that moment he ceased fighting and cried out: "For whom do I have to fight now? You, warriors of the east, see how the mightiest warrior in Japan puts an end to himself!" Thrusting the point of his sword into his mouth, he flung himself headlong from his horse so that the sword pierced his head.

Yoshinaka and Kanehira died valiant deaths at Awazu. Could there have been a more heroic battle?

2. A SAMURAI INSTRUCTS HIS SON

The men under your command . . . must be carefully chosen for your service. Do not take "difficult" fellows. If men under your orders, however loyal, are wanting in intelligence, you must not trust them with important duties, but rely upon experienced older men. If you are in doubt refer to me, Shigetoki.

In dealing with subordinates do not make an obvious distinction between good and not-good. Use the same kind of language, give the same kind of treatment to all, and thus you will get the best out of the worst. But you yourself must not lose sight of the distinction between good character and bad character, between capable and incapable. You must be fair, but in practice you must not forget the difference between men who are useful and men who are not. Remember that the key to discipline is fair treatment in rewards and in punishments. But make allowance for minor misdeeds in young soldiers and others, if their conduct is usually good.

Do not be careless or negligent in the presence of subordinates, especially of older men. Thus do not spit or snuffle or lounge about on a chest with your legs dangling. This only gives men the impression that you do not care for their good opinion. Preserve your dignity. If you behave rudely, they will tell their families and gossip will spread. You must treat all servants with proper consideration and generosity, not only your own people but also those of your parents and other superiors. If you do not, they will scorn you and say to one another: "He thinks he is very important, but he doesn't amount to much."

Remember, however, that there are times when a commander must exercise his power of deciding questions of life or death. In those circumstances since human life is at stake you must give most careful thought to your action. Never kill or wound a man in anger, however great the provocation. Better get somebody else to administer the proper punishment. Decisions made in haste before your feelings are calm can only lead to remorse. Close your eyes and reflect carefully when you have a difficult decision to make.

When accusations are brought to you, always remember that there must be another side to the question. Do not merely indulge in anger. To give fair decisions is the most important thing not only in commanding soldiers but also in governing a country.

STUDY QUESTIONS

1. What virtues do the warriors in the *Tale of the Heike* display?
2. What is the nature of the relationship between Yoshinaka and Kanehira? How strong is the emotional bond between them?
3. In what ways is Tomoe important in the *Tale of the Heike?* What does the role of Tomoe suggest about gender relations among the early samurai?
4. What advice does the samurai father give to his son?
5. To what extent did the virtues displayed by the samurai warriors conflict with the requirements of becoming effective administrators?
6. To what extent does the *Tale of the Heike* romanticize both the reality of war and the nature of the samurai class? Compare the *Tale of the Heike* with the Chinese poems from the Tang dynasty with regard to the issue of war (see Chapter 21).
7. In what ways did Japan become different from China in the twelfth and thirteenth centuries?
8. What similarities do you see between the samurai and the Mongols? (See Chapter 33.) What are the important differences?

24

The Early Stages of the Byzantine Empire

The sixth-century reign of Justinian, one of Byzantium's most illustrious emperors, witnessed an attempt to recover many of the western territories of the recently collapsed Roman Empire. This effort was short-lived. More important was the tone Justinian set for the vigorous eastern portion of the empire, centered around Constantinople (Byzantium) in southeastern Europe and Asia Minor. Justinian codified the Roman legal system, introduced financial and administrative reforms, and tightened imperial control of the Eastern Orthodox Church. His desire to recapture Roman splendor prompted great expenditure on a public building program, particularly at Constantinople. Fearing that "posterity, beholding the enormous size and number of [buildings], should deny their being the work of one man," Justinian ordered a Palestinian historian, Procopius, to compose a treatise on his new program.

Procopius's *On Justinian's Buildings,* written in 555 C.E., predictably exaggerated Justinian's prowess, but it did capture the emperor's ambition. Procopius focused on the Church of the Holy Wisdom (Hagia Sophia) in Constantinople, completed in 537 as Christendom's largest and most beautiful edifice. (The church would later be converted to a mosque, when Turks captured Constantinople [Istanbul] in 1453; it is now a museum.) Justinian is said to have boasted of the great church, "Solomon, I have surpassed you!" Like the Byzantine Empire itself, the new building combined Roman and Middle Eastern (particularly Persian) styles, setting up a new culture closely related to that of the late Roman Empire.

The following selection, from Procopius, suggests key elements of the political as well as artistic program of early Byzantium. How does Byzantium compare with ancient Rome (see Chapter 15)? Why would Byzantium prove to be such an important cultural and political example to other East European peoples, particularly the

From Procopius, *Of the Buildings of Justinian,* translated by Aubrey Stewart (London: Palestine Pilgrims' Text Society, 1888), pp. 2–5, 9–11.

Slavs as they established their civilization to the north? What elements of Byzantine civilization would these imitators be most likely to copy?

The lowest dregs of the people in Byzantium once assailed the Emperor Justinian in the rebellion called Nika, which I have clearly described in my "History of the Wars." To prove that it was not merely against the Emperor, but no less against God that they took up arms, they ventured to burn the church of the Christians. (This church the people of Byzantium call Sophia, *i.e.,* . . . *Wisdom;* a name most worthy of God.) God permitted them to effect this crime, knowing how great the beauty of this church would be when restored. Thus the church was entirely reduced to ashes; but the Emperor Justinian not long afterwards adorned it in such a fashion, that if anyone had asked the Christians in former times if they wished their church to be destroyed and thus restored, showing them the appearance of the church which we now see, I think it probable that they would have prayed that they might as soon as possible behold their church destroyed, in order that it might be turned into its present form.

• • •

The Emperor Justinian was born in our time, and succeeding to the throne when the state was decayed, added greatly to its extent and glory by driving out from it the barbarians, who for so long a time had forced their way into it, as I have briefly narrated in my "History of the Wars." They say that Themistocles, the son of Neocles, prided himself on his power of making a small state great, but our Emperor has the power of adding others states to his own, for he has annexed to the Roman Empire many other states which at his accession were independent, and has founded innumerable cities which had no previous existence. As for religion, which he found uncertain and torn by various heresies, he destroyed everything which could lead to error, and securely established the true faith upon one solid foundation. Moreover, finding the laws obscure through their unnecessary multitude, and confused by their conflict with one another, he firmly established them by reducing the number of those which were unnecessary, and in the case of those that were contradictory, by confirming better ones. He forgave of his own accord those who plotted against him, and, by loading with wealth those who were in want, and relieving them from the misfortunes which had afflicted them, he rendered the empire stable and its members happy. By increasing his armies he strengthened the Roman Empire, which lay everywhere exposed to the attacks of barbarians, and fortified its entire frontier by building strong places.

• • •

Now, as I said before, we must turn out attention to the buildings of this monarch, lest posterity, beholding the enormous size and number of them, should deny their being the work of one man; for the works of many men of former times, not being confirmed by history, have been disbelieved through their own excessive greatness.

• • •

It is, indeed, a proof of the esteem with which God regarded the Emperor, that He furnished him with men who would be so useful in effecting his designs,

Interior of Saint Sophia. In the domed style characteristic of Eastern Orthodox churches and cathedrals, calligraphy and other appointments show the church's conversion to a mosque. *How do the basic architectural features compare with Procopius's description? What impression would they make on visitors?* (Giraudon/Art Resource, NY.)

and we are compelled to admire the intelligence of the Emperor, in being able to choose the most suitable of mankind to carry out the noblest of his works.

The church consequently presented a most glorious spectacle, extraordinary to those who beheld it, and altogether incredible to those who are told of it. In height it rises to the very heavens, and overtops the neighbouring buildings like a ship anchored among them: it rises above the rest of the city, which it adorns, while it forms a part of it, and it is one of its beauties that being a part of the city, and growing out of it, it stands so high above it, that from it the whole city can be beheld as from a watchtower. Its length and breadth are so judiciously arranged that it appears to be both long and wide without being disproportioned. It is distinguished by indescribable beauty, for it excels both in its size and in the harmony of its proportion, having no part excessive and none deficient; being more magnificent than ordinary buildings, and much more elegant than those which are out of proportion. It is singularly full of light and sunshine; you would declare that the place is not lighted by the sun from without, but that the rays are produced within itself, such an abundance of light is poured into this church. . . . Thus far I imagine the building is not incapable of being described, even by a weak and feeble tongue. As the arches are arranged in a quadrangular figure, the stonework between them takes the shape of a triangle; the lower angle of each triangle, being compressed between the shoulders of the arches, is slender, while the upper part becomes wider as it rises in the space between them, and ends against the circle which rises from thence, forming there its remaining angles. A spherical-shaped dome standing upon this circle makes it exceedingly beautiful; from the lightness of the building it does not appear to rest upon a solid foundation, but to cover the place beneath as though it were suspended from heaven by the fabled golden chain. All these parts surprisingly joined to one another in the air, suspended one from another, and resting only on that which is next to them, form the work into one admirably harmonious whole, which spectators do not care to dwell upon for long in the mass, as each individual part attracts the eye and turns it to itself. The sight causes men to constantly change their point of view, and the spectator can nowhere point to any part, which he admires more than the rest, but having viewed the art which appears everywhere, men contract their eyebrows as they look at each point, and are unable to comprehend such workmanship, but always depart thence stupified through their incapacity to comprehend it.

· · ·

The entire ceiling is covered with pure gold, which adds glory to its beauty, though the rays of light reflected upon the gold from the marble surpass it in beauty; there are two porticos on each side, which do not in any way dwarf the size of the church, but add to its width. In length they reach quite to the ends, but in height they fall short of it; these also have a domed ceiling and are adorned with gold. Of these two porticos, the one is set apart for male, and the other for female worshippers; there is no variety in them, nor do they differ in any respect from one another, but their very equality and similarity add to the beauty of the church. Who could describe the galleries of the portion set apart for women, or the numerous porticos and cloistered courts with which the church is surrounded? who could tell of the beauty of the columns and marbles with which the church is adorned? one would think that one had come upon a meadow full of flowers in bloom: who would not admire the purple tints of some and the green of others, the glowing red and glittering white, and those, too, which nature, like a painter, has marked with the strongest contrasts of colour? Whoever enters there to worship perceives at once that it is not by any human strength or skill, but by the favour of God that this work has been perfected; his mind rises sublime to commune with God, feeling that He cannot be far off, but must especially love to dwell in the place which He has chosen; and this takes place not only when a man sees it for the first time, but it always makes the same impression upon him, as though he had never beheld it before. No one ever became weary of this spectacle, but those who are in the Church delight in what they see, and, when they leave it, magnify it in their talk about it; moreover, it is impossible accurately to describe the treasure of gold and silver plate and gems, which the Emperor Justinian has presented to it; but by the description of one of them, I leave the rest to be inferred. That part of the church which is especially sacred, and where the priests alone are allowed to enter, which is called the Sanctuary, contains forty thousand pounds' weight of silver.

STUDY QUESTIONS

1. What were the main architectural features of the church? What did the building suggest about religious attitudes among Byzantine leaders? Why would such a church be built?
2. How did Procopius link the cathedral's opulence to true Christian values?
3. What relationship between church and state does the passage suggest?

25

Russia Converts to Christianity

The conversion of the Slavs to Orthodox Christianity was one of the formative steps in the development of Slavic civilization, as the Orthodox Church assumed a major role in the transmission and assimilation of Byzantine culture into Eastern Europe. Byzantine emperors employed judicious diplomacy, international trade, and the church to transform their hostile and barbaric neighbors into cultural satellites. Kievan Russia, following King Vladimir's conversion to Orthodox Christianity in the late tenth century C.E., proved especially receptive to Byzantine culture and used the empire as a prototype in evolving its own governmental institutions. Provided with a modified Greek alphabet (Glagolithic or Cyrillic), created expressly in about 863 for the translation of biblical and liturgical works into Slavic by Saint Cyril (also known as Constantine), Russian scholars began to record their history and to produce a remarkable native literature. Having no need to master the Greek and Latin languages, which proved essential for full reception of Byzantium's classical heritage, Russian scholars remained somewhat outside the mainstream of traditional classical thought.

The selections below appear in the *Russian Primary Chronicle* ("The Tale of Bygone Years"), our principal historical source for the history of Kievan Russia during the tenth to twelfth centuries. Originally compiled in about 1110, the earliest surviving copy is a 1377 version (Laurentian). The account of the conversion of the Slavs by Saints Cyril and Methodius in the ninth century is probably of Moravian origin and may be dependent on old texts and the oral tradition. The account of Vladimir's conversion and baptism in 988 is undoubtedly a Russian legend.

Although the conversion to Christianity was certainly a major step in the Slavic civilization, it also raises questions: Why, according to the *Chronicle* account, did most Slavs pick Orthodox Christianity? Why did they bother to convert to a new religion at all, and what impact would this new religion have on their culture?

There was at that time but one Slavic race, including the Slavs who settled along the Danube and were subjugated by the Magyars, as well as the Moravians, the Czechs, the Lyakhs [Poles], and the Polianians, the last of whom are now called Russians. It

From *A Source Book for Russian History from Early Times to 1917*, 2 vols., edited by George Vernadsky, (New Haven: Yale University Press, 1972), Vol. I, pp. 12–13, 25–26. Copyright © Yale University Press, 1972. Reprinted by permission.

was for these Moravians that Slavic books were first written, and this writing prevails also among the Russians and the Danubian Bulgarians.

When the Moravian Slavs and their princes were living in baptism, the Princes Rostislav, Sviatopolk, and Kotsel sent messengers to the emperor Michael, saying, "Our nation is baptized, and yet we have no teacher to direct and instruct us and to interpret the Sacred Scriptures. We understand neither Greek nor Latin. Some teach us one thing and some another. Furthermore, we do not understand written characters nor their meaning. Therefore send us teachers who can make known to us the words of the Scriptures and their sense." The Emperor Michael, upon hearing their request, called together all the scholars and reported to them the message of the Slavic princes. . . . The emperor prevailed upon them [Constantine and Methodius] to undertake the mission and sent them into the Slavic country to Rostislav, Sviatopolk, and Kotsel. When they arrived [in 863], they undertook to compose a Slavic alphabet and translated the Acts and the Gospels. The Slavs rejoiced to hear the greatness of God extolled in their native tongue. The apostles afterward translated the Psalter, the Oktoechos, and other books.

Now some zealots began to condemn the Slavic books, contending that it was not right for any other nation to have its own alphabet, apart from the Hebrews, the Greeks, and the Latins, according to Pilate's superscription, which he composed for the Lord's cross. When the pope at Rome heard of this situation, he rebuked those who murmured against the Slavic books. . . . Constantine then returned again and went to instruct the people of Bulgaria, but Methodius remained in Moravia.

Prince Kotsel appointed Methodius bishop of Pannonia in the see of Saint Andronicus, one of the Seventy, a disciple of the holy apostle Paul. Methodius chose two priests who were very rapid writers and translated the whole Scriptures in full from Greek into Slavic in six months. . . . Now Andronicus is the apostle of the Slavic race. He traveled among the Moravians, and the apostle Paul taught there likewise. . . . Since Paul is the teacher of the Slavic race, from which we Russians too are sprung, even so the apostle Paul is the teacher of us Russians, for he preached to the Slavic nation and appointed Andronicus as bishop and successor to himself among them. But the Slavs and the Russians are one people, for it is because of the Varangians that the latter became known as Russians, though originally they were Slavs. While some Slavs were termed Polianians, their speech was still Slavic, for they were known as Polianians because they lived in the fields [*pole* means "field" in Russian]. But they had the same Slavic language.

• • •

[In the year 980] Vladimir began to reign alone in Kiev, and he set up idols on the hills outside the castle: one of Perun, made of wood with a head of silver and a moustache of gold, and others of Khors, Dazh'bog, Stribog, Simar'gl, and Mokosh'. The people sacrificed to them, calling them gods, and brought their sons and their daughters to sacrifice them to these devils. They desecrated the earth with their offerings, and the Russian land and this hill were defiled with blood.

• • •

In the year 6495 [987] Vladimir summoned together his boyars [nobles] and the city elders and said to them, "Behold, the Bulgars came before me, saying,

'Accept our religion.' Then came the Germans and praised their own faith. After them came the Jews. Finally the Greeks appeared, disparaging all other faiths but praising their own, and they spoke at length, telling the history of the whole world from its beginning. Their words were wise, and it was marvelous to listen and pleasant for anyone to hear them. They preached about another world. 'Anyone,' they said, 'who adopts our religion and then dies shall arise and live forever. But anyone who embraces another faith shall in the next world be consumed by fire.' What is your opinion on this subject, and what do you answer?" The boyars and the elders replied, "You know, Prince, that no man condemns what is his own but praises it instead. If you desire to make certain, you have servants at your disposal. Send them to inquire about the ritual of each and how he worships God."

Their counsel pleased the prince and all people, so that they chose ten good and wise men.

[They visited foreign lands, and] then they returned to their country. The prince called together his boyars and the elders, and he said: "The envoys who were sent out have returned. Let us hear what took place." He said, "Speak in the presence of my retinue." The envoys then reported, "When we journeyed among the Bulgars, we observed how they worship in their temple. . . . Their religion is not good. Then we went among the Germans and saw them performing many ceremonies in their temples, and we saw no beauty there. Then we went to Greece, and the Greeks led us to where they worship their God, and we did not know whether we were in heaven or on earth. For on earth there is no such splendor or such beauty, and we are at a loss to describe it. We know only that God dwells there among men, and their service is better than the ceremonies of other nations. For we cannot forget that beauty. Every man, after tasting something sweet, is afterward unwilling to accept that which is bitter, and therefore we can no longer remain here [in paganism]." Then the boyars said in reply, "If the Greek faith were evil, it would not have been adopted by your grandmother Olga, who was wiser than anyone else." Vladimir then responded, asking, "Where shall we accept baptism?" and they replied, "Wherever you wish." . . .

After a year had passed, in 6496 [988], Vladimir proceeded with an armed force against Kherson, a Greek city [by the Black Sea]. . . . [After a siege] the inhabitants . . . surrendered.

Vladimir and his retinue entered the city, and he sent messages to the emperors Basil and Constantine, saying, "Behold, I have captured your glorious city. I have also heard that you have an unwedded sister. Unless you give her to me in marriage, I shall deal with your own city as I have with Kherson." When the emperors heard this message they were troubled, and they issued this statement: "It is not proper for Christians to give women in marriage to pagans. If you are baptized, you shall have her for your wife, inherit the kingdom of God, and be our co-believer. If you do not do so, however, we cannot give you our sister in marriage." When Vladimir learned of their response, he said to the emperors' envoys, "Tell the emperors I will accept baptism, since I have already given some study to your religion, and the Greek faith and ritual, as described by the emissaries I sent to examine it, has pleased me well." When the emperors heard this report they rejoiced and persuaded their sister Anna [to consent to the match]. They then sent word to Vladimir, "Be baptized, and then we shall send you our sister." But Vladimir said,

"Let your sister herself come [with the priests] to baptize me." The emperors complied with his request and sent their sister, accompanied by some dignitaries and priests. . . . The bishop [episkop] of Kherson, together with the princess's priests . . . baptized Vladimir. . . .

As a bride price in exchange for the princess, he gave Kherson back to the Greeks and then went back to Kiev.

When the prince arrived at his capital, he directed that the idols should be overturned and that some should be cut to pieces and others burned up. . . .

Thereupon Vladimir sent heralds throughout the whole city, proclaiming, "If anyone, whether rich or poor, beggar or slave, does not come tomorrow to the river, he will be an enemy of mine." When the people heard this they went gladly, rejoicing and saying, "If this were not good, the prince and his boyars would not have accepted it." On the morrow the prince went forth to the Dnieper with the priests of the princess and those from Kherson, and a countless multitude assembled. They all went into the water; some stood up to their necks, others to their breasts, and the younger up to their breasts near the bank, some people holding children in their arms, while the adults waded farther out. The priests stood by and offered prayers. There was joy in heaven and upon earth at the sight of so many souls saved. But the Devil groaned, "Woe is me! They are driving me out of here!" . . .

He [Vladimir] ordered that wooden churches should be built and established where [pagan] idols had previously stood. He founded the Church of Saint Basil on the hill where the idol of Perun and the other images had been set, and where the prince and the people had offered their sacrifices. He began to found churches, to assign priests throughout the cities and towns, and to bring people in for baptism from all towns and villages. He began to take the children of the best families and send them for instruction from books.

STUDY QUESTIONS

1. What kinds of causes for historical change does this account emphasize?
2. How is Vladimir's conversion explained?
3. What relationship is suggested between king and nobles? Between king and ordinary subjects?
4. What church-state relationship is implied by this account?
5. Given obvious distortions and simplifications in this account, what is its value as a historical source? What does it say about Russian politics, religion, and society at this time?

26

Feudalism: Contemporary Descriptions and the Magna Carta

Although imperial or royal rule received great attention in postclassical Eastern Europe, feudalism was more characteristic in Western Europe. Western feudalism, evolving in turbulent eighth-century France, offered aristocratic landowners potential security in the absence of law and order. By concession or usurpation, major landowners assumed substantial legal and governmental powers from the central government and proceeded through private arrangements with lesser landowners (their vassals) to create local militias for defensive purposes. Inherently particularistic and initially undisciplined, feudalism enveloped the monarchy itself. Feudalism evolved its own system of law and code of ethics for its members as it spread throughout Europe to assume a dominant role in the political and cultural history of the Middle Ages. Introduced to England in 1066 by William the Conqueror—who substantially curbed the powers of all feudal vassals while retaining considerable central authority—feudalism emphasized mutual obligations within the military elite, often including the king. All members, including the monarchs who headed the feudal system, enjoyed specific rights but were also bound by feudal law to perform fixed obligations.

The first document was written by a well-known French bishop, who offers a general description—obviously somewhat idealized—of what feudalism involved. The second, from a ninth-century feudal contract, describes conditions of separation; these should be compared with the ideal statement and also with the less legalistic values in Japanese feudalism. The third document shows how the

Selections 1 and 2 from Brian Tierney, *Sources of Medieval History* (New York: Alfred A. Knopf, 1978), Vol. I, pp. 131, 133. Permission granted by the McGraw-Hill Companies. Selection 3 from *Documents Illustrating the History of Civilization in Medieval England* (1066–1600), edited by R. Trevor Davis (New York: Dutton & Co., 1926) pp. 39-52. Reprinted from *Statutes of the Realm*, 1810, Vol. 1, pp. 5ff.

contractual emphases in Western feudalism—I'll live up to my obligations if you live up to yours—could lead to innovations in the system of monarchy, innovations that would have durable importance in the Western political tradition. The only available means for feudal vassals to force an obstinate royal overlord to observe the binding feudal law was to resort to arms. Such means were used in 1215 by secular and ecclesiastical vassals under the leadership of Stephen Langton, archbishop of Canterbury, against King John of England. John was forced to place his seal on the Magna Carta, a charter of sixty chapters listing arbitrary royal encroachments on the feudal law as well as violations against traditional rights and liberties. Although the charter exerted little real impact on medieval English law and government because John died nine weeks after signing the document, its rediscovery and use by seventeenth-century opponents of royal absolutism allowed it to take a fundamental position in the English constitution. Contrary to popular belief, the original charter did not establish the individual right to trial by jury.

The Magna Carta must be interpreted as a feudal document: how does it define rights and government, and who participates in what kind of rights? Feudalism was a political response to the extremely chaotic conditions of the early Middle Ages in Western Europe. The feudal system could be bent toward more centralized rule only with difficulty, and the Magna Carta reveals some of the resulting tensions. Feudalism did, however, generate the beginnings of political principles, based on the concept of mutuality, that would be used in later political systems, as the subsequent revival of the Magna Carta attests (see Volume 2 for later concepts of limited government). The Western feudal concept must also be compared with that of Japan (see Chapter 23).

1. FULBERT, BISHOP OF CHARTRES, ON FEUDAL OBLIGATIONS (1020)

To William most glorious duke of the Aquitanians, bishop Fulbert the favor of his prayers.

Asked to write something concerning the form of fealty, I have noted briefly for you on the authority of the books the things which follow. He who swears fealty to his lord ought always to have these six things in memory; what is harmless, safe, honorable, useful, easy, practicable. Harmless, that is to say that he should not be injurious to his lord in his body: safe, that he should not be injurious to him in his secrets or in the defenses through which he is able to be secure; honorable, that he should not be injurious to him in his justice or in other matters that pertain to his honor; useful, that he should not be injurious to him in his possessions; easy or practicable, that that good which his lord is able to do easily, he make not difficult, nor that which is practicable he make impossible to him.

However, that the faithful vassal should avoid these injuries is proper, but not for this does he deserve his holding: for it is not sufficient to abstain from evil, unless what is good is done also. It remains, therefore, that in the same six things mentioned above he should faithfully counsel and aid his lord, if he wishes to be looked upon as worthy of his benefice and to be safe concerning the fealty which he has sworn.

The lord also ought to act toward his faithful vassal reciprocally in all these things. And if he does not do this he will be justly considered guilty of bad faith, just as the former, if he should be detected in the avoidance of or the doing of or the consenting to them, would be perfidious and perjured.

I would have written to you at greater length, if I had not been occupied with many other things, including the rebuilding of our city and church which was lately entirely consumed in a great fire; from which loss though we could not for a while be diverted, yet by the hope of the comfort of God and of you we breathe again.

2. LORDS AND VASSALS (816)

If anyone shall wish to leave his lord (*seniorem*), and is able to prove against him one of these crimes, that is, in the first place, if the lord has wished to reduce him unjustly into servitude; in the second place, if he has taken counsel against his life; in the third place, if the lord has committed adultery with the wife of his vassal; in the fourth place, if he has wilfully attacked him with a drawn sword; in the fifth place, if the lord has been able to bring defence to his vassal after he has commended his hands to him, and has not done so; it is allowed to the vassal to leave him. If the lord has perpetrated anything against the vassal in these five points it is allowed the vassal to leave him.

3. THE MAGNA CARTA

John, by the grace of God, king of England, lord of Ireland, duke of Normandy and Aquitaine, and count of Anjou, to the archbishops, bishops, abbots, earls, barons, justiciars, foresters, sheriffs, stewards, servants, and to all his bailiffs and loyal persons, greeting. Know that, having regard to God and for the salvation of our souls, and those of all our predecessors and heirs, and unto the honour of God and the advancement of Holy Church, and for the reform of our realm, by the counsel of our venerable fathers . . . we have granted:

I. In the first place we have granted to God, and by this our present charter confirmed for us and our heirs for ever that the English Church shall be free, and shall have her rights entire and her liberties inviolate; and we will that it be thus observed; which is apparent from this, that the freedom of elections, which is reckoned most important and very essential to the English Church, we, of pure and unconstrained will, did grant, and did by our charter confirm and did obtain the ratification of the same from our Lord, Pope Innocent III., before the quarrel arose between us and our barons: and this we will observe, and our will is that it be observed in good faith by our heirs for ever. We have also granted to all freemen of our kingdom, for us and our heirs for ever, all the underwritten liberties, to be had and held by them and their heirs, of us and our heirs for ever.

· · ·

XII. No scutage [tax] or aid shall be imposed on our kingdom, unless by common counsel of our kingdom, except for ransoming our person, for making our eldest son a knight, and for marrying our eldest daughter once; and for them there shall not be levied more than a reasonable aid. In like manner it shall be done concerning aids from the city of London.

XIII. And the city of London shall have all its ancient liberties and free customs, as well by land as by water; furthermore we decree and grant that all other cities, boroughs, and towns, and ports shall have all their liberties and free customs.

XIV. And for obtaining the common counsel of the kingdom about the assessing of an aid (except in the three cases aforesaid) or of a scutage, we will cause to be summoned the archbishops, bishops, abbots, earls, and greater barons, individually by our letters; and we will moreover cause to be summoned generally through our sheriffs and bailiffs, all others who hold of us in chief, for a definite date, namely after the expiry of at least forty days, and at a definite place; and in all letters of such summons we will specify the reason of the summons. And when the summons has thus been made, the business shall proceed on the day appointed, according to the counsel of such as are present, although not all who are summoned have come.

. . .

XXIII. No village or individual shall be compelled to make bridges at river banks, except those who were from old times rightfully compelled to do so.

XXIV. No sheriff, constable, coroners, or others of our bailiffs, shall hold pleas of our crown.

. . .

XXVIII. No constable or other bailiff of ours shall take corn or other provisions from anyone without immediately tendering money in exchange, unless by permission of the seller he is allowed to postpone payment.

XXIX. No constable shall compel any knight to give money in stead of castle guard, when he is willing to perform it in his own person, or (if he himself cannot do it from any reasonable cause) then by another reliable man; and if we have led him or sent him upon military service, he shall be quit of guard, in proportion to the time during which he has been on service because of us.

XXX. No sheriff or bailiff of ours, or other person, shall take the horses or carts of any freeman for transport duty, against the will of the said freeman.

XXXI. Neither we nor our bailiffs shall take for our castles or for any other work of ours, timber which is not ours, against the will of the owner of that timber.

XXXII. We will not retain beyond one year and one day, the lands of those who have been convicted of felony, and the lands shall thereafter be handed over to the lords of the fiefs.

. . .

XXXVIII. No bailiff for the future shall, upon his own unsupported complaint, put anyone to his "law" without reputable witnesses brought for this purpose.

XXXIX. No freeman shall be taken or imprisoned or disseised or exiled or in anyway destroyed, nor will we go upon him nor send upon him, except by the lawful judgement of his peers or by the law of the land.

XL. To no one will we sell, to no one will we refuse right or justice.

XLI. All merchants shall have safe and secure exit from England, and entry to England, with right to tarry there and to move about as well by land as by water, for buying and selling by the ancient and right customs, quit from all evil tolls, except, in time of war, such merchants as are of the land at war with us. And if such are found in our land at the beginning of the war, they shall be detained, without injury to their bodies or goods, until information be received by us or by our chief justiciar how the merchants of our land found in the land at war with us are treated; and if our men are safe there the others shall be safe in our land.

XLII. It shall be lawful in future for anyone to leave our kingdom and to return safe and secure by land and water, except for a short period in time of war on grounds of public policy—reserving always the allegiance due to us—excepting always those imprisoned or outlawed in accordance with the law of the kingdom, and natives of any country at war with us, and merchants, who shall be treated as is above provided.

. . .

XLV. We will appoint as justices, constables, sheriffs, or bailiffs only such as know the law of the kingdom and mean to observe it well.

. . .

LII. If anyone has been dispossessed or removed by us, without the legal judgement of his peers, from his lands, castles, franchises, or from his right, we will immediately restore them to him; and if a dispute arise over this, then let it be decided by the five-and-twenty barons, of whom mention is made below in the clause for securing the peace. Moreover, for all those possessions, from which anyone has, without the lawful judgement of his peers been disseised or removed, by our father, King Henry, or by our brother, King Richard, and which we retain in our hand—or which are possessed by others, to whom we are bound to warrant them—we shall have respite until the usual term of crusaders; excepting those things about which a plea has been raised, or an inquest made by our order, before our taking of the cross; but as soon as we return from our pilgrimage—or if by chance we desist from our pilgrimage—we will immediately grant full justice therein.

. . .

LV. All fines made by us unjustly and against the law of the land, shall be entirely remitted, or else it shall be done concerning them according to the decision of the five-and-twenty barons of whom mention is made below in (the clause for) securing the peace, or according to the judgement of the majority of the same, along with the aforesaid Stephen, archbishop of Canterbury, if he can be present, and such others as he may wish to bring with him for this purpose; and if he cannot be present the business shall nevertheless proceed without him, provided always that if any one or more of the aforesaid five-and-twenty barons are in a similar suit, they shall be removed as far as shall concern this particular judgement, others being substituted in their places after having been selected by the rest of the five-and-twenty for this purpose only, and after having been sworn.

. . .

LX. Moreover, all these aforesaid customs and liberties, the observance of which we have granted in our kingdom as far as pertains to us towards our men, shall be observed by all of our kingdom, as well clergy as laymen, as far as pertains to them towards their men.

LXI. Since, moreover, for God and the amendment of our kingdom and for the better allaying of our quarrel that has arisen between us and our barons, we have granted all these concessions, desirous that they should enjoy them in complete and firm stability for ever, we give and grant to them the underwritten security, namely, that the barons choose five-and-twenty barons of the kingdom, whomsoever they will, who shall be obliged, to observe and hold, and cause to be observed, with all their might, the peace and liberties which we have granted and confirmed to them by this our present Charter, so that if we, or our justiciar, or our bailiffs or any one of our officers, shall in anything be at fault towards anyone, or shall have broken any one of the articles of the peace or of this security, and the offence be notified to four barons of the aforesaid five-and-twenty, the said four barons shall come to us (or to our justiciar, if we are out of the realm) and, laying the transgression before us, petition to have that transgression redressed without delay. And if we shall not have corrected the transgression (or, in event of our being out of the kingdom, if our justiciar shall not have corrected it) within forty days, reckoning from the time it has been notified to us (or to our justiciar, if we should be out of the kingdom), the four barons aforesaid shall refer the matter to the rest of the five-and-twenty barons, and those five-and-twenty barons shall, together with the community of the whole land, distrain and distress us in all possible ways, namely, by seizing our castles, lands, possessions, and in any other way they can, until redress has been obtained as they deem fit, saving our own person and the persons of our queen and children; and when redress has been obtained, they shall resume their former relations toward us. . . .

STUDY QUESTIONS

1. What were the basic characteristics of European feudalism? What did lords and vassals gain from a feudal tie? What were their respective obligations?
2. In what ways is it clear that vassals, although required to be loyal to their lords, were basically in the same social class?
3. In what ways was the Magna Carta a feudal document? How had the king violated feudalism, and what remedies were proposed?
4. Why were the Magna Carta's principles (though not the document itself) important in Western political history? How did feudal ideas about restrictions on a king compare with more modern ideas of limited government?
5. What were the main differences between Japanese and European feudalism? What was the long-term significance of these differences? Would Japanese vassals have approved of an approach such as that suggested in the Magna Carta?
6. What would a Confucian bureaucrat have thought of the feudal system? Would he have preferred the European or the Japanese version?

27

Medieval Theology: Thomas Aquinas Blends Faith and Reason

The dominant role of the Christian religion in all aspects of European civilization during the Middle Ages has led some historians to label the period an "age of faith." A hierarchical society appointed by God and governed by his vice-regents, the pope and king, focused concern on preparation for life after death and devoted considerable energy toward the honor and glorification of God. By the mid-twelfth century C.E. the theological rationale of the nature of God, man, and the universe—based on revelation and patristic traditions—encountered a serious challenge from the previously unknown logical and philosophical works of Aristotle, which offered a conflicting worldview including the primacy of reason as a means for establishing truth. Western thinkers eagerly recaptured Greek learning, and also Arab and Jewish philosophies about nature and reason. Leading theologians successfully met the challenge by applying Aristotelian methodology and by incorporating many of Aristotle's philosophical concepts to construct a Christian theological and philosophical system, called scholasticism, which brought their views into agreement.

The reconciliation of Christian traditions and Aristotelian precepts was a major concern of Thomas Aquinas (1225–1274), who determined that correct reasoning offered a means for establishing Christian truths. As professor of theology at the University of Paris, the Dominican theologian constructed a synthesis of natural theology in his *Summa Theologica* using logical reasoning and a reliance on authoritative sources. An analysis of the existence of God and of human ability to know God in that work is presented in the following extracts. Omitted in this selection are authoritative opinions that conflict with Aquinas's conclusions and his arguments against them, which are standard in the rationalistic methodology of the period. The extracts demonstrate his method of interrelating faith and reason, his use of Aristotle's *Physics* and *Metaphysics* in proving the existence of God, and his views that when reason proves insufficient in establishing Christian truths, it must yield to faith.

From Thomas Aquinas, *The Summa Theologica*, P. 1, Q. 2 and 12, in *Basic Writing of Saint Thomas Aquinas*, edited by Anton C. Pegis (New York: Random House, 1945), Vol. I, pp. 19, 20, 22–23, 92, 93–94, 95, 97, 101–102. Copyright © Random House, Inc., 1945. Reprinted by permission of Hackett Publishing Co., Inc. All rights reserved.

Called scholasticism, this rationalistic theology as put forth by Aquinas was a striking intellectual creation that allowed its supporters to believe that they possessed a comprehensive framework by which everything that could be understood was understood. Scholasticism was also, however, a key point in a larger intellectual history that ran from the ancient Greeks to modern Western science. How did Aquinas's system resemble, as well as differ from, later Western intellectual assumptions? (See Volume II, Chapter 2.)

The Existence of God

. . . A thing can be self-evident in either of two ways: on the one hand, self-evident in itself, though not to us; on the other, self-evident in itself, and to us. A proposition is self-evident because the predicate is included in the essence of the subject: *e.g., Man is an animal,* for animal is contained in the essence of man. If, therefore, the essence of the predicate and subject be known to all, the proposition will be self-evident to all; as is clear with regard to the first principles of demonstration, the terms of which are certain common notions that no one is ignorant of, such as being and non-being, whole and part, and the like. If, however, there are some to whom the essence of the predicate and subject is unknown, the proposition will be self-evident in itself, but not to those who do not know the meaning of the predicate and subject of the proposition. Therefore, it happens, as Boethius says, that there are some notions of the mind which are common and self-evident only to the learned, as that incorporeal substances are not in space. Therefore I say that this proposition, *God exists*, of itself is self-evident, for the predicate is the same as the subject, because God is His own existence as will be hereafter shown. Now because we do not know the essence of God, the proposition is not self-evident to us, but needs to be demonstrated by things that are more known to us, though less known in their nature—namely, by His effects. . . .

Demonstration can be made in two ways: One is through the cause, and is called *propter quid*, and this is to argue from what is prior absolutely. The other is through the effect, and is called a demonstration *quia;* this is to argue from what is prior relatively only to us. When an effect is better known to us than its cause, from the effect we proceed to the knowledge of the cause. And from every effect the existence of its proper cause can be demonstrated, so long as its effects are better known to us; because, since every effect depends upon its cause, if the effect exists, the cause must preexist. Hence the existence of God, in so far as it is not self-evident to us, can be demonstrated from those of His effects which are known to us. . . .

The existence of God can be proved in five ways. The first and more manifest way is the argument from motion. It is certain, and evident to our senses, that in the world some things are in motion. Now whatever is moved is moved by another, for nothing can be moved except it is in potentiality to that towards which it is moved; whereas a thing moves inasmuch as it is in act. For motion is nothing else than the reduction of something from potentiality to actuality. But nothing can be reduced from potentiality to actuality, except by something in a state of actuality. Thus that which is actually hot, as fire, makes wood, which is potentially hot, to be actually hot, and thereby moves and changes it. Now it is not possible that the same thing should be at once in actuality and potentiality in the same respect, but only in different respects. For what is actually hot cannot simultaneously be poten-

Gothic Architecture. The interior (nave) of the cathedral in Rheims, France. The Gothic style is often compared to the scholastic philosophy of scholars like Thomas Acquinas, in presenting a distinctive mastery in praise of God. (Lauros-Giraudon/Art Resource, NY.)

tially hot; but it is simultaneously potentially cold. It is therefore impossible that in the same respect and in the same way a thing should be both mover and moved, *i.e.,* that it should move itself. Therefore, whatever is moved must be moved by another. If that by which it is moved be itself moved, then this also must needs be moved by another, and that by another again. But this cannot go on to infinity, because then there would be no first mover, and, consequently, no other mover, seeing that subsequent movers move only inasmuch as they are moved by the first mover; as the staff moves only because it is moved by the hand. Therefore it is necessary to arrive at a first mover, moved by no other; and this everyone understands to be God.

The second way is from the nature of efficient cause. In the world of sensible things we find there is an order of efficient causes. There is no case known (neither is it, indeed, possible) in which a thing is found to be the efficient cause of itself; for so it would be prior to itself, which is impossible. Now in efficient causes it is not possible to go on to infinity, because in all efficient causes following in order, the first is the cause of the intermediate cause, and the intermediate is the cause of the ultimate cause, whether the intermediate cause be several, or one only. Now to take away the cause is to take away the effect. Therefore, if there be no first cause among efficient causes, there will be no ultimate, nor any intermediate, cause. But if in efficient causes it is possible to go on to infinitely, there will be no first efficient cause, neither will there be an ultimate effect, nor any intermediate efficient causes; all of which is plainly false. Therefore it is necessary to admit a first efficient cause, to which everyone gives the name of God.

The third way is taken from possibility and necessity, and runs thus. We find in nature things that are possible to be and not to be, since they are found to be generated, and to be corrupted, and consequently, it is possible for them to be and not to be. But it is impossible for these always to exist, for that which can not-be at some time is not. Therefore, if everything can not-be, then at one time there was nothing in existence. Now if this were true, even now there would be nothing in existence, because that which does not exist begins to exist only through something already existing. Therefore, if at one time nothing was in existence, it would have been impossible for anything to have begun to exist; and thus even now nothing would be in existence—which is absurd. Therefore, not all beings are merely possible, but there must exist something the existence of which is necessary. But every necessary thing either has its necessity caused by another, or not. Now it is impossible to go on to infinity in necessary things which have their necessity caused by another, as has been already proved in regard to efficient causes. Therefore we cannot but admit the existence of some being having of itself its own necessity, and not receiving it from another, but rather causing in others their necessity. This all men speak of as God.

The fourth way is taken from the gradation to be found in things. Among beings there are some more and some less good, true, noble, and the like. But *more* and *less* are predicated of different things according as they resemble in their different ways something which is the maximum, as a thing is said to be hotter according as it more nearly resembles that which is hottest: so that there is something which is truest, something best, something noblest, and, consequently, something which is most being, for those things that are greatest in truth are greatest in being, as it is written in [Aristotle's] *Metaph.* ii. Now the maximum in any genus is the cause of all in that genus, as fire, which is the maximum of heat, is the cause of all hot things, as is said in the same book. Therefore there must also be something which is to all beings the cause of their being, goodness, and every other perfection; and this we call God.

The fifth way is taken from the governance of the world. We see that things which lack knowledge, such as natural bodies, act for an end, and this is evident from their acting always, or nearly always, in the same way, so as to obtain the best result. Hence it is plain that they achieve their end, not fortuitously, but designedly. Now whatever lacks knowledge cannot move towards an end, unless it be directed by some being endowed with knowledge and intelligence; as the arrow is directed by the archer. Therefore some intelligent being exists by whom all natural things are directed to their end; and this being we call God. . . .

How God Is Known by Us

Since everything is knowable according as it is actual, God, Who is pure act without any admixture of potentiality, is in Himself supremely knowable. But what is supremely knowable in itself may not be knowable to a particular intellect, because of the excess of the intelligible object above the intellect; as, for example, the sun, which is supremely visible, cannot be seen by the bat by reason of its excess of light.

Therefore, some who considered this held that no created intellect can see the essence of God. This opinion, however, is not tenable. For the ultimate beatitude of man consists in the use of his highest function, which is the operation of the intellect. Hence, if we suppose that a created intellect could never see God, it would either never attain to beatitude, or its beatitude would consist in something else beside God; which is opposed to faith. For the ultimate perfection of the rational creature is to be found in that which is the source of its being; since a thing is perfect so far as it attains to its source. Further, the same opinion is also against reason. For there resides in every man a natural desire to know the cause of any effect which he sees. Thence arises wonder in men. But if the intellect of the rational creature could not attain to the first cause of things, the natural desire would remain vain.

Hence it must be granted absolutely that the blessed see the essence of God. . . .

Two things are required both for sensible and for intellectual vision—*viz.,* power of sight, and union of the thing seen with the sight. For vision is made actual only when the thing seen is in a certain way in the seer. Now in corporeal things it is clear that the thing seen cannot be by its essence in the seer, but only by its likeness; as the likeness of a stone is in the eye, whereby the vision is made actual, whereas the substance of the stone is not there. But if the source of the visual power and the thing seen were one and the same thing, it would necessarily follow that the seer would possess both the visual power, and the form whereby it sees, from that one same thing.

Now it is manifest both that God is the author of the intellectual power and that He can be seen by the intellect. And since the intellectual power of the creature is not the essence of God, it follows that it is some kind of participated likeness of Him Who is the first intellect. Hence also the intellectual power of the creature is called an intelligible light, as it were, deprived from the first light, whether this be understood of the natural power, or of some superadded perfection of grace or of glory. Therefore, in order to see God, there is needed some likeness of God on the part of the visual power, whereby the intellect is made capable of seeing God. But on the part of the thing seen, which must in some way be united to the seer, the essence of God cannot be seen through any created likeness. First, because, as Dionysius says, *by the likenesses of the inferior order of things, the superior can in no way be known;* as by the likeness of a body the essence of an incorporeal thing cannot be known. Much less therefore can the essence of God be seen through any created species whatever. Secondly, because the essence of God is His very being, as was shown above, which cannot be said of any created form. Hence, no created form can be the likeness representing the essence of God to the seer. Thirdly, because the divine essence is uncircumscribed, and contains in itself supereminently whatever can be signified or understood by a created intellect. Now this cannot in any way be represented by any created species, for every created form is determined according to some aspect of wisdom, or of power, or of being itself, or of some like thing. Hence, to say that God is seen through some likeness is to say that the divine essence is not seen at all; which is false.

Therefore it must be said that to see the essence of God there is required some likeness in the visual power, namely, the light of glory strengthening the intellect to see God, which is spoken of in the *Psalm* (xxxv. 10): *In Thy light we shall see light.* The essence of God, however, cannot be seen by any created likeness representing the divine essence as it is in itself. . . .

. . . It is impossible for God to be seen by the sense of sight, or by any other sense or power of the sensitive part of the soul. For every such power is the act of a corporeal organ, as will be shown later. Now act is proportioned to the being whose act it is. Hence no power of that kind can go beyond corporeal things. But God is incorporeal, as was shown above. Hence, He cannot be seen by the sense or the imagination, but only by the intellect. . . .

. . . It is impossible for any created intellect to see the essence of God by its own natural power. For knowledge takes place according as the thing known is in the knower. But the thing known is in the knower according to the mode of the knower. Hence the knowledge of every knower is according to the mode of its own nature. If therefore the mode of being of a given thing exceeds the mode of the knower, it must result that the knowledge of that thing is above the nature of the knower. Now the mode of being of things is manifold. For some things have being only in this individual matter; such are all bodies. There are other beings whose natures are themselves subsisting, not residing in matter at all, which, however, are not their own being, but receive it: and these are the incorporeal substances called angels. But to God alone does it belong to be His own subsistent being.

Therefore, what exists only in individual matter we know naturally, since our soul, through which we know, is the form of some particular matter. Now our soul possesses two cognitive powers. One is the act of a corporeal organ, which naturally knows things existing in individual matter; hence sense knows only the singular. But there is another kind of cognitive power in the soul, called the intellect; and this is not the act of any corporeal organ. Therefore the intellect naturally knows natures which exist only in individual matter; not indeed as they are in such individual matter, but according as they are abstracted therefrom by the consideration of the intellect. Hence it follows that through the intellect we can understand these things in a universal way; and this is beyond the power of sense. Now the angelic intellect naturally knows natures that are not in matter; but this is beyond the power of the intellect of the human soul in the state of its present life, united as it is to the body.

It follows, therefore, that to know self-subsistent being is natural to the divine intellect alone, and that it is beyond the natural power of any created intellect: for no creature is its own being, since its being is participated. Therefore, a created intellect cannot see the essence of God unless God by His grace unites Himself to the created intellect, as an object made intelligible to it. . . .

. . . It is impossible for any created intellect to comprehend God; but *to attain to God with the mind in some degree is great beatitude,* as Augustine says.

In proof of this we must consider that what is comprehended is perfectly known; and that is perfectly known which is known so far as it can be known. Thus, if anything which is capable of scientific demonstration is held only by an opinion resting on a probable proof, it is not comprehended. For instance, if anyone knows by scientific demonstration that a triangle has three angles equal to two right angles, he comprehends that truth; whereas if anyone accepts it as a probable opinion because wise men or most men teach it, he does not comprehend the thing itself, because he does not attain to that perfect mode of knowledge of which it is intrinsically capable. But no created intellect can attain to that perfect mode of the knowledge of the divine intellect whereof it is intrinsically capable. Here is the proof. Everything is knowable according to its actuality. But God, Whose being is infinite, as was shown above, is infinitely knowable. Now no created intellect can know God infinitely. For a created intellect knows the divine essence more or less perfectly in proportion as it receives a greater or lesser light of glory. Since therefore the created light of glory received into any created intellect cannot be infinite, it is clearly impossible for any created intellect to know God in an infinite degree. Hence it is impossible that it should comprehend God. . . .

STUDY QUESTIONS

1. How does Aquinas use logic to prove God's existence?
2. How did he reconcile his enthusiasm for Greek logic with his Christian faith? How does he establish the need for faith?
3. Why did some Christian thinkers criticize this rationalistic approach, in terms of its implications about human powers and about God's nature?
4. What were Aquinas's views about the relationship between human reason and objective reality? How might this affect the approach to science, as it began to to win new interest in Europe during this period?
5. Could the tense but fruitful relationship between rationalism and religion advanced by Aquinas have developed also in Islam, or was this a purely Christian development?

28

Ideals of Courtly Love:
A New Definition of "Relationships"

Christianity and the church dominated many aspects of life in Western Europe during the postclassical centuries, but other important themes emerged as well. Growing trade was one example. So was the emergence of a new literary genre from the twelfth century C.E. onward, around themes of chivalry and courtly love. Poets and singers developed many courtly love romances, which they used to entertain aristocrats in their increasingly attractive castles.

Chivalry and courtly love signified a broadening of interests and refinement of manners among aristocrats, no longer feudal warriors alone. This kind of refinement, which included a growing taste for art and luxury, was not unusual in aristocratic history, as initial military exploits led to successes that broadened horizons. Feudal warfare was dying down, and the aristocracy was partially redefining itself.

The emphasis on love is interesting in its own right. Here was a new theme in European literature, at least since the advent of Christianity, which some historians have seen as a forerunner of more modern emphasis on love. How was earthly love reconciled with Christian insistence on control of earthly passions—or was it?

Courtly love idealized women and can be seen as a cultural improvement in women's status—compared, for example, with other cultures, such as that of India, that valued love. But other aspects of Europe in these centuries suggest a deterioration in women's roles—for example, a reduction in the range of urban jobs available. Was the idealization of women in courtly love a gain or a constriction? How does it compare with other cultures (including the West in more recent times) that emphasized women as sources of love and beauty?

Evolving at the court of the counts of Champagne, the art of courtly love incorporated its own set of rules and code of etiquette and provided its practitioners special courts that adjudicated disputes and provided formal, binding judgments. A codification of its principles appeared about 1174 in *De Arte Honeste Amandi,* a treatise by Andreas Capellanus, who served as chaplain to Marie, the countess of Champagne and daughter of Eleanor of Aquitaine. The selections here provide

Capellanus's definition of "romantic" love and the rules that govern it. Many themes he advanced have provided inspiration and subject matter to writers for over 800 years.

Courtly love ideals were literary standards—they may not have described real life even for the nobility. They did, however, describe some real changes in aristocratic culture away from an earlier warrior emphasis. They also suggested some Western themes about emotions and male-female relations that demand analysis. How much was women's situation improved through an emphasis on receiving and exchanging love? Was the West, through the redefinition of male-female emotions—at least at the level of ideals—beginning to move away from other patriarchal societies? How do the courtly love standards compare with ideals in China, India, and the Islamic world? (See Chapters 5, 12, and 18.)

Love is a certain inborn suffering derived from the sight of and excessive meditation upon the beauty of the opposite sex, which causes each one to wish above all things the embraces of the other and by common desire to carry out all of love's precepts in the other's embrace.

That love is suffering is easy to see, for before the love becomes equally balanced on both sides there is no torment greater, since the lover is always in fear that his love may not gain its desire and that he is wasting his efforts. He fears, too, that rumors of it may get abroad, and he fears everything that might harm it in any way, for before things are perfected a slight disturbance often spoils them. If he is a poor man, he also fears that the woman may scorn his poverty; if he is ugly, he fears that she may despise his lack of beauty or may give her love to a more handsome man; if he is rich, he fears that his parsimony in the past may stand in his way. To tell the truth, no one can number the fears of one single lover. This kind of love, then, is a suffering which is felt by only one of the persons and may be called "single love." But even after both are in love the fears that arise are just as great, for each of the lovers fears that what he has acquired with so much effort may be lost through the effort of someone else, which is certainly much worse for a man than if, having no hope, he sees that his efforts are accomplishing nothing, for it is worse to lose the things you are seeking than to be deprived of a gain you merely hope for. The lover fears, too, that he may offend his loved one in some way; indeed he fears so many things that it would be difficult to tell them.

• • •

Now, in love you should note first of all that love cannot exist except between persons of opposite sexes. Between two men or two women love can find no place, for we see that two persons of the same sex are not at all fitted for giving each other the exchanges of love or for practicing the acts natural to it. Whatever nature forbids, love is ashamed to accept.

• • •

An excess of passion is a bar to love, because there are men who are slaves to such passionate desire that they cannot be held in the bonds of love—men who, after they have thought long about some woman or even enjoyed her, when they see another woman straightway desire her embraces, and they forget about the services they have received from their first love and they feel no gratitude for them. Men of this kind lust after every woman they see; their love is like that of a shameless dog. They should rather, I believe, be compared to asses, for they are moved only by that low nature which shows that men are on the level of the other animals rather than by that true nature which sets us apart from all the other animals by the difference of reason.

· · ·

The readiness to grant requests is, we say, the same thing in women as over-voluptuousness in men—a thing which all agree should be a total stranger in the court of Love. For he who is so tormented by carnal passion that he cannot embrace anyone in heartfelt love, but basely lusts after every woman he sees, is not called a lover but a counterfeiter of love and a pretender, and he is lower than a shameless dog. Indeed the man who is so wanton that he cannot confine himself to the love of one woman deserves to be considered an impetuous ass. It will therefore be clear to you that you are bound to avoid an overabundance of passion and that you ought not to seek the love of a woman who you know will grant easily what you seek.

· · ·

Furthermore a lover ought to appear to his beloved wise in every respect and restrained in his conduct, and he should do nothing disagreeable that might annoy her. And if inadvertently he should do something improper that offends her, let him straightway confess with downcast face that he has done wrong, and let him give the excuse that he lost his temper or make some other suitable explanation that will fit the case. And every man ought to be sparing of praise of his beloved when he is among other men; he should not spend a great deal of time in places where she is. When he is with other men, if he meets her in a group of women, he should not try to communicate with her by signs, but should treat her almost like a stranger lest some person spying on their love might have opportunity to spread malicious gossip. Lovers should not even nod to each other unless they are sure that nobody is watching them. Every man should also wear things that his beloved likes and pay a reasonable amount of attention to his appearance—not too much because excessive care for one's looks is distasteful to everybody and leads people to despise the good looks that one has. If the lover is lavish in giving, that helps him retain a love he has acquired, for all lovers ought to despise all worldly riches and should give alms to those who have need of them. Also, if the lover is one who is fitted to be a warrior, he should see to it that his courage is apparent to everybody, for it detracts very much from the good character of a man if he is timid in a fight. A lover should always offer his services and obedience freely to every lady, and he ought to root out all his pride and be very humble. Then, too, he must keep in mind the general rule that lovers must not neglect anything that good manners demand or good breeding suggests, but they should be very careful to do everything of this sort. Love may also be retained by indulging in the sweet and delightful solaces of the flesh, but only in such manner and in such number that they may never seem wearisome to be the loved one. Let the lover strive to practice gracefully and manfully any act or mannerism which he has noticed is pleasing to his beloved. A clerk should not, of course, affect the manners or the dress of the laity, for no one is likely to please his beloved, if she is a wise woman, by wearing strange clothing or by practicing manners that do not suit his status. Furthermore a lover should make every attempt to be constantly in the company of good men and to avoid completely the society of the wicked. For association with the vulgar makes a lover who joins them a thing of contempt to his beloved.

. . .

Too many opportunities for exchanging solaces, too many opportunities of seeing the loved one, too much chance to talk to each other all decrease love, and so does an uncultured appearance or manner of walking on the part of the lover or the sudden loss of his property. Love decreases, too, if the woman finds that her lover is foolish and indiscreet, or if he seems to go beyond reasonable bounds in his demands for love, or if she sees that he has no regard for her modesty and will not forgive her bashfulness. Love decreases, too, if the woman considers that her lover is cowardly in battle, or sees that he is unrestrained in his speech or spoiled by the vice of arrogance.

Other things which weaken love are blasphemy against God or His saints, mockery of the ceremonies of the Church, and a deliberate withholding of charity from the poor. We find that love decreases very sharply if one is unfaithful to his friend, or if he brazenly says one thing while he deceitfully conceals a different idea in his heart. Love decreases, too, if the lover piles up more wealth than is proper, or if he is too ready to go to law over trifles.

. . .

. . . [L]ove comes to an end if one of the lovers breaks faith or tries to break faith with the other, or if he is found to go astray from the Catholic religion. It comes to an end also after it has been openly revealed and made known to men. So, too, if one of the lovers has plenty of money and does not come to the aid of the other who is in great need and lacks a great many things, then love usually becomes very cheap and comes to an ignominious end. An old love also ends when a new one begins, because no one can love two people at the same time. Furthermore, inequality of love and a fraudulent and deceitful duplicity of heart always drive out love, for a deceitful lover, no matter how worthy he is otherwise, ought to be rejected by any woman. Again, if by some chance one of the lovers becomes incapable of carrying out love's duties, love can no longer last between them and deserts them and deserts them completely. Likewise if one of the lovers becomes insane or develops a sudden timidity, love flees and becomes hateful.

These are the rules.

    I. Marriage is no real excuse for not loving.
    II. He who is not jealous cannot love.
    III. No one can be bound by a double love.
    IV. It is well known that love is always increasing or decreasing.
    V. That which a lover takes against his will of his beloved has no relish.
    VI. Boys do not love until they arrive at the age of maturity.
    VII. When one lover dies, a widowhood of two years is required of the survivor.
    VIII. No one should be deprived of love without the very best of reasons.

IX. No one can love unless he is impelled by the persuasion of love.

X. Love is always a stranger in the home of avarice.

XI. It is not proper to love any woman whom one should be ashamed to seek to marry.

XII. A true lover does not desire to embrace in love anyone except his beloved.

XIII. When made public love rarely endures.

XIV. The easy attainment of love makes it of little value; difficulty of attainment makes it prized.

XV. Every lover regularly turns pale in the presence of his beloved.

XVI. When a lover suddenly catches sight of his beloved his heart palpitates.

XVII. A new love puts to flight an old one.

XVIII. Good character alone makes any man worthy of love.

XIX. If love diminishes, it quickly fails and rarely revives.

XX. A man in love is always apprehensive.

XXI. Real jealousy always increases the feeling of love.

XXII. Jealousy, and therefore love, are increased when one suspects his beloved.

XXIII. He whom the thought of love vexes, eats and sleeps very little.

XXIV. Every act of a lover ends in the thought of his beloved.

XXV. A true lover considers nothing good except what he thinks will please his beloved.

XXVI. Love can deny nothing to love.

XXVII. A lover can never have enough of the solaces of his beloved.

XXVIII. A slight presumption causes a lover to suspect his beloved.

XXIX. A man who is vexed by too much passion usually does not love.

XXX. A true lover is constantly and without intermission possessed by the thought of his beloved.

XXXI. Nothing forbids one woman being loved by two men or one man by two women.

STUDY QUESTIONS

1. What was the definition of love in this new literature? How does it compare with modern ideas of love? Why was love valued?

2. How did Cappellanus reconcile love and religion? Do you think the reconciliation would have persuaded religious leaders at the time? What was the relationship between this love ideal and sexuality?

3. Why might aristocrats have been open to these new themes by the twelfth and thirteenth centuries?

4. What implications did these love ideals have for upper-class women? Were they more likely to improve women's status or to impose new cultural constraints?

29

African Kingdoms and Islam

The postclassical period formed a crucial stage in African history. Early civilization in Africa had focused in the northeast, in Egypt and the areas south of it (Kush, Axum, ultimately Ethiopia) where major kingdoms formed. Agriculture and iron-working were widespread throughout much of the continent by the classical period. By the fifth century C.E., a second center of active trade and state building was developing in West Africa, in kingdoms such as Ghana and later Mali that stretched along the southern rim of the Sahara Desert. These "Sudanic kingdoms" (from the Arab world for black) built large regional holdings, with kings who claimed divine powers but who also maintained careful relations with more local rulers and military leaders. Extensive trade ran from the Sudanic kingdoms to North Africa and the Middle East, involving exchanges of gold, salt, some slaves, and other products in return for more manufactured goods and horses. Growing sophistication was applied to mining technology and other activities relating to commerce, and kings profited greatly from their ability to tax international trade from the region.

Contacts with North Africa included growing awareness of Islam. Mass conversions to Islam did not occur in sub-Saharan Africa at this point, but there was important interaction. Many Sudanic kings used Muslims as bureaucrats, benefiting among other things from their education and literacy. Many kings of Mali and other domains converted to Islam, establishing major educational centers and in one case making an elaborate pilgrimage to Mecca. At the same time, sub-Saharan Africa did not become a full part of Islamic civilization as North Africa did. Political institutions, popular religion, art, and gender roles were among the features of African society that remained partly distinct.

The society that was created during this period in many parts of Africa proved highly durable. Regional kingdoms, a mixture of Islam and popular religion, active

From *Ibn Battuta in Black Africa*, edited by Said Hamdum and Noel King (London: Rex Collings, 1975), 27–29, 36–39, 47–48. Reprinted by permission of Markus Wiener Publishers, Inc.

West African Art. A bronze head of a Benin king, dating from the 1500s. Leaders in Benin still wear caps and chokers similar to those worn by this figure. (The Metropolitan Museum of Art, The Michael C. Rockefeller Memorial Collection. Bequest of Nelson A. Rockefeller, 1979 [1979.206.86].)

internal trade, and strong family institutions continued to characterize this civilization for many centuries, surviving easily into the nineteenth century even amid additional new influences.

The following document is from an Arab traveler, who visited many African kingdoms during the fourteenth century. His observations indicate the range of contacts sub-Saharan Africa enjoyed with the Muslim world but also some of the differences that defined a separate civilization. Ibn Battuta (1304–1369), one of the great voyagers in world history, had been born in Morocco. He journeyed for almost 30 years in Asia, Europe, and Africa. His African accounts are extremely valuable, for no other comparable written sources exist for the period. He visited several parts of Africa, mainly through contacts with existing Arab communities—the whites, in his account—in what was an established part of the Muslim trading orbit. This was a brave traveler, with some biases and a definite love of comfort, but also with an eager curiosity about the places he visited.

I went to the house of ibn Baddā', an excellent man of the people of Salā. I had written to him to rent a house for me and he had done that. Then the Overseer of Iwālātan, whose name was Manshā Jū, invited those who had come in the caravan to his hospitality. I refused to attend that affair, but my friends insisted very much; so I went with the rest. Then the meal was brought out: a concoction of *anlī* mixed with a drop of honey and milk, which they placed in a half calabash like a deep wooden bowl. Those present drank and went away. I said to them, 'Was it for this the black invited us?' They said, 'Yes, this is great entertainment in their country.' I became sure then that there was no good to be expected from them. I wanted to travel back with the pilgrims of Iwālātan. Then it seemed good to me to go to see the capital [or: residence, presence] of their King. My residence in Iwālātan was about fifty days. Its people were generous to me and entertained me. Among my hosts was its *qādī*, Muhammad ibn 'Abd Allāhibn Yanū-mar and his brother, the *faqīh* [qādī and faqīh were Muslim legal authorities] and teacher Yahyä. The town of Iwālātan is very hot and there are in it a few small date palms in whose shade they plant melons. They obtain water from the ground which exudes it. Mutton is obtainable in quantity there. The clothes of its people are of fine Egyptian material. Most of the inhabitants belong to the Massufa, and as for their women—they are extremely beautiful and are more important than the men.

Anecdote Concerning the Massūfa Who Inhabit Iwālātan

The condition of these people is strange and their manners outlandish. As for their men, there is no sexual jealousy in them. And none of them derives his genealogy from his father but, on the contrary, from his maternal uncle. A man does not pass on inheritance except to the sons of his sister to the exclusion of his own sons. Now that is a thing I never saw in any part of the world except in the country of the unbelievers of the land of Mulaībār [Malabar] among the Indians. As to the former [the Massūfa], they are Muslims keeping to the prayers, studying *fiqh* [Islamic jurisprudence], and learning the Qur'ān by heart. With regard to their women, they are not modest in the presence of men, they do not veil themselves in spite of their perseverance in the prayers. He who wishes to marry among them can marry, but the women do not travel with the husband, and if one of them wanted to do that, she would be prevented by her family. The women there have friends and companions amongst men outside the prohibited degrees of marriage [i.e., other than brothers, fathers, etc.]. Likewise for the men, there are companions from amongst women outside the prohibited degrees. One of them would enter his house to find his wife with her companion and would not disapprove of that conduct. . . .

The sultan [emperor of Mali] has a raised cupola which is entered from inside his house. He sits in it a great part of the time. It has on the audience side a chamber with three wooden arches, the woodwork is covered with sheets of beaten silver and beneath these, three more covered with beaten gold, or, rather, it is silver covered with gilt. The windows have woollen curtains which are raised on a day when the sultan will be in session in his cupola: thus it is known that he is holding a session. When he sits, a silken cord is put out from the grill of one of the arches with a scarf of Egyptian embroidery tied to it. When the people see the scarf, drums are beaten and bugles sounded. Then from the door of the palace come out about three hundred slaves. Some have bows in their hands and some small spears and shields. Some of the spearmen stand on the right and some on the left, the bowmen sit likewise. Then they bring two mares saddled and bridled, and with them two rams. They say that these are effective against the evil eye. When the sultan has sat down three of his slaves go out quickly to call his deputy, Qanjā Musā. The *farāriyya* [commanders] arrive, and they are the *amīrs* [officers], and among them are the preacher and the men of *fiqh,* who sit in front of the armed men on the right and left of the place of audience. The interpreter Dūghā stands at the door of the audience chamber wearing splendid robes of *zardkhuāna* [official] and others. On his head is a turban which has fringes, they have a superb way of tying a turban. He is girt with a sword whose sheath is of gold, on his feet are light boots and spurs. And nobody wears boots that day except he. In his hands there are two small spears, one of gold and one of silver with points of iron. The soldiers, the district governors, the pages and the Massūfa and others are seated outside the place of audience in a broad street which has trees in it. Each *farārī* [commander] has his followers before him with their spears, bows, drums and bugles made of elephant tusks. Their instruments of music are made of reeds and calabashes, and they beat them with sticks and produce a wonderful sound. Each *farārī* has a quiver which he places between his shoulders. He holds his bow in his hand and is mounted on a mare. Some of his men are on foot and some on mounts.

Inside the audience chamber under the arches a man is standing, he who wants to speak to the sultan speaks to Dūghā, Dūghā speaks to the man who is standing, and he speaks to the sultan.

An Account of the Sessions in the Place of Audience

The sultan sits on certain days in the palace yard to give audience. There is a platform under a tree with three steps which they call *banbī*. It is covered with silk and has pillows placed on it. The *shatr* [umbrella] is raised, this is a shelter made of silk with a golden bird like a sparrowhawk above it. The sultan comes out from a gate in the corner of the palace, bow in hand, his quiver between his shoulders, and on his head a cap of gold tied with a golden band which has fringes like thin-bladed knives more than a span long. He often wears a robe which is soft and red, made from Roman cloth called *mutanfas*. The singers go out before him carrying gold and silver *qanābir* [guitars] and behind him come three hundred armed slaves. The sultan walks slowly and pauses often and sometimes he stops completely. When he comes to the *banbī* he stops and looks at the people. Then he mounts the steps with dignity in the manner of a preacher getting into the pulpit. When he sits down they beat the drums, blow the bugles and the horns, and three of the slaves go out in haste and call the deputy and the *farāriyya* [commanders]. They enter and sit down. The two mares are brought in with the two rams. Damughā stands at the door while the rest of the people are in the street under the tree. The blacks are the most humble of men before their king and the most extreme in their self-abasement before him. They swear by his name, saying 'Mansā Sulaimānkī' [the law of Mansā Sulaimānkī]. When he calls one of them while he is in session in his cupola which we described above, the man invited takes off his clothes and wears patched clothes, takes off his turban, puts on a dirty cap, and goes in raising his clothes and trousers up his legs half-way to his knees. He advances with humility looking like a beggar. He hits the ground with his elbows, he hits it hard. He stands bowed, like one in the *ruku'* position in prayer, listening to what the king says. When one of them speaks to the sultan and he gives him an answer, he removes his clothes from his back and throws dust on his head and back, as a person does when bathing with water. I used to wonder how they do not blind their eyes. When the sultan speaks in his council, at his word those present take their turbans off their heads and listen to the speech. . . .

Amongst their good qualities is the small amount of injustice amongst them, for of all people they are the furthest from it. Their sultan does not forgive anyone in any matter to do with justice. Among these qualities there is also the prevalence of peace in their country, the traveller is not afraid in it nor is he who lives there in fear of the thief or of the robber by violence. They do not interfere with the property of the white man who dies in their country even though it may consist of great wealth, but rather they entrust it to the hand of someone dependable among the white men until it is taken by the rightful claimant.

Another of the good habits amongst them is the way they meticulously observe the times of the prayers and attendance at them, so also it is with regard to their congregational services and their beating of their children to instill these things in them.

When it is Friday, if a man does not come early to the mosque he will not find a place to pray because of the numbers of the crowd. It is their custom for every man to send his boy with his prayer mat. He spreads it for him in a place commensurate with his position and keeps the place until he comes to the mosque. Their prayer-mats are made of the leaves of a tree like a date palm but it bears no fruit.

Among their good qualities is their putting on of good white clothes on Friday. If a man among them has nothing except a tattered shirt, he washes and cleans it and attends the Friday prayer in it. Another of their good qualities is their concern for learning the sublime Qur'ān by heart. They make fetters for their children when they appear on their part to be falling short in their learning of it by heart, and they are not taken off from them till they do learn by heart. I went in to visit the *qādī* on an 'Id day and his children were tied up. I said to him, 'Why do you not release them?' He said, 'I shall not do so until they learn the Qur'ān by heart.' One day I passed by a handsome youth from them dressed in fine clothes and on his feet was a heavy chain. I said to the man who was with me, 'What has this youth done—has he killed someone?' The youth heard my remark and laughed. It was told me, 'He has been chained so that he will learn the Qur'ān by heart.'

Among the bad things which they do—their serving women, slave women and little daughters appear before people naked, exposing their private parts. I used to see many of them in this state in Ramaḍān, for it was the custom of the *farāriyya* [commanders] to break the fast in the sultan's house. Everyone of them has his food carried in to him by twenty or more of his slave girls and they are naked, every one. Also among their bad customs is the way women will go into the presence of the sultan naked, without any covering; and the nakedness of the sultan's daughters—on the night of the twenty-seventh of Ramaḍān, I saw about a hundred slave girls coming out of his palace with food, with them were two of his daughters, they had full breasts and no clothes on. Another of their bad customs is their putting of dust and ashes on their heads as a sign of respect. And another is the laughing matter I mentioned of their poetic recitals. And another is that many of them eat animals not ritually slaughtered, and dogs and donkeys.

STUDY QUESTIONS

1. How is it clear that Ibn Battuta assumes the presence of standard institutions of civilization in sub-Saharan Africa?
2. What kinds of government does Ibn Battuta describe?
3. What did he find strange? Are his observations likely to have been accurate, and if not, what might explain his exaggerations?
4. What are the advantages and disadvantages of using travelers' accounts for information about a past society?
5. What kind of ties did sub-Saharan Africa maintain with the Islamic world? What were the major differences between the two societies? Why did African leaders maintain distinctions along with their genuine appreciation of Islam?

The Americas

30

The Mayan Creation Story

Popol Vuh relates the Mayan story of creation. Literally translated as the "Council Book," it also served as a source of advice for the Lords of Quiché, a Mayan center of civilization of the postclassical era about 1000 C.E. located northwest of Guatemala City. At meetings, the lords used the Council Book to interpret signs, particularly omens related to death, famine, and conflict. The only extant version of *Popol Vuh* was written between 1554 and 1558 by descendants of these ancient lineages. They wrote in the Mayan language, using the Roman alphabet. Francisco Ximénez, a member of the Dominican Order, discovered and translated the manuscript into Spanish about 1701.

As related in the story, the gods of sky and water created the earth in one attempt. By contrast, the creation of humans took four attempts. The first three were defective and spawned other types of creatures. Even on the successful fourth try, the gods later changed the outcome because the humans were too perfect. Between the three failures and the fourth try, *Popol Vuh* relates numerous adventures of the gods and how they influenced cosmic and earthly conditions. They created the planets, sun, animals, trees, corn planting, artisan activities, and ball games. The following is the story of human creation.

And here is the beginning of the conception of humans, and of the search for the ingredients of the human body. So they spoke, the Bearer, Begetter, the Makers, Modelers named Sovereign Plumed Serpent:

"The dawn has approached, preparations have been made, and morning has come for the provider, nurturer, born in the light, begotten in the light. Morning has come for humankind, for the people of the face of the earth," they said. It all

From *Popol Vuh: The Mayan Book of the Dawn of Life,* translated by Dennis Tedlock (New York: Simon and Schuster, 1985), pp. 163–167. Reprinted with permission of Simon & Schuster, Inc.

came together as they went on thinking in the darkness, in the night, as they searched and they sifted, they thought and they wondered.

And here their thoughts came out in clear light. They sought and discovered what was needed for human flesh. It was only a short while before the sun, moon, and stars were to appear above the Makers and Modelers. Broken Place, Bitter Water Place is the name: the yellow corn, white corn came from there.

And these are the names of the animals who brought the food: fox, coyote, parrot, crow. There were four animals who brought the news of the ears of yellow corn and white corn. They were coming from over there at Broken Place, they showed the way to the break.

And this was when they found the staple foods.

And these were the ingredients for the flesh of the human work, the human design, and the water was for the blood. It became human blood, and corn was also used by the Bearer, Begetter.

And so they were happy over the provisions of the good mountain, filled with sweet things, thick with yellow corn, white corn, and thick with pataxte and cacao, countless zapotes, anonas, jocotes, nances, matasanos, sweets—the rich foods filling up the citadel named Broken Place, Bitter Water Place. All the edible fruits were there: small staples, great staples, small plants, great plants. The way was shown by the animals.

And then the yellow corn and white corn were ground, and Xmucane did the grinding nine times. Corn was used, along with the water she rinsed her hands with, for the creation of grease; it became human fat when it was worked by the Bearer, Begetter, Sovereign Plumed Serpent, as they are called.

After that, they put it into words:

the making, the modeling of our first mother-father,
with yellow corn, white corn alone for the flesh,
food alone for the human legs and arms,
for our first fathers, the four human works.

It was staples alone that made up their flesh.

. . .

These are the names of the first people who were made and modeled.
This is the first person: Jaguar Quitze.
And now the second: Jaguar Night.
And now the third: Mahucutah.
And the fourth: True Jaguar.
And these are the names of our first mother-fathers. They were simply made and modeled, it is said; they had no mother and no father. We have named the men by themselves. No woman gave birth to them, nor were they begotten by the builder, sculptor, Bearer, Begetter. By sacrifice alone, by genius alone they were made, they were modeled by the Maker, Modeler, Bearer, Begetter, Sovereign Plumed Serpent. And when they came to fruition, they came out human:
They talked and they made words.
They looked and they listened.
They walked, they worked.

They were good people, handsome, with looks of the male kind. Thoughts came into existence and they gazed; their vision came all at once. Perfectly they saw, perfectly they knew everything under the sky, whenever they looked. The moment they turned around and looked around in the sky, on the earth, everything was seen without any obstruction. They didn't have to walk around before they could see what was under the sky; they just stayed where they were.

As they looked, their knowledge became intense. Their sight passed through trees, through rocks, through lakes, through seas, through mountains, through plains. Jaguar Quitze, Jaguar Night, Mahucutah, and True Jaguar were truly gifted people.

And then they were asked by the builder and mason:

"What do you know about your being? Don't you look, don't you listen? Isn't your speech good, and your walk? So you must look, to see out under the sky. Don't you see the mountain-plain clearly? So try it," they were told.

And then they saw everything under the sky perfectly. After that, they thanked the Maker, Modeler:

> "Truly now,
> double thanks, triple thanks
> that we've been formed, we've been given
> our mouths, our faces,
> we speak, we listen,
> we wonder, we move,
> our knowledge is good, we've understood
> what is far and near,
> and we've seen what is great and small
> under the sky, on the earth.
> Thanks to you we've been formed,
> we've come to be made and modeled,
> our grandmother, our grandfather,"

they said when they gave thanks for having been made and modeled. They understood everything perfectly, they sighted the four sides, the four corners in the sky, on the earth, and this didn't sound good to the builder and sculptor:

"What our works and designs have said is no good:

'We have understood everything, great and small,' they say." And so the Bearer, Begetter took back their knowledge:

"What should we do with them now? Their vision should at least reach nearby, they should see at least a small part of the face of the earth, but what they're saying isn't good. Aren't they merely 'works' and 'designs' in their very names? Yet they'll become as great as gods, unless they procreate, proliferate at the sowing, the dawning, unless they increase."

"Let it be this way: now we'll take them apart just a little, that's what we need. What we've found out isn't good. Their deeds would become equal to ours, just because their knowledge reaches so far. They see everything," so said

> the Heart of Sky, Hurricane,
> Newborn Thunderbolt, Raw Thunderbolt,
> Sovereign Plumed Serpent,
> Bearer, Begetter,

Xpiyacoc, Xmucane,
Maker, Modeler,

as they are called. And when they changed the nature of their works, their designs, it was enough that the eyes be marred by the Heart of Sky. They were blinded as the face of a mirror is breathed upon. Their eyes were weakened. Now it was only when they looked nearby that things were clear.

And such was the loss of the means of understanding, along with the means of knowing everything, by the four humans. The root was implanted.

And such was the making, modeling of our first grandfather, our father, by the Heart of Sky, Heart of Earth.

STUDY QUESTIONS

1. Of what substance did the Mayan gods make humans? Given such a belief, how might the ancient Mayans, and their descendants, view this substance? What does this suggest about their world view?
2. Why and how did the Mayan gods alter their human creatures? What does this imply about the relationship between humans and gods?
3. Compare this story with creation stories from other civilizations. What are the similarities and differences?

31

Tribute Under the Aztecs

Aztec warriors created a military empire in Central Mexico between 1420 and 1480 C.E. When the Spaniards arrived in 1519, the Aztecs governed an area inhabited by about 18 million people. Despite their recent impressive military success, the Aztecs, when they first appeared on the historical scene about 1250, were uncouth barbarian invaders from the north. They were not responsible for creating civilization in Central Mexico but were its inheritors. Approximately twelve centuries before the Aztec appearance, the essential features of civilization had already been established by the rulers of Teotihuacan (1–900 C.E.) and Toltec (1000–1200 C.E.) empires. Cultivation of maize was highly developed, particularly through the use of irrigation channels. Surplus production was obtained from local villages through a tribute system that funneled grain, and other products, to central government warehouses. This surplus supported a hierarchy of officials who not only ran the government and the military but also devised calendars, built monumental shrines, created a religious literature, and led ritual observances that bound society together. Although these individual empires succumbed to barbarian invasions, civilization itself did not disappear. The invaders adapted elements of civilization for their own benefit. Later, when the Aztecs entered the civilized area of Central Mexico, they repeated the experience of previous intruders. Specifically, the Aztecs took control of a centuries-old tribute system. A Spanish observer, Gonzalo Fernández de Oviedo y Valdés (1478–1557), described that system and the poverty it caused.

The Indians of New Spain, I have been told by reliable persons who gained their information from Spaniards who fought with Hernando Cortés in the conquest of that land, are the poorest of the many nations that live in the Indies at the present time. In their homes they have no furnishings or clothing other than the poor garments which they wear on their persons, one or two stones for grinding maize, some pots in which to cook the maize, and a sleeping mat. Their meals consist chiefly of vegetables cooked with chili, and bread. They eat little—not that they would not eat more if they could get it, for the soil is very fertile and yields bountiful harvests, but the common people and plebeians suffer under the tyranny of their Indian lords, who tax away the greater part of their produce in a manner that I shall describe. Only the lords and their relatives, and some principal men and merchants, have estates and lands of their own; they sell and gamble with their lands as they please, and they sow and harvest them but pay no tribute. Nor is any tribute paid by artisans, such as masons, carpenters, feather-workers, or silver-smiths, or by singers and kettle-drummers (for every Indian lord has musicians in his household, each according to his station). But such persons render personal service when it is required, and none of them is paid for his labor.

Each Indian lord assigns to the common folk who come from other parts of the country to settle on his land (and to those who are already settled there) specific fields, that each may know the land that he is to sow. And the majority of them have their homes on their land; and between twenty and thirty, or forty and fifty houses have over them an Indian head who is called *tiquitlato,* which in the Castilian tongue means "the finder (or seeker) of tribute." At harvest time this *tiquitlato* inspects the cornfield and observes what each one reaps, and when the reaping is done they show him the harvest, and he counts the ears of corn that each has reaped, and the number of wives and children that each of the vassals in his charge possesses. And with the harvest before him he calculates how many ears of corn each person in that household will require till the next harvest, and these he gives to the Indian head of that house; and he does the same with the other produce, namely kidney beans, which are a kind of small beans, and chili, which is their pepper; and *chia,* which is as fine as mustard seed, and which in warm weather they drink, ground and made into a solution in water and used for medicine, roasted and ground; and cocoa, which is a kind of almond that they use as money, and which they grind, make into a solution, and drink; and cotton, in those places where it is raised, which is in the hot lands and not the cold; and pulque, which is their wine; and all the various products obtained from the maguey plant, from which they obtain food and drink and footwear and clothing. This plant grows in the cold regions, and the leaves resemble those of the cinnamon tree, but are much larger. Of all these and other products they leave the vassal only enough to sustain him for a year. And in addition the vassal must earn enough to pay the tribute of mantles, gold, silver, honey, wax, lime, wood, or whatever products it is customary to pay as tribute in that country. They pay this tribute every forty, sixty, seventy, or ninety days, according to the terms of the agreement. This tribute also the *tiquitlato* receives and carries to his Indian lord.

Ten days before the close of the sixty or hundred days, or whatever is the period appointed for the payment of tribute, they take to the house of the Indian lord the produce brought by the *tiquitlatos;* and if some poor Indian should prove unable to pay his share of tribute, whether for reasons of health or poverty, or lack of work, the *tiquitlato* tells the lord that such-and-such will not pay the proportion of the tribute that had been assigned to him; then the lord tells the *tiquitlato* to take the recalcitrant vassal to a *tianguez* or market, which they hold every five days in all the towns of the land, and there sell him into slavery, applying the proceeds of the sale to the payment of his tribute. . . .

All the towns have their own lands, long ago assigned for the provision of the *orchilobos* or *ques* or temples where they kept their idols; and these lands were and are the best of all. And they have this custom: At seeding time all would go forth at

Aztec sculpture: Coatlicue. Coatlicue was the Aztec earth goddess and mother of the Aztec war god and chief deity, Huitzilipochtli. Through an outward display of terror, the eight foot statue was designed to show the power of gods over mortals. Two snakes arise out of her neck to form her face. Blood serpents emerge from her wrists. She wears a skirt of snakes and a necklace of several human hands, disembodied human hearts, and a human skull pendant. Of all the parts, the necklace, communicated clearly that communicated clearly that human sacrifice sustained the gods and maintained cosmic order. That was the purpose of Aztec rule. (Corbis/Bettmann.)

the summons of the town council to sow these fields, and to weed them at the proper time, and to cultivate the grain and harvest it and carry it to a house in which lived the pope and the *teupisques, pioches, exputhles* and *piltoutles* (or, as we would say, the bishops, archbishops, and canons and prebendaries, and even choristers, for each major temple had these five classes of officials). And they supported themselves from this harvest, and the Indians also raised chickens for them to eat.

In all the towns Montezuma had his designated lands, which they sowed for him in the same way as the temple lands; and if no garrison was stationed in their towns, they would carry the crops on their backs to the great city of Temestitan [Tenochtitlán]; but in the garrison towns the grain was eaten by Montezuma's soldiers, and if the town did not sow the land, it had to supply the garrison with food, and also give them chickens and all other needful provisions.

STUDY QUESTIONS

1. What evidence can you find in this selection that shows social stratification prior to the arrival of the Spaniards?
2. How did the pre-Columbian tribute system work? What does such a tribute system indicate about social organization in ancient Mexico?
3. After the conquest, how would the Spaniards view the operation of the tribute system? How might that view contribute to the structure of a new society?
4. For whom did the sculptor carve the statute of Coatlicue? Or who hired the sculptor and what does that imply about his work?
5. What was the sculptor attempting to convey?
6. Compare the Coatlicue statue with statues of earth mothers from other civilizations. What do statues say about their respective civilizations?

32

Merchants and Trade: Sources and Comparisons

The postclassical period witnessed an important expansion of trade, within many civilizations and across their fluid boundaries. Merchants gained a growing role in West Africa, throughout the Islamic world, in Europe (both east and west), and in East Asia. Many traded locally, although international merchants made the biggest impression. Chinese commercial centers grew rapidly, supporting a more urban environment. The search for wealth had never been so extensive, the willingness to take risks had never been so great, and the desire to promote commercial interests in government circles had never been so strong. At the same time, many societies had reservations about merchants. Aristocrats worried about their social claims; rulers might envy their wealth; priests and philosophers questioned their motives. The clash of cultures, between religion and materialism, was particularly intense because of the complex new forces at work in these centuries. A genuine ambivalence about merchants was common throughout the postclassical world—and it could affect merchants themselves, as well as how they were treated, and it could also shift. Comparison and assessment of change over time are both essential analytical approaches to the issue of the merchant's role. Christian tradition was uneasy with merchants' motives, fearing that they diverted people from religion; as trade increased, Christian concern relaxed somewhat. But efforts to find ways to accommodate the very different goals of capitalist trade and the holy life continued. Islam was initially more favorable to merchants, whose activities seemed compatible with religious obligations so long as they obeyed basic rules of fairness and gave to charity. It

Selection 1 from *An Arab Philosophy of History: Selections from the Prolegomena of Ibn Khaldun*, edited and translated by Charles Issawi (London: John Murray, 1950), 68–70, 78, 80, 81. Reprinted by permission of the publisher. Selection 2 from Reginald of Durham, "Life of St. Godric," in *Social Life in Britain from the Conquest to the Reformation*, edited by G. G. Coulton (Cambridge: Cambridge University Press, 1918), 415–420.

was no accident that Islam had up to that time sponsored the most intense merchant activity known in world history. The Middle East had long been a center of trade, even in the classical period. Muhammad, originally a merchant, praised the life of commerce, so long as it did not violate the primacy of religious goals, and so long as it was accompanied by active chants. But experience introduced greater caution, and toward the end of the postclassical period, as Muslim trade continued, though with slightly less dynamism, ambivalence became more obvious. What value did Muslim thinkers see in trade? What were the danger signals? How do Christian and Muslim views compare at this point?

Given the attitudes and policies suggested for the two societies—Western Europe and the Middle East—which society in your judgment was becoming most favorable for merchant activity, and why? Do cultural values really shape trade activities, or is a universal desire for profit more significant?

The values tensions surrounding merchant activity were very real in the postclassical period in both civilizations. They translated into individual ambiguities. Many European merchants—even some less holy than Godric—repented of their goals later in life and gave money away or entered a monastery.

The tensions also reflected a fascinating interaction between economic opportunities and cultural norms. None of the civilizations yielded entirely to one extreme or the other—which is why comparison must be subtle; a search for stark contrasts would be overly simple. The fact that some civilizations changed their balance over time adds another complexity. Nevertheless, certain of the differences were real, and they mattered in world history. China, to take the most obvious example, could have played a far larger trade role than it did, but it deliberately held back because of its own internal success—it did not need the outside world—and because of its cultural hostility to trade. Europe's growing commercial role required an adjustment of religious concerns, which did prove possible but caused wide anxiety about moral directions.

The description of the twelfth-century British merchant Godric was written by a biographer attracted to his saintly life (most merchants did not, it should be emphasized, become saints). It suggests both actual activities and cultural values. The Muslim description of merchants' vices and merits comes from the great historian and philosopher Ibn Khaldun, a North African who wrote in the fourteenth century.

1. A MUSLIM VIEW: IBN KHALDUN

Characteristics of Traders

Commerce, as we have said before, is the increasing of capital by buying goods and attempting to sell them at a price higher than their cost. This is done either by waiting for a rise in the market price; or by transporting the goods to another place where they are more keenly demanded and therefore fetch a higher price; or, lastly, by selling them on a long-term credit basis. Commercial profit is small, relatively to the capital invested, but if the capital is large, even a low rate of profit will produce a large total gain.

In order to achieve this increase in capital, it is necessary to have enough initial capital to pay in cash the sellers from whom one buys goods; it is also necessary to sell for cash, as honesty is not widespread among people. This dishonesty leads on the one hand to fraud and the adulteration of goods, and on the other to delays in payment which diminish profits because capital remains idle during the interval. It also induces buyers to repudiate their debts, a practice which is very injurious to the merchant's capital unless he can produce documentary evidence or the testimony of eyewitness. Nor are magistrates of much help in such cases, because they necessarily judge on evident proofs.

As a result of all this, the trader can only secure his meagre profits by dint of much effort and toil, or indeed he may well lose not only profits but capital as well. Hence, if he is known to be bold in entering law suits, careful in keeping accounts, stubborn in defending his point of view, firm in his attitude towards magistrates, he stands a good chance of getting his due. Should he not have these qualities, his only chance is to secure the support of a highly placed protector who will awe his debtors into paying him and the magistrates into meting justice out to him. Thus he gets justice spontaneously in the first case, and by compulsion in the second. Should a person, however, be lacking in boldness and the spirit of enterprise and at the same time have no protector to back him up, he had better avoid trade altogether, as he risks losing his capital and becoming the prey of other merchants. The fact of the matter is that most people, especially the mob and the trading classes, covet the goods of others; and but for the restraint imposed by the magistrates all goods would have been taken away from their owners. . . . The manners of trademen are inferior to those of rulers and far removed from manliness and uprightness. We have already stated that traders must buy and sell and seek profits. This necessitates flattery, and evasiveness, litigation and disputation, all of which are characteristic of this profession. And these qualities lead to a decrease and weakening in virtue and manliness. For acts inevitably affect the soul; thus good acts produce good and virtuous effects in the soul while evil or mean acts produce the opposite. Hence the effects of evil acts will strike root and strengthen themselves, if they should come early in life and repeat themselves; while if they come later they will efface the virtues by imprinting their evil effects on the soul; as is the case with all habits resulting from actions.

These effects will differ according to the conditions of the traders. For those of them who are of mean condition and in direct contact with the cheating and extortion of sellers will be more affected by these evils and further removed from manliness. . . . The other kind of traders are those who are protected by prestige and do not have to undertake directly such operations. Such persons are very rare indeed and consist of those who have acquired wealth suddenly, by inheritance or by other, unusual means. This wealth enables them to get in touch with the rulers and thus to gain prestige and protection so that they are released from practising these things [viz. buying and selling] themselves; instead, they entrust such business to their agents. Moreover the rulers, who are not indifferent to the wealth and liberality of such traders, protect them in their right and thus free them from certain unpleasant actions and their resulting evil effects. Hence they will be more manly and honourable than the other kind of trader; yet certain effects will still make themselves felt behind the veil, inasmuch as they still have to supervise their agents and employees in their doings—but this only takes place to a limited extent and its effects are hardly visible. . . .

Consider, as an example, the lands of the East, such as Egypt, Syria, Persia, India, or China; or the lands lying North of the Mediterranean. Because social life is flourishing there, notice how wealth has increased, the state has grown stronger, towns have multiplied, trade has prospered, conditions have improved. . . .

As for Trade, although it be a natural means of livelihood, yet most of the methods it employs are tricks aimed at making a profit by securing the difference between the buying and selling prices, and by appropriating the surplus. This is why Canon Law allows the use of such methods, which, although they come under the heading of gambling, yet do not constitute the taking without return of other people's goods. . . .

Should their standard of living, however, rise, so that they begin to enjoy more than the bare necessities, the effect will be to breed in them a desire for repose and tranquillity. They will therefore co-operate to secure superfluities; their food and clothing will increase in quantity and refinement; they will enlarge their houses and plan their towns for defence. A further improvement in their conditions will lead to habits of luxury, resulting in extreme refinement in cooking and the preparation of food; in choosing rich clothing of the finest silk; in raising lofty mansions and castles and furnishing them luxuriously, and so on. At this stage the crafts develop and reach their height. Lofty castles and mansions are built and decorated sumptuously, water is drawn to them and a great diversity takes place in the way of dress, furniture, vessels, and household equipment.

Such are the townsmen, who earn their living in industry or trade. Their gains are greater than those working in agriculture or animal husbandry and their standard of living higher, being in line with their wealth. We have shown, then, that both the nomadic and the urban stages are natural and necessary.

2. A CHRISTIAN VIEW: REGINALD OF DURHAM ON SAINT GODRIC

This holy man's father was named Ailward, and his mother Edwenna; both of slender rank and wealth, but abundant in righteousness and virtue. They were born in Norfolk, and had long lived in the township called Walpole. . . . When the boy had passed his childish years quietly at home; then, as he began to grow to manhood, he began to follow more prudent ways of life, and to learn carefully and persistently the teachings of worldly forethought. Wherefore he chose not to follow the life of a husbandman, but rather to study, learn and exercise the rudiment of more subtle conceptions. For this reason, aspiring to the merchant's trade, he began to follow the chapman's [peddler's] way of life, first learning how to gain in small bargains and things of insignificant price; and thence, while yet a youth, his mind advanced little by little to buy and sell and gain from things of greater expense. For, in his beginnings, he was wont to wander with small wares around the villages and farmsteads of his own neighborhood; but, in process of time, he gradually associated himself by compact with city merchants. Hence, within a brief space of time, the youth who had trudged for many weary hours from village to village, from farm to farm, did so profit by his increase of age and wisdom as to travel with associates of his own age through towns and boroughs, fortresses and cities, to fairs and to all the various booths of the market-place, in pursuit of his public chaffer. He went along the high-way, neither puffed up by the good testimony of his conscience nor downcasting the nobler part of his soul by the reproach of poverty. . . .

Yet in all things he walked with simplicity; and, in so far as he yet knew how, it was ever his pleasure to follow in the footsteps of the truth. For, having learned the Lord's Prayer and the Creed from his very cradle, he oftentimes turned them over in his mind, even as he went alone on his longer journeys; and, in so far as the truth was revealed to his mind, he clung thereunto most devoutly in all his thoughts concerning God. At first, he lived as a chapman for four years in Lincolnshire, going on foot and carrying the smallest wares; then he travelled abroad, first to St. Andrews in Scotland and then for the first time to Rome. On his return, having formed a familiar friendship with certain other young men were eager for merchandise, he began to launch upon bolder courses, and to coast frequently by sea to the foreign lands that lay around him. Thus, sailing often to and fro between Scotland and Britain, he traded in many divers wares and, amid these occupations, learned much worldly wisdom. . . . He fell into many perils of the sea, yet by God's mercy he was never wrecked; for He who had upheld St Peter as he walked upon the waves, by that same strong right arm kept this His chosen vessel from all misfortune amid these perils. Thus, having learned by frequent experience his wretchedness amid such dangers, he began to worship certain of the Saints with more ardent zeal, venerating and calling upon their shrines, and giving himself up by wholehearted service to those holy names. In such invocations his prayers were oftentimes answered by prompt consolation; some of which prayers he learned from his fellows with whom he shared these frequent perils; others he collected from faithful hearsay; others again from the custom of the place, for he saw and visited such holy places with frequent assiduity. Thus aspiring ever higher and higher, and yearning upward with his whole heart, at length his great labours and cares bore much fruit of worldly gain. For he laboured not only as a merchant but also as a shipman . . . to Denmark and Flanders and Scotland; in all which lands he found certain rare, and therefore more precious, wares, which he carried to other parts wherein he knew them to be least familiar, and coveted by the inhabitants beyond the price of gold itself; wherefore he exchanged these wares for others coveted by men of other lands; and thus he chaffered most freely and assiduously. Hence he made great profit in all his bargains, and gathered much wealth in the sweat of his brow; for he sold dear in one place the wares which he had bought elsewhere at a small price.

Then he purchased the half of a merchant-ship with certain of his partners in the trade; and again by his prudence he bought the fourth part of another ship. At length, by his skill in navigation, wherein he excelled all his fellows, he earned promotion to the post of steersman. . . .

For he was vigorous and strenuous in mind, whole of limb and strong in body. He was of middle stature, broad-shouldered and deep-chested, with a long face, grey eyes most clear and piercing, bushy brows, a broad forehead, long and open nostrils, a nose of comely curve, and a pointed chin. His beard was thick, and longer than the ordinary, his mouth well-shaped, with lips of moderate thickness; in youth his hair was black, in age as white as snow; his neck was short and thick, knotted with veins and sinews; his legs were somewhat slender, his instep high, his knees hardened and horny with frequent kneeling; his whole skin rough beyond the ordinary, until all this roughness was softened by old age. . . . In labour he was strenuous, assiduous above all men: and, when by chance his bodily strength proved insufficient, he compassed his ends with great ease by the skill which his daily labours had given, and by a prudence born of long experience. . . . He knew, from the aspect of sea and stars, how to foretell fair or foul weather. In his various voyages he visited many saints' shrines, to whose protection he was wont most devoutly to commend himself; more especially the church of St Andrew in Scotland, where he most frequently made and paid his vows. On the way thither, he oftentimes touched at the island of Lindisfarne, wherein St Cuthbert had been bishop, and at the isle of Farne, where that Saint had lived as an anchoret, and where St Godric (as he himself would tell afterwards) would meditate on the Saint's life with abundant tears. Thence he began to yearn for solitude, and to hold his merchandise in less esteem than heretofore. . . .

And now he had lived sixteen years as a merchant, and began to think of spending on charity, to God's honour and service, the goods which he had so laboriously acquired. He therefore took the cross as a pilgrim to Jerusalem, and, having visited the Holy Sepulchre, came back to England by way of St James [of Compostella]. Not long afterwards he became steward to a certain rich man of his own country, with the care of his whole house and household. But certain of the younger household were men of iniquity, who stole their neighbours' cattle and thus held luxurious feasts, whereat Godric, in his ignorance, was sometimes present. Afterwards, discovering the truth, he rebuked and admonished them to cease; but they made no account of his warnings, wherefore he concealed not their iniquity, but disclosed it to the lord of the household, who, however, slighted his advice. Wherefore he begged to be dismissed and went on a pilgrimage, first to St Gilles and thence to Rome the abode of the Apostles, that thus he might knowingly pay the penalty for those misdeeds wherein he had ignorantly partaken. I have often seen him, even in his old age, weeping for this unknowing transgression. . . .

On his return from Rome, he abode awhile in his father's house; until, inflamed again with holy zeal, he purposed to revisit the abode of the Apostles and made his desire known unto his parents. Not only did they approve his purpose, but his mother besought his leave to bear him company on this pilgrimage; which he gladly granted, and willingly paid her every filial service that was her due. They came therefore to London; and they had scarcely departed from thence when his mother took off her shoes, going thus barefooted to Rome and back to London. Godric, humbly serving his parent, was wont to bear her on his shoulders. . . .

Godric, when he had restored his mother safe to his father's arms, abode but a brief while at home; for he was now already firmly purposed to give himself entirely to God's service. Wherefore, that he might follow Christ the more freely, he sold all his possessions and distributed them among the poor. Then, telling his parents of this purpose and receiving their blessing, he went forth to no certain abode, but whithersoever the Lord should deign to lead him; for above all things he coveted the life of a hermit.

STUDY QUESTIONS

1. What kinds of uneasiness did Muslim observers have about trade?
2. How did Islam offer a distinctive combination of trade and cultural goals—a combination relatively favorable to trade without slighting religion? In what

ways did Islam and Christianity, such similar religions in many respects, differ over the validity of trade? Would a story like Godric's have been probable in Islam?

3. What exceptions do the sources suggest, even as they emphasize high ideals? What kinds of activities in Europe clearly represented crasser motives than those of a holy merchant like Godric? Why, in fact, did Godric not enter a holy calling initially—what kinds of motives drew him to trade?

4. Do the sources demonstrate that Europe was becoming wealthier than the Islamic world by the late postclassical period?

5. In light of the postclassical sources and comparisons, how would you rate the argument that no matter what their professed values, most people and societies are motivated by a desire for profit and will expand commercially whenever they can? Is a desire for economic gain an inherent part of human nature?

6. Which came first in world history: concern about trade or economic limitations? Did Christianity cause Western Europe's initial commercial lag in the postclassical period, or did economic decline encourage Christian concerns? How did Islam affect actual Middle Eastern economic patterns in the postclassical period?

33

Chinggis Khan and the Rise of the Mongols

The sudden rise of the Mongols, the greatest of the pastoral nomadic conquerors to come galloping out of the grasslands of central Asia, has long excited the imagination of historians. In 1206 C.E., a thousand years after Mo-tun had united the Hsiung-nu (see Chapter 16), Chinggis Khan established a new and powerful confederation of horseriding nomads under the leadership of the Mongols. During the next half-century the Mongol leader and his successors created the largest empire in world history. By the middle of the thirteenth century the Mongols controlled all of central Asia, all of Persia and Iraq (ancient Mesopotamia), and much of Russia. Moreover, by the end of the century the Mongols had succeeded where all of their central Asian predecessors had failed—they had conquered China. The Mongol's military success was truly unprecedented.

For historians the classic question that the Mongols have always presented is causation: What explains the extraordinary military success of this relatively small and rather underequipped army? The documents that follow provide some tentative answers to this old but still interesting (and unresolved) question. Present-day historians are also raising new questions about the meaning of the Mongol conquests. To what extent did the Mongols facilitate cross-cultural trade, the blending of cultures, the spread of technology, and the spread of diseases? How did Mongol gender structures compare with those elsewhere?

A final issue raised by the Mongols is the short-lived nature of their conquests. The key Mongol states flourished for about a century, from 1250 to 1350, and then vanished (except for Russia, where the Mongols clung to power for another century). Why did the Mongol states unravel so quickly?

As in the case of the Hsiung-nu, scholars of the Mongols must rely largely on documentation produced by writers who were not themselves nomads. To be sure,

Selection 1 from 'Ala-ad-Din 'Ata-Malik Juvaini, *Genghis Kahn: The History of the World Conqueror* by J. A. Boyle, 1997. Manchester University Press, Manchester, UK.. Selection 2 from "Mongol Conquest of Northern Russia in 1237–1238" in *Medieval Russia: A Source Book, 850–1700,* Third Edition by Basil Dmytryshyn, copyright © 1991 by Holt, Rinehart and Winston. Reprinted by permission of the publisher. Selection 3 from *History of the Mongols: Based on Eastern and Western Accounts of the Thirteenth and Fourteenth Centuries,* edited by Bertold Spuler and translated by Helga and Stuart Drummond (Berkeley: University of California Press, 1972), pp. 57–58. Selection 4 from *The Mission of Friar William of Rubruck: His Journey to the Court of the Great Khan Mongke 1253–1255,* translated by Peter Jackson (London: Hakluyt Society, 1990), pp. 74, 90–92.

unlike the Hsiung-nu, the Mongols did have a system of writing (as the Persian historian Juvaini notes in the first selection). However, apart from the rather obscure *Secret History of the Mongols,* the Mongols produced very little writing of their own. Our most valuable evidence about them comes from writings by the people they conquered and ruled and from visitors to the khans. The selections that follow are a mixture of this kind of evidence.

1. JUVAINI: A PERSIAN HISTORIAN ON CHINGGIS KHAN AND THE MONGOLS

['Ala-ad-Din 'Ata-Malik Juvaini (1226–1283) wrote one of the most valuable histories of the Mongols, from which the following passages have been taken. The book was written just prior to Juvaini's appointment in 1259 as governor of Baghdad by the Mongol Il Khan Hulegu.]

The home of the Tartars [the Mongols], and their origin and birthplace, is an immense valley, whose area is a journey of seven or eight months both in length and breadth. . . .

Before the appearance of Chingiz-Khan they had no chief or ruler. Each tribe or two tribes lived separately; they were not united with one another, and there was constant fighting and hostility between them. Some of them regarded robbery and violence, immorality and debauchery as deeds of manliness and excellence. The Khan of Khitai [ruler of northern China] used to demand and seize goods from them. Their clothing was of the skins of dogs and mice, and their food was the flesh of those animals and other dead things . . .

The sign of a great emir amongst them was that his stirrups were of iron; from which one can form a picture of their other luxuries. And they continued in this indigence, privation and misfortune until the banner of Chingiz-Khan's fortune was raised and they issued forth from the straits of hardship into the amplitude of well-being. . . .

In accordance and agreement with his own mind he [Chinggis Khan] established a rule for every occasion and a regulation for every circumstance; while for every crime he fixed a penalty. And since the Tartar peoples had no script of their own, he gave orders that Mongol children should learn writing from the Uighur; and that these *yasas* and ordinances should be written down on rolls. These rolls are called the *Great Book of Yasas* and are kept in the treasury of the chief princes. Wherever a khan ascends the throne, or a great army is mobilized, or the princes assemble and begin [to consult together] concerning affairs of state and the administration thereof, they produce these rolls and model their actions thereon; and proceed with the disposition of armies or the destruction of provinces and cities in the manner therein prescribed. . . .

Being the adherent of no religion and the follower of no creed, he eschewed bigotry, and the preference of one faith to another, and the placing of some above others; rather he honoured and respected the learned and pious of every sect, recognizing such conduct as the way to the Court of God. And as he viewed the Moslems with the eye of respect, so also did he hold the Christians and idolaters in high esteem. As for his children and grandchildren, several of them have chosen a religion according to their inclination, some adopting Islam, others embracing Christianity, others selecting idolatry and others again cleaving to

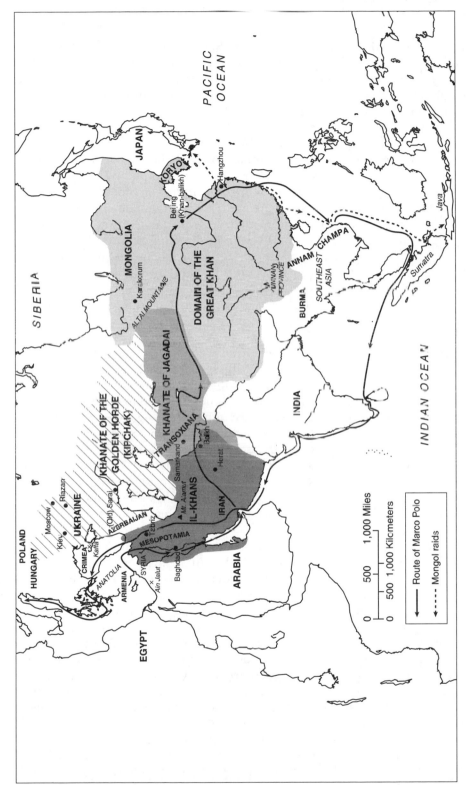

Mongol Territories

the ancient canon of their fathers and forefathers and inclining in no direction; but these are now a minority. But though they have adopted some religion they still for the most part avoid all show of fanaticism and do not swerve from the *yasa* of Chingiz-Khan, namely, to consider all sects as one and not to distinguish them from one another.

It is one of their laudable customs that they have closed the doors of ceremony, and preoccupation with titles, and excessive aloofness and inaccessibility; which things are customary with the fortunate and the mighty. When one of them ascends the throne of the Khanate, he receives one additional name, that of Khan or Qa'an, than which nothing more is written [in official documents]; while the other sons and his brothers are addressed by the name they were given at birth, both in their presence and in their absence; and this applies both to commoners and to the nobility. And likewise in directing their correspondence they write only the simple name, making no difference between Sultan and commoner; and write only the gist of the matter in hand, avoiding all superfluous titles and formulas. . . .

The reviewing and mustering of the army has been so arranged that they have abolished the registry of inspection and dismissed the officials and clerks. For they have divided all the people into companies of ten, appointing one of the ten to be the commander of the nine others; while from among each ten commanders one has been given the title of 'commander of the hundred,' all the hundred having been placed under his command. And so it is with each thousand men and so also with each ten thousand, over whom they have appointed a commander whom they call 'commander of the *tümen*.' In accordance with this arrangement, if in an emergency any man or thing be required, they apply to the commanders of *tümen;* who in turn apply to the commanders of thousands, and so on down to the commanders of tens. There is a true equality in this; each man toils as much as the next, and no difference is made between them, no attention being paid to wealth or power. If there is a sudden call for soldiers an order is issued that so many thousand men must present themselves in such and such a place at such and such an hour of that day or night.

And they arrive not a twinkling of an eye before or after the appointed hour. Their obedience and submissiveness is such that if there be a commander of a hundred thousand between whom and the Khan there is a distance of sunrise and sunset, and if he but commit some fault, the Khan dispatches a single horseman to punish him after the manner prescribed: if his head has been demanded, he cuts it off, and if gold be required, he takes it from him. . . .

Again, when the extent of their territories became broad and vast and important events fell out, it became essential to ascertain the activities of their enemies, and it was also necessary to transport goods from the West to the East and from the Far East to the West. Therefore throughout the length and breadth of the land they established *yams* [rest stops], and made arrangements for the upkeep and expenses of each *yam,* assigning thereto a fixed number of men and beasts as well as food, drink and other necessities. All this they shared out amongst the *tümen,* each two *tümen* having to supply one *yam.* Thus, in accordance with the census, they so distribute and exact the charge, that messengers need make no long detour in order to obtain fresh mounts while at the same time the peasantry and the army are not placed in constant inconvenience. Moreover strict orders were issued to the messengers with regard to the sparing of the mounts, etc., to recount all of which would delay us too long. Every year the *yams* are inspected, and whatever is missing or lost has to be replaced by the peasantry.

Since all countries and peoples have come under their domination, they have established a census after their accustomed fashion and classified everyone into tens, hundreds and thousands; and required military service and the equipment of *yams* together with the expenses entailed and the provision of fodder—this in addition to ordinary taxes; and over and above all this they have fixed the *qupchur* charges also.

They have a custom that if an official or a peasant die, they do not interfere with the estate he leaves, be it much or little, nor may anyone else tamper with it. And if he have no heir, it is given to his apprentice or his slave. On no account is the property of a dead man admitted to the treasury, for they regard such a procedure as inauspicious.

When Hülegü appointed me to [the governorship of] Baghdad, the inheritance taxes were in force in all that region; I swept away that system and abolished the imposts that had been levied in the countries of Tustar and Bayat. . . .

2. RUSSIAN CHRONICLES ON MONGOL CONQUESTS

It happened in 1237. That winter, the godless Tatars [i.e., the Mongols], under the leadership of Batu, came to the Riazan principality from the East through the forests. Upon arriving they encamped at Onuza, which they took and burned. From here they despatched their emissaries—a woman witch and two men—to the princes of Riazan demanding a tithe from the princes and complete armor and horses from the people. The princes of Riazan, Iurii Igorevich and his brother Oleg, did not allow the emissaries to enter the city, and [together with] the Murom and Pronsk princes [they] moved against the Tatars in the direction of Voronezh. The princes replied: "When we are gone, everything will be yours." . . . The princes of Riazan sent a plea to Prince Iurii of Vladimir, begging him to send aid or to come in person. Prince Iurii, however, did not go; neither did he listen to the plea of the princes of Riazan, as he wanted to fight the Tatars alone. . . .

The princes of Riazan, Murom, and Pronsk moved against the godless and engaged them in a battle. The struggle was fierce, but the godless Mohammedans emerged victorious with each prince fleeing toward his own city. Thus angered, the Tatars now began the conquest of the Riazan land with great fury. They destroyed cities, killed people, burned, and took [people] into slavery. On December 6 [1237], the cursed strangers approached the capital city of Riazan, besieged it, and surrounded it with a stockade. The princes of Riazan shut themselves up with the people of the city, fought bravely, but succumbed. On December 21 [1237], the Tatars took the city of Riazan, burned it completely, killed Prince Iurii Igorevich, his wife, slaughtered other princes, and of the captured men, women, and children, some they killed with their swords, others they killed with arrows and [then] threw them into the fire; while some of the captured they bound, cut, and disemboweled their bodies. The Tatars burned many holy churches, monasteries, and villages, and took their property.

On Tuesday February 3 [1238], . . . the Tatars approached Vladimir. The inhabitants of Vladimir, with their princes and military commander, Peter Osliadiukovich, shut themselves up in the city. The Tatars came to the Golden Gates, brought with them Prince Vladimir, the son of the Grand Prince Iurii Vsevolodovich, and inquired: "Is the Grand Prince Iurii in the city?" But the inhabitants of Vladimir began to shoot at them. They, however, shouted: "Do not shoot!" And, having approached very close to the gates, they showed the inhabitants of Vladimir their young Prince Vladimir, son of Iurii, and asked: "Do you recognize your young Prince?" As a result of privation and misfortune, his face was sad and he looked weak. Vsevolod and Mstislav stood atop the Golden Gates and recognized their brother Vladimir. Oh, how sad and tearful it is to see one's brother in such a condition! Vsevolod and Mstislav, with their *boyars* and all the inhabitants, wept as they looked at Vladimir. And the Tatars departed from the Golden Gates, circled the entire city, examined it, and encamped at Zremany in front of the Golden Gates and about the entire city; and there were many of them. . . .

After they made camp around Vladimir, the Tatars went and occupied the city of Suzdal. . . . They brought a multitude of prisoners into their camp, approached the city of Vladimir on Saturday, and from early morning till evening they built scaffolds and set up rams, and during the night they surrounded the entire city with a fence. In the morning, the princes, Bishop Mitrophan, military leader Peter Osliadiukovich, and all the *boyars* and the people realized that their city would be taken and they all began to weep. . . . On Sunday, February 8 [1238], . . . early in the morning the Tatars approached the city from all sides and began to hit the city [walls] with rams, and began to pour great stones into the center of the city from far away, as if by God's will, as if it rained inside the city; many people were killed inside the city and all were greatly frightened and trembled. The Tatars broke through the wall at the Golden Gates, also from the Lybed [side] at the Orininy and the Copper Gates, and from the Kliazma [direction] at the Volga Gates, and in other places; they destroyed the whole city, threw stones inside, and . . . entered it from all sides like demons. Before dinner they took the new city which they set on fire; and there they killed Prince Vsevolod with his brother, many *boyars* and people, while other princes and all the people fled into the middle city. Bishop Mitrophan and the Grand Duchess with her sons and daughters, daughters-in-law, grandchildren, *boyars*, and their wives, and many people fled into a church, locked the church gates, and climbed inside the church to the choir loft. The Tatars took this city too, and began to search after the princes and their mother, and found that they were inside the church. . . . The Tatars broke the gates of the church and slaughtered those who were inside and resisted. And they began to ask the whereabouts of the princes and their mother and found they were in the choir loft. They began to entice them to come down. But they did not listen to them. The Tatars then brought many fire logs inside the church and set it on fire. Those present in the choir loft, praying, gave their souls to God; they were burned and joined the list of martyrs. And the Tatars pillaged the holy church, and they tore the miracle-making icon of the Mother of God.

Chinggis Khan Leads the Charge Against the Enemy. Illustration from the *History of the Mongols,* by Rashid al-Din, a Persian historian who served as a high Mongol official. (Note how the anonymous artist was careful to depict the equipment and fighting skill of these horseriders. (Bibliothèque Nationale de France.)

3. KARAKORUM: BUILDING A MONGOL CAPITAL

[Rashid al-Din (ca. 1247–1317) was a Persian historian and the author of a massive world history, from which the following passage comes. Like Juvaini, Rashid served the Mongols as a high official. Ogedei, the subject of this reading, was the son of Chinggis Khan and succeeded his father as Great Khan, 1229–1241.]

During the seven years [between 1234/35 and 1240/41] . . . [Ogedei] enjoyed life and amused himself. He moved from summer to winter camp and vice versa, serene and happy, and took permanent delight in beautiful women and moonfaced enchantresses.

At every opportunity, he allowed his sublime thoughts to overflow lavishly into the most just and charitable of good deeds, into the eradication of injustice and enmity, into the development of cities and districts, as well as into the construction of various buildings. He never neglected any measure designed to strengthen the framework of peace, and to lay the foundations of prosperity. In earlier years, he had already brought with him from China various craftsmen and masters skilled in the arts. Therefore in his main camp ('yurt') in Karakorum, where he content-edly resided most of the time, he now had erected his palace with a very high base and columns as befits the lofty thoughts of such a ruler. Each side of the palace was an arrow-shot long. In the centre, a sumptuous high pavilion ('kiosk') was built; the building was handsomely decorated with paintings and representations, and it was called *qarshi* [Mongolian = Palace]. The Khan designated it his sublime residence. [Thereafter] the order was put out, that each of his brothers, sons and the other princes residing close to him should build a handsome house near the palace. Everybody obeyed the order. When these buildings were completed and snuggled one against the other they formed a whole settlement. [Furthermore the Great Khan] ordered that experienced goldsmiths should make for the drinking house a centerpiece of gold and silver in the shape of animals such as elephants, tigers, horses, and the like. They were set up, together with large drinking vessels which were filled with wine and fermented mare's milk (*qumys*). In front of each figure a silver basin was set up: from the orifices of these figures wine and mare's milk poured into the basins.

[Once, the ruler] asked: 'Which is the best city on earth?' The reply was: 'Baghdad.' He therefore had a great city built on the banks of the river Orkhon, and he called it Karakorum.

4. A REPORT ON MONGOL GENDER RELATIONS

[The author of the following passage, William of Rubruck, was a Franciscan friar who visited the Mongols during the 1250s on behalf of King Louis IX of France.]

The married women make themselves very fine wagons, which I could describe to you only by drawing—and indeed I should have drawn everything for you had I known how to draw. One rich Mo'al [Mongol or Tartar] has easily a hundred or two hundred such wagons with chests. Baatu has twenty-six wives, each of whom has a large dwelling, not counting the other, smaller ones placed behind the large one, which are chambers, as it were, where the maids live: to each of these dwellings be-long a good two hundred wagons. When they unload the dwellings, the chief wife pitches her residence [*curia*] at the westernmost end, and the others follow accord-ing to rank, so that the last wife will be at the eastern end: there is a space of a stone's throw between the residence of one lady and the next. Hence the court [*cu-ria*] of one wealthy Mo'al will have the appearance of a large town, though there will be very few males in it.

One woman will drive twenty or thirty wagons, since the terrain is level. The ox- or camel-wagons are lashed together in sequence, and the woman will sit at the front driving the ox, while all the rest follow at the same pace. If at some point the going happens to become difficult, they untie them and take them through one at a time. For they move slowly, at the pace at which a sheep or an ox can walk. . . .

It is the women's task to drive the wagons, to load the dwellings on them and to unload again, to milk the cows, to make butter and *grut* [curds or cheese], and to dress the skins and stitch them together, which they do with a thread made from sinew. They divide the sinew into tiny strands, and then twist them into a single long thread. In addition they stitch shoes, socks and other garments. They never wash clothes, for they claim that this makes God angry and that if they were hung out to dry it would thunder: in fact, they thrash anyone doing laundry and confiscate it. (They are extraordinarily afraid of thunder. In that event they turn out of their dwellings all strangers, and wrap themselves up in black felt, in which they hide until it has passed.) They never wash dishes either, but instead, when the meat is cooked, rinse the bowl in which they are to put it with boiling broth from the cauldron and then pour it back into the cauldron. In addition [the women] make the felt and cover the dwellings.

The men make bows and arrows, manufacture stirrups and bits, fashion saddles, construct the dwellings and the wagons, tend the horses and milk the mares, churn the *comos* (that is, the mare's milk), produce the skins in which it is stored, and tend and load the camels. Both sexes tend the sheep and goats, and they are milked on some occasions by the men, on others by the women. The skins are dressed with curdled ewe's milk, thickened and salted.

When they want to wash their hands or head, they fill their mouths with water, and let it trickle slowly from their mouths onto their hands, using it to wet their hair and wash their heads.

Regarding their marriages, you should know that the only way to have a wife there is to purchase her, and for this reason the girls are sometimes very mature before they are married, for the parents always keep them until they sell them. They observe the first and second degrees of consanguinity, but none of affinity, for they can have two sisters at the same time or in succession. Widows among them do not marry, on the grounds of their belief that all who serve them in this life will do so in the one to come; and so in the case of a widow they think that after death she will always revert to her first husband. Consequently, there is to be found among them the shameful practice whereby a son sometimes marries all his father's wives except his own mother. The residence [*curia*] of the father and mother always devolves upon the youngest son, and so he himself is obliged to provide for all his father's wives who pass to him along with his father's household; then, if he wishes, he treats them as his own wives, since he reckons he has made no loss if they revert to his father after death.

So, then, when someone makes a contract with someone else to take his daughter, the girl's father holds a banquet, and she flees to her relatives in order to lie in hiding. Then the father says, 'Behold, my daughter is yours; take her, wherever you may find her.' At this the man searches for her with his friends until he discovers her, and he is required to take her by force and carry her off with a semblance of violence to his own home.

STUDY QUESTIONS

1. What are the most important points that Juvaini makes about Chinggis Khan and the Mongols?
2. How are the Mongols portrayed in the Russian Chronicles?
3. According to Rashid al-Din, what were the chief attributes of Ogedei?
4. What does William of Rubruck report about gender structures among the Mongols?

5. Based on your reading of these sources, how do you explain the Mongol's military success?

6. In seeking to understand the Mongols, what are the advantages and disadvantages of relying on Persian writers who served as high officials under the Mongols? On Russian chroniclers who identified with the victims of the Mongols? On a Western European friar who visited the Mongols?

7. Review the selections from Ssu-ma Ch'ien on the Hsiung-nu in Chapter 16. What similarities and differences do you see between the Mongols and the Hsiung-nu? When you compare the Mongols with the Hsiung-nu, what evidence of changes in the way of life of the nomads do you see?

8. How do the writers on the Mongols compare with Ssu-ma Ch'ien as sources for our understanding of pastoral nomads?

9. Did life on the steppe adequately prepare the Mongols to successfully govern agrarian societies such as Persia and China?

10. How did the Mongols contribute to cross-cultural trade, the spread of technology, the blending of cultures, and the spread of diseases? (See the excerpts from Marco Polo in Chapter 22 for suggestions.)

34

Global Contacts: Travelers to Holy Places

Buddhist, Christian, and Muslim Pilgrims

Buddhism, Christianity, and Islam spread widely in Afro-Eurasia during the first millennium. As the number of converts increased, the tradition of pilgrimage—that is, travel to holy places—became increasingly important. For Buddhists the sacred places were in northern India. As we have seen, this is the region where the Buddha was born, where he achieved enlightenment under the branches of the *bodhi* tree, and where he subsequently taught (see Chapter 10). For Christian pilgrims the most important destination was Jerusalem, the city where Jesus taught and was crucified and buried. Muslims were under the special injunction of the fifth pillar of Islam to make a pilgrimage (*hajj*) to the Arabian cities of Mecca and Medina. Mecca was the city where Muhammad was born and first taught; Medina was the city to which Muhammad fled in 622 (the *hegira*) and where he was buried (see Chapters 18 to 20).

Pilgrim narratives, which are the records of journeys to holy places left by religious travelers or their contemporaries, help historians to appreciate the strength of religious ideals in the past. In addition, by examining narratives from different religions historians can begin to obtain an understanding of religious ideals and practices in comparative perspective.

But pilgrim narratives are valuable for other reasons too. Despite having been written essentially for religious purposes, the stories told by pilgrims often contain valuable information about travel conditions, trade routes, and contacts between people from different cultures. Some of the narratives are also quite interesting to the

Selection 1 from *Egeria: Diary of a Pilgrimage,* translated by George E. Gingras (New York: Newman Press, 1970), p. 88–89, 91–95, 125–126. Reprinted by permission of Paulist Press. Selection 2 from Shaman Hwui-Li, *The Life of Huien-Tsiang* [Hsuang Tsang], translated by Samuel Beal (Westport, Conn.: Hyperion Press, 1973), pp. 102–105, 110–112. Selection 3 from Ibn Jubayr, *The Travels of Ibn Jubayr,* translated by R. J. C. Broadhurst (London: Jonathan Cape, 1952), pp. 77–78, 85, 116–117. Selection 4 from *Corpus of Early African Sources for West African History,* edited by N. Levtzion and J. F. P. Hopkins and translated by J. F. P. Hopkins (Cambridge: Cambridge University Press, 1981), pp. 269–271.

historian for the light they throw on matters such as political structures, economic and social conditions, gender relations, and cultural life in the regions that the pilgrims came from or traveled through.

The documents that follow come from the experiences of four pilgrims: one Christian, one Buddhist, and two Muslims. (Two Muslim pilgrims are included because of the special importance of pilgrimage in Islam.) Egeria, the author of the first selection, was either a laywoman or a nun who traveled to Jerusalem from her home in Gaul or Spain during the 380s. The second document is a contemporary account of the journey to India made by the Chinese Buddhist monk Hsuan Tsang from 629 to 645. Ibn Jubayr, the author of the third selection, traveled from Muslim Spain to Mecca in the 1180s. The final document is a contemporary record of the pilgrimage to Mecca made by the West African ruler of the early fourteenth century, Mansa Musa.

1. EGERIA: A CHRISTIAN PILGRIM FROM THE FOURTH CENTURY

[Many of the early Christian pilgrims were women. Egeria's narrative, which is a long letter to her co-religionists in Gaul or Spain, was written in the 380s from Constantinople, the Roman capital and leading center of Christianity.]

After arriving there [in Constantinople], I did not cease giving thanks to Jesus our God, who had deigned to bestow His grace upon me, in the various churches, that of the apostles and the numerous shrines that are here. As I send this letter to Your Charity and to you, reverend ladies, it is already my intention to go, in the name of Christ our God, to Asia, that is, to Ephesus, to pray at the shrine of the holy and blessed apostle John. If, after this, I am still living, I will either tell Your Charity in person—if God will deign to grant that—about whatever other places I shall have come to know, or certainly I will write you of it in letters, if there is anything else I have in mind. You, my sisters, my light, kindly remember me, whether I live or die. . . .

On the seventh day, however, that is, on Sunday, before the cockcrow, a whole multitude, whatever number can be accommodated in this place [in Jerusalem] and as many as at Easter, gathering outside in the forecourt adjoining the Anastasis [i.e., the Church of the Resurrection which was built over the grotto of the Holy Sepulcher, the reputed burial place of Jesus] where for this reason there are lamps hanging. Fearing that they will not arrive in time for cockcrow, the people come beforehand and sit there, singing hymns and antiphons and reciting prayers after each hymn and antiphon. Because of the multitude which assembles, there are always priests and deacons ready to hold the vigil, for, by custom, the holy places are not opened before cockcrow.

As soon as the first cock has crowed, the bishop immediately comes down to the church and goes into the grotto at the Anastasis. All the doors are then opened, and the multitude goes into the Anastasis, where countless lights are already glowing. And as soon as the people have entered, one of the priests sings a Psalm and they all make the response; afterwards, a prayer is said. Next one of the deacons sings a Psalm, and again a prayer is said, whereupon a third Psalm is sung by one of the minor ministers, followed by a third prayer and a commemoration of all. When the three Psalms and prayers have been said, then the censers are

Buddhist Monastery with Pagoda. Located near Xi'an (formerly Chang'an), China, seventh century C.E. The shape of Chinese pagodas was partly inspired by Indian stupas (hemispherical-shaped structures containing relics of the Buddha). This pagoda contains the remains of Huzsan Tsang. (Stephen S. Gosch.)

brought into the grotto of the Anastasis, with the result that the whole basilica of the Anastasis is filled with odors of incense. Then the bishop stands within the railings, takes up the Gospel, and goes toward the door; there the bishop himself reads the Resurrection of the Lord. As soon as the reading of it has begun, so much moaning and groaning is heard, and there is so much weeping among all the people, that the hardest of men would be moved to tears because the Lord has endured so much on our behalf.

Once the Gospel has been read, the bishop goes out, and singing hymns they lead him to the [Church of the] Cross, and with him go the people. There another Psalm is sung and a prayer said. Then he blesses the faithful, and the dismissal is given. As the bishop leaves, all come forth to kiss his hand. The bishop then withdraws to his house, and from that time on all the monks return to the Anastasis to sing Psalms and antiphons until dawn, and to recite a prayer after each Psalm or antiphon. Each day priests and deacons take turns in holding the vigil at the Anastasis with the people. Among the laity there are men and women who wish to remain there until dawn, while others, not wishing to do so, return to their homes to sleep and to rest.

Since it is Sunday, at dawn they assemble for the liturgy in the major church built by Constantine and located on Golgotha [i.e., the reputed site of the crucifixion of Jesus] behind the [Church of the] Cross; and whatever is done all over customarily on Sundays is done here. Indeed it is the practice here that as many of the priests who are present and are so inclined may preach; and last of all, the bishop preaches. These sermons are given every Sunday so that the people may be instructed in the Scriptures and the love of God. Because of the sermons that are preached, there is a great delay in giving the dismissal from the church; therefore, the dismissal is not given before the fourth or fifth hour.

However, once the dismissal from the church has been given in the manner which is followed everywhere, then the monks, singing hymns, lead the bishop to the Anastasis. When the bishop, to the accompaniment of hymns, approaches, all the doors of the basilica of the Anastasis are opened, and all the people enter, the faithful, that is, but not the catechumens. Once the people have entered, then the bishop enters and he proceeds immediately to within the railings of the grotto shrine. First, they give thanks to God, and so the sacrifice is offered; and then a prayer is said for everyone. Afterwards, the deacon cries out that all should bow their heads, wherever they are standing, and then the bishop, standing within the inner railings, blesses them; afterwards, he goes out. As he is leaving, all come forth to kiss his hand. And so it is that the dismissal is delayed until as late as the fifth or sixth hour. Later at vespers everything is done exactly according to the daily ritual.

This ritual is observed each day throughout the year, except on solemn feast days—and we shall take note of what is done on those days later. . . .

However, after the people have rested, everyone gathers together again in the major church on Golgotha at the beginning of the second hour. It would be superfluous to describe how the churches—the Anastasis, the Cross, and the church in Bethlehem—are decorated on that day. You see nothing there but gold and gems and silk. If you look at the hangings, they are made of silk with gold stripes; if you look at the curtains, they are also made of silk with gold stripes. Every kind of sacred vessel brought out on that day is of gold inlaid with precious stones. How could the number and weight of the candle holders, the candelabra, the lamps, and the various sacred vessels be in any way estimated and noted down? And what can I say about the decoration of this building which Constantine, with his mother on hand, had embellished with as much gold, mosaics, and marble as the resources of his empire permitted—and not only the major church, but the Anastasis as well, and the Cross and the other holy places in Jerusalem? . . .

A portion of the population in this province [i.e., Syria-Palestine] knows both Greek and Syriac; another segment knows only Greek; and still another, only Syriac. Even though the bishop may know Syriac, he always speaks Greek and never

Syriac; and, therefore, there is always present a priest who, while the bishop speaks in Greek, translates into Syriac so that all may understand what is being explained. Since whatever scriptural texts are read must be read in Greek, there is always someone present who can translate the readings into Syriac for the people, so that they will always understand. So that those here who are Latins, those consequently knowing neither Greek nor Syriac, will not be bored, everything is explained to them, for there are other brothers and sisters who are bilingual in Greek and Latin and who explain everything to them in Latin. But this above all is very pleasing and very admirable here, that whatever hymns and antiphons are sung, whatever readings and prayers are recited by the bishop, they are said in such a manner as to be proper and fitting to the feast which is being observed and to the place where the service is being held. . . .

2. HSUAN TSANG: THE CHINESE BUDDHIST IN INDIA

[Hsuan Tsang's journey to India in the seventh century has long fascinated Chinese of all ages. One of the great classics of Chinese fiction, Journey to the West, *is loosely based on the monk's travels. In the following document one of Hsuan Tsang's colleagues describes the monk's visit to the Buddhist holy places.]*

To the south-east of the old city are the ruins of the Kukkutârama convent, which was built by Aśôka râja [i.e., Ashoka, the Mauryan emperor, r. 268–232 B.C.E.]: it was here he convoked the 1000 priests and supplied them with the four kinds of religious offerings.

The Master of the Law [Hsuan Tsang] paid reverence to all these sacred traces, during seven days, visiting them severally.

Then going south-west six or seven *yôjanas* he came to the Tiladaka convent. In this convent were several tens of priests of the three pitakas (*i.e., Buddhist priests*), who hearing of the arrival of the Master of the Law came out in a body to meet and escort him.

From this, again, proceeding southwards 100 *li* or so, we come to the Bôdhi tree [in Bodh Gaya]. The tree is protected by high and very solid brick walls; the wall stretching east and west is long, but narrower from north to south.

The principal gate faces the east looking towards the river Nairanjana. The southern gate borders on a great flower-tank. The west a mountain side protects. The north gate leads into the great Sanghârâma. Within this on every side are the sacred traces of religion, vihâras, stûpas, and so on, all of which kings and great ministers and rich nobles have constructed from a principle of reverence, and for the perpetual memory (*of their religion*).

In the centre of the whole enclosure is the Diamond throne, which was perfected at the beginning of the Bhadra Kalpa, and rose up from the ground when the world was formed. It is the very central point of the universe, and goes down to the golden wheel, from whence it rises upwards to the earth's surface. It is perfected of diamond, and is about 100 paces round. In using the word *diamond* we mean that it is firm and indestructible, and able to resist all things. If it were not for its support the earth could not remain; if the seat were not so strong as diamond, then no part of the world could support one who has entered the samâdhi of *perfect fixedness (vajra samadh)*. . . .

The Bôdhi tree is the same as the Pippala tree (*Ficus religiosa*) [a fig tree].

Whilst Buddha was in the world the height of the tree was several hundred feet; but as wicked kings have continually cut it down and destroyed it, the tree is now only about fifty feet high. As Buddha, whilst sitting beneath this tree, reached perfect wisdom (*anuttara Bôdhi*), it is therefore called the Bôdhi tree. The bark is of a yellowish white colour, and its leaves of a shining green; it retains its leaves through the autumn and winter; only, when the day of Buddha's Nirvâna comes, the leaves all fall off, but when the day has passed, they all grow again. Every year on this day the kings of the countries, the ministers and magistrates, assemble beneath the tree, and pour milk on its roots and light lamps and scatter flowers, then collecting the leaves, they retire.

The Master of the Law when he came to worship the Bodhi tree and the figure of Tathâgata [the Buddha] at the time of his reaching perfect wisdom, made (*afterwards*) by (*the interposition of*) Mâitrôya Bôdhisattva, gazed on these objects with the most sincere devotion, he cast himself down with his face to the ground in worship, and with much grief and many tears in his self-affliction, he sighed, and said: "At the time when Buddha perfected himself in wisdom, I know not in what condition I was, in the troublous whirl of birth and death; but now, in this latter time of image (*worship*), having come to this spot and reflecting on the depth and weight of the body of my evil deeds, I am grieved at heart, and my eyes filled with tears."

At this time there happened to come to the spot, from different quarters, a body of priests who had just broken up from their religious retreat, numbering several thousand men; these persons, when they beheld (*? the Master*) were all moved to pity and sorrow.

For a *yôjana* around this spot the space is full of sacred traces. The Master therefore remained here for eight or nine days to pay his worship at each spot successively.

On the tenth day he went to the Nâlanda temple [the great Indian center of Buddhist worship and study]; the congregation there had selected four of their number, of distinguished position, to go and meet him. . . .

The place [Nâlanda temple] was originally the garden of the lord Âmra: Five hundred merchants bought it for ten lacs of gold pieces, and presented it to Buddha. Here Buddha preached the law for three months, and most of the merchants obtained the fruit of Arhatship, in consequence. . . .

Moreover, the whole establishment is surrounded by a brick wall, which encloses the entire convent from without. One gate opens into the great college, from which are separated eight other halls, standing in the middle (*of the Saṅghârâma*). The richly adorned towers, and the fairy-like turrets, like pointed hill-tops, are congregated together. The observatories seem to be lost in the vapours (*of the morning*), and the upper rooms tower above the clouds.

From the windows one may see how the winds and the clouds (*produce new forms*), and above the soaring eaves the conjunctions of the sun and moon (*may be observed*).

And then we may add how the deep, translucent ponds, bear on their surface the blue lotus, intermingled with the *Kanaka* flower, of deep red colour, and at intervals the the Âmra groves spread over all, their shade.

All the outside courts, in which are the priests' chambers, are of four stages. The stages have dragon-projections and coloured eaves, the pearl-red pillars, carved and ornamented, the richly adorned balustrades, and the roofs covered with tiles that reflect the light in a thousand shades, these things add to the beauty of the scene. . . .

3. IBN JUBAYR: PILGRIMAGE TO MECCA IN THE 1180s

We entered Mecca—God protect it—at the first hour of of Rabi', being the 4th of August, by the 'Umrah Gate. As we marched that night, the full moon had thrown its rays upon the earth, the night had lifted its veil, voices struck the ears with the *Talbiyat*[1] ['Here am I, O God, here am I'], from all sides, and tongues were loud in invocation, humbly beseeching God to grant them their requests, sometimes re-doubling their *Talbiyat,* and sometimes imploring with prayers. Oh night most happy, the bride of all the nights of life, the virgin of the maidens of time.

And so, at the time and on the day we have mentioned, we came to God's ven-erable Haram, the place of sojourn of Abraham the Friend (of God), and found the Ka'bah, the Sacred House, the unveiled bride conducted (like a bride to her groom) to the supreme felicity of heaven, encompassed by the deputations [pil-grims] of the All-Merciful. We performed the *tawaf*[2] of the new arrival, and then prayed at the revered Maqam.[3] We clung to the covering of the Ka'bah near the Multazam, which is between the Black Stone and the door, and is a place where prayers are answered. We entered the dome of Zamzam[4] and drank of its waters which is 'to the purpose for which it is drunk,' as said the Prophet—may God bless and preserve him—and then performed the *sa'i*[5] between al-Safa and al-Marwah. After this we shaved and entered a state of *halal*.[6] Praise be to God for generously including us in the pilgrimage to Him and for making us to be of those on whose behalf the prayers of Abraham reach. Sufficient He is for us and the best Manager. We took lodging in Mecca at a house called al-Halal near to the Haram and the Bab al-Suddah, one of its gates, in a room having many domestic conveniences and overlooking the Haram and the sacred Ka'bah. . . .

The blessed Black Stone is enchased in the corner facing east. The depth to which it penetrates it is not known, but it is said to extend two cubits into the wall. Its breadth is two-thirds of a span, its length one span and a finger joint. It has four pieces, joined together, and it is said that it was the Qarmata [Carmathians]—may God curse them—who broke it. Its edges have been braced with a sheet of silver whose white shines brightly against the black sheen and polished brilliance of the Stone, presenting the observer a striking spectacle which will hold his looks. The

1. *Talbiyat.* The cry which pilgrims must utter as they approach Mecca.
2. *Tawaf.* The rite of walking around the Ka'bah seven times.
3. *Maqam.* A sacred building associated with Abraham, the Hebrew patriarch who Muslims believe built the Ka'bah.
4. *Zamam.* The sacred well, which was made by the Angel Gabriel, whose water saved Ishmael from dying of thirst (see Sa'i below) and is used to wash the Ka'bah.
5. *Sa'i.* The ceremony of running seven times between the hills of al-Safa and al-Marwah in commemoration of Hagar, who in doing so attracted the attention of the Angel Gabriel and saved her son Ishmael from dying of thirst.
6. *Halal.* That which is lawful.

Stone, when kissed, has a softness and moistness which so enchants the mouth that he who puts his lips to it would wish them never to be removed. This is one of the special favours of Divine Providence, and it is enough that the Prophet—may God bless and preserve him—declare to be a covenant of God on earth. May God profit us by the kissing and touching of it. By His favour may all who yearn fervently for it be brought to it. In the sound piece of the stone, to the right of him who presents himself to kiss it, is a small white spot that shines and appears like a mole on the blessed surface. Concerning this white mole, there is a tradition that he who looks upon it clears his vision, and when kissing it one should direct one's lips as closely as one can to the place of the mole. . . .

The *Kiswah* [lit. 'robe,' covering] of the sacred Ka'bah is of green silk as we have said. There are thirty-four pieces: nine on the side between the Yemen and Syrian corners, nine also on the opposite side between the Black corner and the 'Iraq corner, and eight on both the side between the 'Iraq and Syrian corners and on that between the Yemen and the Black. Together they come to appear as one single cover comprehending the four sides. The lower part of the Ka'bah is sur-rounded by the projecting border built of stucco, more than a span in depth and two spans or a little more in width, inside which is wood, not discernible. Into this are driven iron pegs which have at their ends iron rings that are visible. Through these is inserted a rope of hemp, thick and strongly made, which encircles the four sides, and which is sewn with strong, twisted, cotton, thread to a girdle, like that of the *sirwal* [loose cotton trousers], fixed to the hems of the covers. At the juncture of the covers at the four corners, they are sewn together for more than a man's stature, and above that they are brought together by iron hooks engaged in each other. At the top, round the sides of the terrace, runs another projecting border to which the upper parts of the covers are attached with iron rings, after the fashion described. Thus the blessed *Kiswah* is sewn top and bottom, and firmly buttoned, being never removed save at its renewal year by year. Glory to God who perpetuates its honour until the Day of Resurrection. There is no God but He. . . .

This blessed town and its peoples have from ancient times profited from the prayers of the friend of God, Abraham. . . .

The proof of this in Mecca is manifest, and will continue to the Day of Resur-rection, for the hearts of men yearn towards it from far countries and distant re-gions. The road to it is a place of encounter for those, coming and going, to whom the blessed claims (of Islam) have reached. From all parts produce is brought to it, and it is the most prosperous of countries in its fruits, useful requisites, commodi-ties, and commerce. And although there is no commerce save in the pilgrim pe-riod, nevertheless, since people gather in it from east and west, there will be sold in one day, apart from those that follow, precious objects such as pearls, sapphires, and other stones, various kinds of perfume such as musk, camphor, amber and aloes, Indian drugs and other articles brought from India and Ethiopia, the prod-ucts of the industries of 'Iraq and the Yemen, as well as the merchandise of Khurasan, the goods of the Maghrib, and other wares such as it is impossible to enumerate or correctly assess. Even if they were spread over all lands, brisk markets could be set up with them and all would be filled with the useful effects of com-merce. All this is within the eight days that follow the pilgrimage, and exclusive of what might suddenly arrive throughout the year from the Yemen and other countries. Not on the face of the world are there any goods or products but that some of them are in Mecca at this meeting of the pilgrims. This blessing is clear to all, and one of the miracles that God has worked in particular for this city. . . .

4. MANSA MŪSĀ: THE EMPEROR OF MALI ON PILGRIMAGE

[Mansa Mūsā (reigned 1312–1337) was one of the greatest emperors of Mali, a powerful and prosperous West African state in the fourteenth century. The following account of Mansa Mūsā's pilgrimage to Mecca comes from the writings of al-Umari (1301–1349), a historian and geographer who spent many years in Cairo. Much of al-Umari's information about Mansa Mūsā is based on interviews with Egyptian officials who had met the Malian ruler during his visit to Cairo in 1324.]

From the beginning of my coming to stay in Egypt I heard talk of the arrival of this sultan Mūsā on his Pilgrimage and found the Cairenes eager to recount what they had seen of the Africans' prodigal spending. I asked the emir Abū 'l-'Abbās Ahmad b. al-Hāk the *mihmandar* [official guide] and he told me of the opulence, manly virtues, and piety of this sultan. "When I went out to meet him (he said), that is, on behalf of the mighty sultan al-Malik al-Nāsir, he did me extreme honour and treated me with the greatest courtesy. He addressed me, however, only through an interpreter despite his perfect ability to speak in the Arabic tongue. Then he forwarded to the royal treasury many loads of unworked native gold and other valuables. I tried to persuade him to go up to the Citadel to meet the sultan, but he refused persistently, saying: 'I came for the Pilgrimage and nothing else. I do not wish to mix anything else with my Pilgrimage.' He had begun to use this argument but I realized that the audience was repugnant to him because he would be obliged to kiss the ground and the sultan's hand. I continued to cajole him and he continued to make excuses but the sultan's protocol demanded that I should bring him into the royal presence, so I kept on at him till he agreed.

"When we came in the sultan's presence we said to him: 'Kiss the ground!' but he refused outright saying: 'How may this be?' Then an intelligent man who was with him whispered to him something we could not understand and he said: 'I make obeisance to God who created me!' then he prostrated himself and went forward to the sultan. The sultan half rose to greet him and sat him by his side. They conversed together for a long time, then sultan Mūsā went out. The sultan sent to him several complete suits of honour for himself, his courtiers, and all those who had come with him, and saddled and bridled horses for himself and his chief courtiers. His robe of honour consisted of an Alexandrian open-fronted cloak embellished with *tard wahsh* cloth containing much gold thread and miniver fur, bordered with beaver fur and embroidered with metallic thread, along with golden fastenings, a silken skull-cap with caliphal emblems, a gold-inlaid belt, a damascened sword, a kerchief [embroidered] with pure gold, standards, and two horses saddled and bridled and equipped with decorated mule[-type] saddles. He also furnished him with accommodation and abundant supplies during his stay.

"When the time to leave for the Pilgrimage came round the sultan sent to him a large sum of money with ordinary and thoroughbred camels complete with saddles and equipment to serve as mounts for him, and purchased abundant supplies for his entourage and others who had come with him. He arranged for deposits of fodder to be placed along the road and ordered the caravan commanders to treat him with honour and respect.

"On his return I received him and supervised his accommodation. The sultan continued to supply him with provisions and lodgings and he sent gifts from the Noble Hijaz [i.e., the western coast and highlands of Arabia] to the sultan as a blessing. The sultan accepted them and sent in exchange complete suits of honour for him and his courtiers together with other gifts, various kinds of Alexandrian cloth, and other precious objects. Then he returned to his country.

"This man flooded Cairo with his benefactions. He left no court emir nor holder of a royal office without the gift of a load of gold. The Cairenes made incalculable profits out of him and his suite in buying and selling and giving and taking. They exchanged gold until they depressed its value in Egypt and caused its price to fall."

The *mihmandār* spoke the truth, for more than one has told this story. When the *mihmandār* died the tax office found among the property which he left thousands of dinars' worth of native gold which he had given to him, still just as it had been in the earth, never having been worked.

Merchants of Cairo have told me of the profits which they made from the Africans, saying that one of them might buy a shirt or cloak or robe or other garment for five dinars when it was not worth one. Such was their simplicity and trustfulness that it was possible to practice any deception on them. They greeted anything that was said to them with credulous acceptance. But later they formed the very poorest opinion of the Egyptians because of the obvious falseness of everything they said to them and their outrageous behaviour in fixing the prices of the provisions and other good which were sold to them, so much so that were they to encounter today the most learned doctor of religious science and he were to say that he was Egyptian they would be rude to him and view him with disfavour because of the ill treatment which they had experienced at their hands.

[A]l-Ujrumi the guide informed me that he accompanied sultan Mūsā when he made the Pilgrimage and that the sultan was very open-handed towards the pilgrims and the inhabitants of the Holy Places. He and his companions maintained great pomp and dressed magnificently during the journey. He gave away much wealth in alms. "About 200 mithqals of gold fell to me" said Muhanna' "and he gave other sums to my companions." Muhanna' waxed eloquent in describing the sultan's generosity, magnanimity, and opulence.

Gold was at a high price in Egypt until they came in that year. The mithqal did not go below 25 *dirhams* and was generally above, but from that time its value fell and it cheapened in price and has remained cheap till now. The mithqal does not exceed 22 *dirhams* or less. This has been the state of affairs for about twelve years until this day [in the year 1337 or 1338] by reason of the large amount of gold which they brought into Egypt and spent there.

A letter came from this sultan to the court of the sultan in Cairo. It was written in the Maghribī style of handwriting on paper with wide lines. In it he follows his own rules of composition although observing the demands of propriety. It was written by the hand of one of his courtiers who had come on the Pilgrimage. Its contents comprised greetings and a recommendation for the bearer. With it he sent 5,000 mithqals of gold by way of a gift.

STUDY QUESTIONS

1. How does Egeria help us to understand the importance of Jerusalem to fourth-century Christians? What evidence does Egeria provide regarding continuity between Roman and Christian traditions? How does Egeria help us to see the Jerusalem region as a place of cross-cultural encounters?

2. What sacred places made the greatest impact on Hsuan Tsang? What similarities and differences do you see between Jerusalem and Bodh Gaya?

3. What impressed Ibn Jubayr about Mecca? What suggestions of animist, Jewish, and Christian traditions seem to have been incorporated into Muslim practices?

4. How do Jerusalem, Bodh Gaya, and Mecca compare with one another? Which of these three sacred places seems to have been the most important commercial center? (See Chapter 32 for other documents on Islamic and Christian attitudes toward trade.)

5. What impact did Mansa Mūsā have on Cairo? What does the account of Mansa Mūsā's visit suggest about Cairo as a center of trade and cross-cultural interchange?

6. What do these documents tell us about the emotions of pilgrims? Which of them is the most revealing in this regard?

7. How do the narratives help us to understand why these three religions spread so widely?

8. What other kinds of historical evidence—apart from pilgrim narratives—would add to our understanding of the reasons for the spread of religions?

35

Global Contacts: Sailing to Calicut
Chinese and Portuguese Voyages

Contacts between widely separated regions in the world greatly intensified during the fifteenth century C.E. Columbus's first voyage across the Atlantic at the end of the century brought the earth's two great islands—Afro-Eurasia and the Americas—into direct contact with one another for the first time. The changes that resulted from the new transatlantic connections were massive in both the "New World" of the Americas and the "Old World" of Afro-Eurasia.

There was also a great leap forward in contacts between the major regions within Afro-Eurasia, a continuation of the trend that had begun with the establishment of the Silk Road and the Indian Ocean voyages of the classical period (see Chapter 16). Between 1405 and 1433 the Ming emperors in China dispatched seven huge naval expeditions into the Indian Ocean under the admiralship of Cheng Ho. The Chinese ships were the largest and most technologically advanced vessels in the world of the early fifteenth century. They made many successful landings at ports in Southeast Asia, India, Arabia, and the east African coast. Then, for reasons that are somewhat unclear, the Ming government called a halt to the maritime expeditions and cut off funds for shipbuilding, sending the greatest navy in the world into sharp decline.

While the Ming voyages were in full swing, the Portuguese government (which knew nothing about the maritime activities of the Chinese) began to sponsor its own, much smaller, overseas expeditions. During the course of the fifteenth century Portuguese mariners were sent, very tentatively, down the west coast of Africa with the aim of discovering a sea route to Asia. (Powerful Muslim states now blocked the traditional routes from Europe to Asia via the Red Sea and the Persian Gulf.) Finally, in 1497 and 1498, Vasco da Gama led a fleet of three Portuguese ships and a crew of about 170 sailors around the Cape of Good Hope and up the east African coast. Assisted by an experienced Indian Ocean pilot, the Portuguese ships then sailed across the Arabian Sea to Calicut, a major port on the southwest coast of India

Selection 1 from Ma Huan, *Ying-Yai Sheng-Lan: "The Overall Survey of the Ocean's Shores,"* translated by J. V. G. Mills (Cambridge: Cambridge University Press, 1970), pp. 138, 140–141, 143, 146. Reprinted by permission of David Higham Associates. Selection 2 from *A Journal of the First Voyage of Vasco da Gama, 1497–1499,* translated by E. G. Ravenstein (New York: Burt Franklin, n.d.), pp. 49–50, 56–63. Reprinted by permission of the Hakluyt Society.

(which the Chinese fleet had visited several times earlier in the century). Europeans were now able to sail directly to Asian ports. A new era of world history had begun.

The two selections that follow focus on the visits of the Chinese and Portuguese fleets to Calicut at different times in the fifteenth century. In the first reading Ma Huan, who traveled with Cheng Ho on several of the great maritime expeditions, records his impressions of the Indian port in the early fifteenth century. The second selection is taken from the record of the Portuguese voyage made by an anonymous member of da Gama's crew in 1497 and 1498.

1. A CHINESE REPORT ON CALICUT

In the fifth year of the Yung-lo [period] [i.e., 1408] the court ordered: the principal envoy the grand eunuch Cheng Ho and others to deliver an imperial mandate to the king of this country [i.e., Calicut] and to bestow on him a patent conferring a title of honour, and the grant of a silver seal, [also] to promote all the chiefs and award them hats and girdles of various grades

[So Cheng Ho] went there in command of a large fleet of treasure-ships, and he erected a tablet with a pavilion over it and set up a stone which said 'Though the journey from this country to the Central Country [China] is more than a hundred thousand *li*, yet the people are very similar, happy and prosperous, with identical customs. We have here engraved a stone, a perpetual declaration for ten thousand ages.'

The king of the country is a Nan-k'un [upper caste] man; he is a firm believer in the Buddhist religion; [In fact, the king was a Hindu.] [and] he venerates the elephant and the ox.

The population of the country includes five classes, the Muslim people, the Nan-k'un people, the Che-ti people, the Ko-ling people, and the Mu-kua people.

The king of the country and the people of the country all refrain from eating the flesh of the ox. The great chiefs are Muslim people; [and] they all refrain from eating the flesh of the pig. Formerly there was a king who made a sworn compact with the Muslim people, [saying] 'You do not eat the ox; I do not eat the pig; we will reciprocally respect the taboo'; [and this compact] has been honoured right down to the present day. . . .

The king has two great chiefs who administer the affairs of the country; both are Muslims.

The majority of the people in the country all profess the Muslim religion. There are twenty or thirty temples of worship, and once in seven days they go to worship. When the day arrives, the whole family fast and bathe, and attend to nothing else. In the *ssu* and *wu* periods [times of the day], the menfolk, old and young, go to the temple to worship. When the *wei* period arrives, they disperse and return home; thereupon they carry on with their trading, and transact their household affairs.

The people are very honest and trustworthy. Their appearance is smart, fine, and distinguished.

Their two great chiefs received promotion and awards from the court of the Central Country.

If a treasure-ship goes there, it is left entirely to the two men to superintend the buying and selling; the king sends a chief and a Che-ti Wei-no-chi [i.e., a trader or broker] to examine the account books in the official bureau; a broker comes and joins them; [and] a high officer who commands the ships discusses the choice of a certain date for fixing prices. When the day arrives, they first of all take the silk embroideries and the open-work silks, and other such goods which have been brought there, and discuss the price of them one by one; [and] when [the price] has been fixed, they write out an agreement stating the amount of the price; [this agreement] is retained by these persons.

The chief and the Che-ti, with his excellency the eunuch, all join hands together, and the broker then says 'In such and such a moon on such and such a day, we have all joined hands and sealed our agreement with a hand-clasp; whether [the price] be dear or cheap, we will never repudiate it or change it.'

After that, the Che-ti and the men of wealth then come bringing precious stones, pearls, corals, and other such things, so that they may be examined and the price discussed; [this] cannot be settled in a day; [if done] quickly, [it takes] one moon; [if done] slowly, [it takes] two or three moons.

Once the money-price has been fixed after examination and discussion, if a pearl or other such article is purchased, the price which must be paid for it is calculated by the chief and the Wei-no-chi who carried out the original transaction; [and] as to the quantity of the hemp-silk or other such article which must be given in exchange for it, goods are given in exchange according to [the price fixed by] the original hand-clasp—there is not the slightest deviation. . . .

The people of the country also take the silk of the silk-worm, soften it by boiling, dye it in all colours, and weave it into kerchiefs with decorative stripes at intervals; the breadth is four or five *ch'ih,* and the length one *chang* two or three *ch'ih;* [and] each length is sold for one hundred gold coins.

As to the pepper: the inhabitants of the mountainous countryside have established gardens, and it is extensively cultivated. When the period of the tenth moon arrives, the pepper ripens; [and] it is collected, dried in the sun, and sold. Of course, big pepper-collectors come and collect it, and take it up to the official storehouse to be stored; if there is a buyer, an official gives permission for the sale; the duty is calculated according to the amount [of the purchase price] and is paid in to the authorities. Each one *po-ho* of pepper is sold for two hundred gold coins.

The Che-ti mostly purchase all kinds of precious stones and pearls, and they manufacture coral beads and other such things.

Foreign ships from every place come there; and the king of the country also sends a chief and a writer and others to watch the sales; thereupon they collect the duty and pay it in to the authorities.

The wealthy people mostly cultivate coconut trees—sometimes a thousand trees, sometimes two thousand or three thousand—; this constitutes their property.

The coconut has ten different uses. The young tree has a syrup, very sweet, and good to drink; [and] it can be made into wine by fermentation. The old coconut has flesh, from which they express oil, and make sugar, and make a foodstuff for eating. From the fibre which envelops the outside [of the nut] they make ropes for ship-building. The shell of the coconut makes bowls and makes cups; it is also good for burning to ash for the delicate operation of inlaying gold or silver. The trees are good for building houses, and the leaves are good for roofing houses. . . .

On the day when the envoy returned, the king of the country wished to send tribute; [so] he took fifty *liang* of fine red gold and ordered the foreign craftsmen to draw it out into gold threads as fine as a hair; these were strung together to form a ribbon, which was made into a jewelled girdle with incrustations of all kinds of precious stones and large pearls; [and the king] sent a chief, Nai-pang, to present it as tribute to the Central Country.

2. A PORTUGUESE REPORT ON CALICUT

[*A description of Calecut.*] The city of Calecut is inhabited by Christians. [In fact, most of the residents of Calicut were Hindus.] They are of a tawny complexion. Some of them have big beards and long hair, whilst others clip their hair short or shave the head, merely allowing a tuft to remain on the crown as a sign that they are Christians. They also wear moustaches. They pierce the ears and wear much gold in them. They go naked down to the waist, covering their lower extremities with very fine cotton stuffs. But it is only the most respectable who do this, for the others manage as best they are able.

The women of this country, as a rule, are ugly and of small stature, They wear many jewels of gold round the neck, numerous bracelets on their arms, and rings set with precious stones on their toes. All these people are well-disposed and apparently of mild temper. At first sight they seem covetous and ignorant.

[*A messenger sent to the King.*] When we arrived at Calecut [in May 1498] the king was fifteen leagues away. The captain-major [Vasco da Gama] sent two men to him with a message, informing him that an ambassador had arrived from the King of Portugal with letters, and that if he desired it he would take them to where the king then was.

The king presented the bearers of this message with much fine cloth. He sent word to the captain bidding him welcome, saying that he was about to proceed to Qualecut (Calecut). As a matter of fact, he started at once with a large retinue. . . .

[*A Royal Audience, May 28.*] The king was in a small court, reclining upon a couch covered with a cloth of green velvet, above which was a good mattress, and upon this again a sheet of cotton stuff, very white and fine, more so than any linen. The cushions were after the same fashion. In his left hand the king held a very large golden cup [spittoon], having a capacity of half an almude [8 pints]. At its mouth this cup was two palmas [16 inches] wide, and apparently it was massive. Into this cup the king threw the husks of a certain herb which is chewed by the people of this country because of its soothing effects, and which they call *atambor* [betel nut]. On the right side of the king stood a basin of gold, so large that a man might just encircle it with his arms: this contained the herbs. There were likewise many silver jugs. The canopy above the couch was all gilt.

The captain, on entering, saluted in the manner of the country: by putting the hands together, then raising them towards Heaven, as is done by Christians when addressing God, and immediately afterwards opening them and shutting the fists quickly. The king beckoned to the captain with his right hand to come nearer, but the captain did not approach him, for it is the custom of the country for no man to approach the king except only the servant who hands him the herbs, and when anyone addresses the king he holds his hand before the mouth, and remains at a distance. When the king beckoned to the captain he looked at us others, and ordered us to be seated on a stone bench near him, where he could see us. He ordered that water for our hands should be given us, as also some fruit, one kind of which resembled a melon, except that its outside was rough and the inside sweet, whilst another kind of fruit resembled a fig, and tasted very nice. There were men who prepared these fruits for us; and the king looked at us eating, and smiled; and talked to the servant who stood near him supplying him with the herbs referred to. . . .

And the captain told him he was the ambassador of a King of Portugal, who was Lord of many countries and the possessor of great wealth of every description, exceeding that of any king of these parts; that for a period of sixty years his ancestors had annually sent out vessels to make discoveries in the direction of India, as they knew that there were Christian kings there like themselves. This, he said, was the reason which induced them to order this country to be discovered, not because they sought for gold or silver, for of this they had such abundance that they needed not what was to be found in this country. He further stated that the captains sent out travelled for a year or two, until their provisions were exhausted, and then returned to Portugal, without having succeeded in making the desired discovery. There reigned a king now whose name was Dom Manuel, who had ordered him to build three vessels, of which he had been appointed captain-major, and who had ordered him not to return to Portugal until he should have discovered this King of the Christians, on pain of having his head cut off. That two letters had been intrusted to him to be presented in case he succeeded in discovering him, and that he would do so on the ensuing day; and, finally, he had been instructed to say by word of mouth that he [the King of Portugal] desired to be his friend and brother.

In reply to this the king said that he was welcome; that, on his part, he held him as a friend and brother, and would send ambassadors with him to Portugal. This latter had been asked as a favour, the captain pretending that he would not dare to present himself before his king and master unless he was able to present, at the same time, some men of this country. . . .

[*Presents for the King.*] On Tuesday [May 29] the captain got ready the following things to be sent to the king, viz., twelve pieces of *lambel* [striped cloth], four scarlet hoods, six hats, four strings of coral, a case containing six wash-hand basins, a case of sugar, two casks of oil, and two of honey. And as it is the custom not to send anything to the king without the knowledge of the Moor, his factor, and of the *bale*, the captain informed them of his intention. They came, and when they saw the present they laughed at it, saying that it was not a thing to offer to a king, that the poorest merchant from Mecca, or any other part of India, gave more, and that if he wanted to make a present it should be in gold, as the king would not accept such things. When the captain heard this he grew sad, and said that he had brought no gold, that, moreover, he was no merchant, but an ambassador; that he gave of that which he had, which was his own [private gift] and not the king's; that if the King of Portugal ordered him to return he would intrust him with far richer presents; and that if King Camolim would not accept these things he would send them back to the ships. Upon this they declared that they would not forward his presents, nor consent to his forwarding them himself. When they had gone there came certain

Moorish merchants, and they all depreciated the present which the captain desired to be sent to the king. . . .

[*A Second Audience, May 30.*] When he had entered, the king said that he had expected him on Tuesday. The captain said that the long road had tired him, and that for this reason he had not come to see him. The king then said that he had told him that he came from a very rich kingdom, and yet had brought him nothing; that he had also told him that he was the bearer of a letter, which had not yet been delivered. To this the captain rejoined that he had brought nothing, because the object of his voyage was merely to make discoveries, but that when other ships came he would then see what they brought him; as to the letter, it was true that he had brought one, and would deliver it immediately.

The king then asked what it was he had come to discover: stones or men? If he came to discover men, as he said, why had he brought nothing? Moreover, he had been told that he carried with him the golden image of a Santa Maria. The captain said that the Santa Maria was not of gold, and that even if she were he would not part with her, as she had guided him across the ocean, and would guide him back to his own country. The king then asked for the letter. The captain said that he begged as a favour, that as the Moors wished him ill and might misinterpret him, a Christian able to speak Arabic should be sent for. The king said this was well, and at once sent for a young man, of small stature, whose name was Quaram. The captain then said that he had two letters, one written in his own language and the other in that of the Moors; that he was able to read the former, and knew that it contained nothing but what would prove acceptable; but that as to the other he was unable to read it, and it might be good, or contain something that was erroneous. As the Christian was unable to *read* Moorish, four Moors took the letter and read it between them, after which they translated it to the king, who was well satisfied with its contents.

The king then asked what kind of merchandise was to be found in his country. The captain said there was much corn [i.e., wheat], cloth, iron, bronze, and many other things. The king asked whether he had any merchandise with him. The captain replied that he had a little of each sort, as samples, and that if permitted to return to the ships he would order it to be landed, and that meantime four or five men would remain at the lodgings assigned them. The king said no! He might take all his people with him, securely moor his ships, land his merchandise, and sell it to the best advantage. Having taken leave of the king the captain returned to his lodgings, and we with him. As it was already late no attempt was made to depart that night. . . .

STUDY QUESTIONS

1. What are the main points that Ma Huan makes about the people of Calicut? What aspects of life in Calicut interested him the most? How do you explain his confusion about religion in Calicut? What seems to have been the purpose of the Chinese visit to Calicut?

2. How does the Portuguese report compare with that of Ma Huan? What similarities and differences do you see?

3. What evidence do you see in these two documents regarding the importance of Indian Ocean commerce during the 1490s and earlier? How does the level of commerce in the fifteenth century compare with that during the classical period? (See Chapter 17.)

4. Do you think the long experience the Chinese had in dealing with pastoral nomads such as the Hsiung-nu was an asset or a liability for Ma Huan and his shipmates when they docked in Calicut? Compare Ssu-ma Ch'ien's report on the Hsiung-nu (in Chapter 16) with Ma Huan's account of Calicut.

5. What do the Chinese decisions to sponsor and then terminate the Cheng Ho voyages suggest about the political leadership of China during the Ming dynasty? Why was the decision to end the voyages significant?

6. Suppose the Portuguese naval program had been ended after da Gama returned home. Would such a decision have been likely to alter the course of world history in important ways?

7. Does the Portuguese document suggest a shift in the European attitude toward trade and merchants? (See Chapter 32.)